F.V.

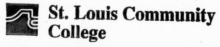
St. Louis Community College

Forest Park
Florissant Valley
Meramec

Instructional Resources
St. Louis, Missouri

Also by A. D. Coleman

CRITICAL SURVEYS

The Grotesque in Photography (Ridge Press/Summit Books, 1977)

CRITICAL ESSAYS

Light Readings: A Photography Critic's Writings, 1968–1978 (Oxford University Press, 1979; second edition, University of New Mexico Press, 1998)

Critical Focus: Photography in the International Image Community (Nazraeli Press, 1995)

Tarnished Silver: After the Photo Boom, Essays and Lectures 1979–1989 (Midmarch Arts Press, 1996)

The Digital Evolution: Photography in the Electronic Age, Essays, Lectures and Interviews 1967–1998 (Nazraeli Press, 1998)

REFERENCE WORKS

The Photography A-V Program Directory (PMI, 1981), with Patricia Grantz and Douglas I. Sheer

FOR CHILDREN

Looking at Photographs: Animals (Chronicle Books, 1995)

Depth of Field

Edward S. Curtis, "Principal Female Shaman of the Hupa," *The North American Indian*, vol. 13 (1924), plate 467.

Depth

of

Field

ESSAYS ON
PHOTOGRAPHY,
MASS MEDIA,
AND LENS CULTURE

A. D. Coleman

University of New Mexico Press
Albuquerque

For permissions and information contact Image/World Syndication Services,
P. O. Box 040078, Staten Island, New York 10304–0002; (718) 447–3091,
coda@nearbycafe. com.

Library of Congress Cataloging-in-Publication Data
Coleman, A. D.
    Depth of field : essays on photography, mass media, and lens
culture / A. D. Coleman. — 1st ed.
        p.   cm.
    Includes bibliographical references and index.
    ISBN 0-8263-1815-0. — ISBN 0-8263-1816-9 (pbk.)
    1. Photographic criticism.   I. Title.
TR187.C63   1998
770'.1 — dc21   98-6965
                                                   CIP

To Marjorie Forman, spirit guide and midwife, who helped me birth it; and to Kathy Vargas and Colleen Thornton, dear friends and close readers.

Contents

Problem: To make what you see be seen, through the intermediary of a machine that does not see it as you see it. And to make what you understand be understood, through the intermediary of a machine that does not understand it as you do.

Robert Bresson, Notes on Cinematography (1977)

The difficulty of literature is not to write, but to write what you mean; not to affect your reader, but to affect him precisely as you wish.

Robert Louis Stevenson, Virginibus Puerisque (1881)

Acknowledgments

For reasons still not entirely clear to me, this book has proved the hardest of all my collections of essays to deliver into the world.

To begin with, it's had several incarnations. I first announced its forthcoming appearance something like fifteen years ago, at a time when it took a quite different, much more expansive form. At that initial stage of its life, it benefitted greatly from the attention, supportiveness, and organizational assistance of Tony Outhwaite of the JCA Literary Agency, then my agent, and subsequently from the enthusiasm and advice of my next agent, Jonathan Silverman of the Scott Meredith Literary Agency.

That version of the book, which I now realize was unwieldy and less than cohesive at best, never found a publisher, so I shelved it for several years to get some distance on it and its problems. Close readings and thoughtful commentary by Richard Kirstel and his late wife, Barbara Kirstel, helped me identify many of its structural difficulties. As a result, I split the book in two. Half of the original version eventually evolved into the volume *Tarnished Silver: After the Photo Boom, Essays and Lectures 1979–1989*.[1] The second half—a set of (mostly) more scholarly essays—formed the core of this meaner, leaner new model. The University of New Mexico Press accepted that book for publication in 1989; I began drafting several new essays for it, and set to work on what I thought would be minor revisions.

But these are substantial commentaries, demanding much research, considerable gestation time, and extensive rewriting. For whatever the reasons, first one and then another of the essays commenced to give me fits. (Some of the subsequent delay is explained—or at least rationalized—in the new opening section of the first essay in this volume, "The Destruction Business.") And life, as is its wont, intruded itself in some major ways to preoccupy me. I learned again the wisdom of the *I Ching*: "Perseverance furthers."

I finally managed a major chunk of the necessary revision of these essays and the editing of this book during a three-month residency as Museum Scholar at the J. Paul Getty Museum in California during the fall of 1993, and as a Fulbright Senior Scholar in the Department of Photography at Gothenberg University in Sweden during the winter and spring of 1994. The support and unbroken stretches of working time provided by these institutions proved invaluable to this project, and I thank all those involved for making those opportunities available to me. Gradually, then and thereafter, what I saw as the essays' various problems began to resolve themselves; at long last, in the late summer of 1996, I found a way to tackle the one remaining hurdle, the meditation on criticism that begins this collection. With its completion, I felt finally that the book had reached its desired form.

My thanks go to the editors, curators, and lecture and conference sponsors who variously commissioned, solicited, and/or welcomed these essays in their original forms, and to those who published subsequent versions of them as I refined and polished my arguments: Jim Hughes at *Camera Arts*, Kathleen Kenyon at the *Center Quarterly*, Thom Harrop and Ana Jones at *Darkroom Photography/Camera & Darkroom*, Neil Postman at *Et cetera: A Journal of General Semantics*, Andreas Müller-Pohle at *European Photography* (Germany), Sue Beardmore at The Ffotogallery (Wales), Joachim Schmid at *Fotokritik* (Germany), Italo Zannier at *Fotologia* (Italy), Jerome Liebling of Hampshire College (Amherst, Mass.), David Spurgeon at *Impact of Science on Society* (France), Jay Black and Ralph D. Barney at the *Journal of Mass Media Ethics*, Henning Hansen at *Katalog* (Denmark), Richard Kostelanetz, Barry Tanenbaum at *Lens' on Campus/Imaging On Campus*, Joan Harrison and Judy Collischan van Wagner of the Hillwood Art Gallery of Long Island University (N.Y.), the photography faculty of Loyola College (Baltimore), Gail Fisher-Taylor at *Photo-Communiqué*/the Holocene Foundation (Canada), Eli Bornstein at *The Structurist* (Canada), Sari Thomas of the Conference on Culture and Communication, Temple University (Philadelphia), and Manuel Vilariño of the University of Santiago de Compostela (Spain). I have indicated in the endnotes and on the Publication Credits page the presentational and publishing history of each essay, so that readers can see something of the process by which they made their way into and through the world and also to facilitate finding them in other languages, since a number of them have been translated.

My indebtedness extends as well to others who played more specific roles in the making of the book in your hands. Between 1990 and 1995 various people —

photographers Linda Troeller and Jennifer Kotter; the late Vilém Flusser, philosopher and media theorist; and film critic Andrew Sarris—provided comments on the book as a whole, or on some of its components, that proved enormously helpful.

The fact that it has at long last appeared I attribute primarily to Marjorie Forman, who helped me find my way through the labyrinths of Jungian analysis during this final version's chrysalis stage; to the artist, curator, and historian Colleen Thornton and the artist and curator Kathy Vargas, whose long-term commitments to my work and ideas, incisive critiques of the individual essays, structural suggestions for the volume as a whole, and other provocations forced me to reconsider and clarify these pieces even further; and to Elizabeth Hadas and Dana Asbury of the University of New Mexico Press, who demonstrated endless patience with me during the final redaction process. I proffer my deepest gratitude to these fine folks.

So I reiterate my heartfelt appreciation to all of the above; and I assure you that none of them are to blame for any of this book's failures, which, after all this time and effort, can only be my own.

—A. D. C.

NOTES

1. Midmarch Arts Press, 1996.

Preface

This volume puts into book form an interlaced group of essays I think of as more scholarly than the running commentary on photography, art, and mass media with which the majority of my readers most commonly associate me. Concerned with issues of theory and history, with those who fall (or are pushed) through the cracks of critical disdain and neglect, with different approaches to praxis and dramatic shifts in the methods and means thereof, with definitions of terms and the function of criticism itself, they were written between 1978 and 1996 and variously, often drastically revised during those years before reaching their present and (I hope) final form.

When I set about my work as a critic of photography and related subjects, in 1968, I thought of myself as anything but a scholar. Having but recently closed the door on the academic context for my own fields of formal study — English literature and creative writing — with a vow never to return, I had at that point no expectation of ever again engaging in anything remotely resembling scholarly activity, especially as a working writer.

So much for good intentions.

I did manage to stay away from just about anything approximating the scholarly (excepting occasional lectures and workshops at colleges, universities, and art institutes, and some teaching of seminars, mostly in adult-education programs) until mid-1976, when I forced myself to spend several months writing what remains my single most cited essay, "The Directorial Mode: Notes Toward a Definition."[1] (Before that, my only notable slip into anything akin to written scholarship was my reluctantly accepting the chore of providing the entry on photography for a revised 1975 edition of *The New Columbia Encyclopedia,*[2] a task into which editor Karen Tweedy-Holmes had to drag me kicking and screaming.)

The essay on the directorial mode was the first to require some footnoting, that defining apparatus of scholarly production. Putting those citations and elaborations in seemed like a tectonic shift at the time. But it also reminded me of how much I'd always enjoyed reading the notes in other people's essays, since often that's where the real action was to be found.[3] So I took great pleasure in planting in my own notes thereto a little ticking time bomb whose explosion took place some years thereafter.[4]

Later that same year I undertook the writing of the first critical survey ever produced of another important mode of photographic activity. The resulting book, *The Grotesque in Photography*,[5] though light on scholarly apparatus (the publishers' choice, not mine), looked and read somewhat like a work of scholarship, and has functioned as a standard reference — indeed, still the only substantial study of its subject — since it appeared in 1977. With the publication of those two works, people began to treat me as if I were a scholar, and I began to doubt my right to disclaim that as an accurate definition of at least a share of my inclinations and energies.

Shortly thereafter, in late 1978, I commenced the earliest essay in this book, "Conspicuous by His Absence: Concerning the Mysterious Disappearance of William Mortensen" — in part because the aforementioned footnote from 1976 and my brief discussion of Mortensen in *The Grotesque in Photography* seemed to demand it, in part because I'd done the spadework for it back in 1974 and didn't want to see that labor go to waste, and in part because I suspected that if I didn't do it no one else would. Those motives — especially the first and last — underlie much of what's in this volume. My perception of problematic gaps in the literature of photography as a whole (as well as within my own body of work), along with my sense of obligation to articulate my operative premises and definitions, serve as the driving forces behind this aspect of my activity.

As this suggests, virtually all of these essays emerged from the process of reconsidering earlier essays and lectures, pursuing issues I'd discovered I had left unresolved therein. At the time I began that essay on Mortensen I'd moved almost entirely away from the reviewing, reportage, and writing of other forms of occasional pieces that had dominated my work for the decade 1968–78, a phase of my professional activity synopsized by my first collection of essays.[6] This meant that space had opened up in my writing life for longer, more meditated, less assignment-driven essays: ruminations whose length was determined by their own inner logic, rather than by editors' needs or the appetites of the publishing market, and of whose production schedule I was the primary —

sometimes the sole — determinant. The kind of projects, that is, usually produced by people who are either independently wealthy or else leading the academic life.

As it happened, by the early 1980s, though I hadn't exactly turned into an academic (at least in my own head), I'd taken on an extensive though not full-time teaching commitment at New York University, and had scaled back my writing for magazines considerably. At that juncture I'd also decided that undertaking a formal course of study in mass media and communications would have developmental value for my work. I found a doctoral program that suited me (headed by Neil Postman) at N.Y.U. and enrolled therein. I chose to concentrate my work within that program on an issue that I'd first raised — in passing, and in a few brief sentences — in that synopsized history of photography for *The New Columbia Encyclopedia*; its barely articulated implications had nagged at me ever since I'd mailed in my typescript. The chronologically second essay contained here, "Lentil Soup: A Meditation on Lens Culture," came out of my research toward that end; addressing the prephotographic history of the lens as a technology, it's the most widely published and translated of my essays to date.

Several of these texts — "On Redaction," "The Destruction Business," "Documentary, Photojournalism and Press Photography Now," and the book's brief epilogue, "Items for An Agenda" — grew out of or were first presented as public lectures or formal papers for symposia, while several others that began as texts for the page turned into such papers: "The Image in Question: Further Notes on the Directorial Mode" and the essay on Edward S. Curtis have both been polished through public performance. Two of the essays — "The Image in Question" and "Mutant Media: Photo/Montage/Collage" — began their lives as commissioned catalogue introductions for survey shows of recent work in their respective modes, directorial imagery and hybrid forms of photographic image-making. In all those cases, the core sections of the first versions turned into building blocks for these further elaborations of the central ideas, which now often bear only a marginal resemblance to their initial appearances.

These essays all link themselves in diverse ways to each other. The last-named pair, for instance, connect to the Mortensen essay, on the one hand, and to "The Vanishing Borderline" — a rumination on the relationship between photography and computer art — on the other. Similarly, the Curtis essay profits from consideration alongside the Mortensen piece, since both address the inevitable excesses of ideologically biased historianship and its consequences; yet it also functions as a case study to which the more general ideas propounded in "Documentary, Photojournalism and Press Photography Now" can be applied.

By the same token, "Mutant Media," "Documentary, Photojournalism and

Press Photography Now," and "On Redaction" strike me as interrelated in that all concern themselves in good part with the absence of clear definitions for such fundamental terms as photomontage, photocollage, the several forms of informationally oriented photography, and the body of work in this medium. They set out to propose and substantiate such definitions — for my own use as a working critic, of course, but also for anyone else who finds them convenient and helpful. (Perhaps they can also even serve as articulated reference points for those who would dispute them, giving them something fixed and carefully reasoned to counter with their own alternatives.) Yet my impulse is far from merely lexicographic; those essays also speak to other, larger issues, for the consideration of which I felt some commitment to a precise vocabulary was vital.

Certainly that applies to my own praxis as well. The book opens with the most recent of these essays, a scrutiny of the process of criticism itself, specifying — as well as I'm able to — what I think I'm about, what standards I set for myself, what I hope to achieve with my work. And it closes with some advice and encouragement — for my readers, of course, but for myself, at this stage of my life and work, as well. I trust in the intelligence of my readers sufficiently to feel confident that they will discern the web of correspondences and cross-references among these separate but related constructs.

If there's an underlying message to all this, it's that it turned out, to my surprise, that I've come to feel comfortable once again within the academic environment and its primary modes of activity. I relish the opportunity to teach, take great pleasure in the less frequent occasions on which I can switch roles and become a student, enjoy scholarship. I love tracking down ideas and leads, spending hours in the library (no news there, actually, as it had been a favorite haunt since childhood), the process of citation, the careful organization of diverse threads of reasoning, the requirements for buttressed argument. Overall, aside from some of its mechanics (citing sources, maintaining bibliographies, and such), it proves not much different from my normal ways of gathering information, checking it, working out ideas, and putting them into written form, even if that wasn't always visible in the results.

So I've either adapted to scholarship or adapted it to me. Or, most likely, both. By now I've produced numerous other such texts, on divers subjects; most have been published, though not yet collected into book form (several can be found in *Tarnished Silver*). I consider its effect on my work absolutely salutory. Just as my professional experience as a working essayist and the resulting imperative of writing an accessible, engaging prose informed my scholarly work, so the rigors of scholarship, and what I'd learned from re-engaging with its disciplines — and, of course, from the specifics of my researches — informed the more fluid, provisional writing I began to generate from mid-1988 onward, when I began reviewing and writing a looser criticism and cultural commentary once again.

Nowadays, they simply seem like alternate hats I wear on different days. Indeed, to my satisfaction and amusement, a number of the essays in this book have appeared both in scholarly journals and (minus their footnotes, but otherwise unchanged in style and tone) in general-audience publications aimed at a broad readership — sometimes simultaneously. Curiously, nowhere in my engagement with serious scholarship did I find a requirement for impenetrability or unclarity of either thought or language; and no editor of the scholarly journals here and abroad in which I've published many of these pieces ever complained about the comparative lack of jargon and trendy locutions, or the absence of most of the fashionable references from my cited sources. As Katha Pollitt noted, in regard to the notorious recent publication of a physicist's blatant parody of such obscurantist writing by the unwitting editors of the journal *Social Text,*

> the comedy of the [Alan] Sokal incident is that it suggests that even the postmodernists don't really understand one another's writing and make their way through the text by moving from one familiar name or notion to the next like a frog jumping across a murky pond by way of lily pads. Lacan . . . performativity . . . Judith Butler . . . scandal . . . (en)gendering (w)holeness . . . Lunch![7]

No lily pads here, I'm afraid; only the clearest water I'm able to supply, in which both I and my readers will have to sink or swim. You're on your own for lunch.

A few words concerning the shape of this book. As the individual essays achieved their final forms, the question of their arrangement in the book became a challenge. The material neither lends itself to chronological ordering nor falls into thematic clusters. No central issue or diegesis emerged as a linear organizing principle. So I shuffled the deck repeatedly. Eventually, a loose sequence suggested itself to me, which I fine-tuned with the input of several of the book's later readers while it was still in typescript.

Looking at the structure that evolved in that fashion, I see that I've constructed it neither as a collage nor as an argument; rather, it is intended as a set of recurring questions, connected and interweaving. Where did photography come from? What has it meant to us until now? What have we scanted, discarded, left out in considering it, and why? How are we presently perceiving it? Where might we be heading with it at the tail end of this century?

My answers to these questions remain necessarily contingent; so, for that matter, do the questions. It may seem odd to have spent so much effort in sculpting queries and responses that may not endure, or may prove wrong-headed. Perhaps it was. My goal was not just to intersect my own thinking on one or another subject at a given moment, but to sum it up.[8] If I felt that, beyond the pleasures of the texts for myself and my readers, I needed to justify such expenditure of energy, I'd simply say that I wanted to see what my own inquiries and lines of reasoning would look like if they were consciously, patiently built to last — even knowing that they won't, because nothing does.

— A. D. Coleman

Staten Island, New York

May 1998

NOTES

1. "The Directorial Mode: Notes Toward a Definition," *Artforum* 15, no. 1 (September 1976): 55–61. Reprinted in A. D. Coleman, *Light Readings: A Photography Critic's Writings, 1968–1978* (New York: Oxford University Press, 1979; Albuquerque: University of New Mexico Press, 1998). For my subsequent thoughts on this subject, see "The Image in Question: Further Notes on the Directorial Mode," elsewhere in this volume.

2. "Photography," *New Columbia Encyclopedia* (New York: Columbia University Press, 1975), pp. 2138–39.

3. Philip Rieff's homage to the footnote in his polemic *Fellow Teachers* (New York: Delta Books, 1975), p. 2, speaks eloquently to its complex function in the life of the mind.

4. See the postscript to the essay "Conspicuous by His Absence: Concerning the Mysterious Disappearance of William Mortensen," elsewhere in this volume.

5. *The Grotesque in Photography* (New York: Ridge Press / Summit Books, 1977).

6. *Light Readings*.

7. Pollitt, "Pomolotov Cocktail," *The Nation* 262, no. 23 (June 10, 1996): 9. For more on this matter, see endnote 24 to the essay "Documentary, Photojournalism and Press Photography Now," elsewhere in this volume. A delicious commentary on this issue is offered in Patricia Nelson Limerick's "Dancing with Professors: The Trouble with Academic Prose," *New York Times Book Review* (October 31, 1993): 3, 23–24.

8. As the composer and saxophonist Wayne Shorter recently put it, "The word 'finished' is artificial. . . . In the end, it's not that anything is finished; it's that the person is finished thinking about it." Ben Ratliff, "With This Composer, the Work Is Never Done," *New York Times* (April 22, 1998): E6.

The Destruction Business

SOME THOUGHTS ON THE FUNCTION OF CRITICISM

Hellhound on my trail, my muse refused to let this essay rest. You didn't know that critics were supervised by muses? Nor did I, though I assumed some oblique connection to Mnemosyne, fount of memory, and through her to Clio, overseer of history. Yet there's no question but that critics, like artists, draw on wellsprings of energy and (for want of a better word) inspiration, though who or what breathes into us may be nothing identified by the Greeks. Indeed, I often suspect an older origin for mine, something from the Hindu perhaps: Shiva, Destroyer of Worlds.

In any event, for three years now this voice has obstinately refused to allow me to publish this essay in the form in which it was initially drafted for this book — which, of course, meant that the book has been stalled for as long. During that period I have managed to publish three other books; and I have taken care of all other preproduction details on this one, in the hope that she might step out for a beer and let me slip this one past her. No such luck; if her attention flagged, I never caught her napping.

Lest you think me mad, let me assure you that this guiding spirit has a current incarnation: a forty-something woman whose level of intelligence (in my estimation) far exceeds my own, an artist and art historian and arts administrator herself, profoundly frustrated because life keeps getting in the way of her exercise of her many gifts, talents, and hard-earned skills. Part of her problem is that she keeps a keener watch on others (myself included) than she does on herself, to their benefit and her own detriment. In any case, she has loomed ominously over this essay, demanding that I push it to extremes that I had until now, for whatever reasons, avoided.

In response, I employed an assortment of my procrastination techniques, the full repertoire of which would probably astonish those who think me prolific. And, needless to say, life interfered in various ways with my plans, as it does with hers, providing endless rationales for whatever needs excusing. (For example, in the midst of this very paragraph my computer went on the blink and lost some earlier version of the past several sentences; shortly thereafter, it evaporated an entire working draft of these prefatory comments.) But, in hindsight, I must 'fess up: the real reason this essay's taken so long is that I wasn't in the mood.

What mood, you ask? Simply put, the labor of destruction (which is, as I will argue, the core of my profession) is best undertaken in a certain mood: a readiness, indeed an eagerness, to lay about one with a will and watch things shatter. As Karl Marx wrote, "[Criticism's] essential sentiment is indignation; its essential activity is denunciation."[1] (Perhaps this is why the Greek novelist and poet Nikos Kazantzakis once said, "One of man's greatest obligations is anger."[2])

And what, might you ask, did it take finally to get me in the mood? A combination of circumstances. To start with, I've spent some time in recent years pondering and savoring the word *citizenship*. This began when my muse, reading the typescript for this very book, on which I'd solicited her commentary, pressed me in conversation to define the public function of criticism more precisely. To my considerable surprise, I heard myself say, "It's the activity of responsible citizenship within a given community." Though I've worked as a professional critic for close to thirty years, I hadn't known I believed that. (As Thoreau once put it, "How can I know what I think till I see what I say?")

But that hardly responded to her primary concern: her conviction that, at least within the confines of this essay as it then stood, I'd let my tender-hearted aspect override my capacity for tough-mindedness. Indeed, she wanted me to go over the top, into berserker fury, hang-'em-high bloody-mindedness, suspecting I'd lost my heart for the battle. In retrospect, it seems to me my thoughts were simply elsewhere at the time. Nonetheless, I couldn't deny she had a point; every month or so I'd reread that version of the essay, note its excessive kindnesses and nice-guyisms, sigh, and put it aside, returning to my brooding on the nature of citizenship.

Eventually, that led me to assessing my fellow citizens in this particular polity, by weighing both the quality and the quantity of the public discourse on photography stimulated by my writings and those of my colleagues. Those of us who publish regularly on this subject do read and, in various ways, respond in print to each other's ideas, of course. But our broader readership persists in an astonishing and disheartening muteness on just about all issues. Rereading such letters to the editor as my own writing had evoked over the past twenty-eight years left me dejected, wondering why I even bothered.

During those three decades, my editors published virtually every letter written to them in response to my essays.[3] Available for my review, therefore, I had almost everything readers had cared to offer as responsive dialogue in the public forums in which I've done my work. Judging from that, the average baseball fan — who cheers on his or her favorite team in public, wears its colors at the ballpark or in the sports bar, and actively debates its strengths and weaknesses with all and sundry, including the sports columnists in the newspapers — shows more articulacy and gumption in this regard than all but a tiny handful of my readers.

Indeed, toward the end of my scrutiny of this slim file of missives I found myself so tired of hearing privately from readers who lacked the elementary sense of civic responsibility required to enter the public debate on any issue that I drafted a form letter intended to discourage any further such communication with me — unless and until they first wrote something to some editor about some issue I raised, the equivalent within this community of voting in a local referendum.[4]

But what brought all this to a head, finally, was the response I received to my fall 1996 commentary in the *New York Observer* on the posthumous publication of a set of photographs of developmentally disabled people made in the last years of her life by the late Diane Arbus.[5] My approach to this project was a version of what the Germans call *ausstellungskritik* — "exhibition critique," aimed primarily at addressing the presentational project, in this case a publication rather than a show. I realized as I researched and wrote this critique that it mattered to me, on some very deep levels, contained something that seemed crucial. Not only did it evolve into a defining structure of thought and function as an important position paper for me, but — since it broached two substantive cans of worms — it seemed likely to stir up some controversy. So I forewarned my supportive editors of that, refined my argument, checked my facts, verified my sources, and let 'er rip.

What resulted was nothing like I'd expected. This painstakingly crafted provocation was met, publicly, with dead silence for four months. Exactly one brief letter to the editor — not a particularly cogent one, unfortunately — came in to the *Observer.* Some commentary on the issues I'd raised made its way into an online discussion group's discourse, not exactly the public arena; and a message board I created for that purpose at my own Website, where I'd posted the original article, began filling up with unilluminating monologues that had everything to do with their authors' feelings and nothing much to do with the matters of principle, both moral and scholarly, on which I'd based my arguments.

Meanwhile, a MacArthur fellow I ran into at a conference indicated full agreement with the principles I'd enunciated but declined my invitation to say so in the *Observer*'s pages or anywhere else. So did a prominent specialist in photography at a major auction house, who felt that my points "were very important, and need to be discussed." The editor of a periodical aimed at collectors e-mailed me a note saying that I was "on the side of the angels" with this piece but did not even mention it in his publication, though one of the issues I raised in the essay pertains directly to the definition of the authentic body of work in photography, and thus to the collecting of photographs. At the same time, a literacy-challenged gent from the Bay Area (where the piece had been reprinted, in my column in *Photo Metro*) decided that my encouragement of reader response meant that I was seeking pen pals, and began bombarding me at home with lengthy private letters, castigating me for my positions and instructing me on the responsibilities of the critic, while adamantly refusing my repeated invitations to put himself on the record by sending his letters to the editor and debating me in public.

Shortly thereafter, I found myself hissed at in passing by Janet Malcolm, of all people, in the pages of the house organ of Random House, *The New York Review of Books*.[6] And someone I once mistakenly considered both a colleague and a friend displayed not only a professional animus of which I'd been unaware but, more disturbingly, some previously unsuspected fascist tendencies — lambasting me in public for my temerity, his counter-arguments incorporating the frightening assertion that "human rights pale beside the necessity of seeing that great art sees the light of day."[7]

And that was it, the sum total a full year after the piece first appeared. Nothing of either the quality or quantity of response I'd assumed my provocation would evoke. Instead, insults, unreasoned hysteria, behind-the-scenes pep talks, amateur psychoanalysis, aimless chatter. Disheartening, to say the least. I found myself variously bored, discouraged, and offended by the low level of the discourse; moreover, I found no nugget of provocation for myself, no substantial challenge that made me rethink my argument, nothing to chew on. The degree of vituperation surprised me, but most of it rolled off, mere *ad hominem* stuff. Except for one: a sneering dismissal of me, in passing, by Mark Power, as "photography's professional scold."[8]

Clearly meant as an insult, that stung. For weeks it smarted. At my muse's urging I pulled the barb out to examine it, turned it over and over in my mind, word by word, separately and together, until I accepted them all as the unintended compliment they were, grappled them to me with hooks of steel, slid that precious amulet into my medicine pouch, and (my muse nodding and smiling now, nodding and smiling) wrote, in rebuttal, "Damn straight, pal. I can live with all three of those terms, separately and in tandem. Carve 'em on my tombstone."[9]

And then, finding myself at long last in the mood, nodding and smiling along with her, sat down under my muse's eye to put this essay into its final form.

Nobody much likes criticism. For that matter, nobody much likes critics — an unfortunate fact demonstrated by countless historical events, the forced suicide of Socrates only one of them.

Artists, in particular, often have an antipathy to critics. Here's Philip Wylie, one of my favorite neglected novelists:

". . . when and if we reach the state of cannibalism, I shall try to eat a critic. There should be good crackling around fat heads."[10]

And Pablo Picasso:

"People who try to explain pictures are usually barking up the wrong tree."[11]

And the painter Max Beckmann:

"Of all the dim-witted enterprises doomed to failure from the start, talking and writing about art is surely the worst."[12]

More sympathetically, there's this insightful comment on the peculiar plight of critics of the nonliterary arts, from the sculptor Henry Moore:

> [Art critics] are at a rather serious disadvantage, you know, relative to literary critics, for they are obliged to express their responses to an art work in a medium altogether different from that of the work they are responding to. The literary critic is after all trained to use the same expressive tool — language — as the poet or novelist he writes about. Not so with art critics. It seems to me they struggle with a heavy burden of translation.[13]

If all of that is true (and I must confess I do not disagree with any of those four opinions), then why would anyone in his or her right mind bother to read criticism — or, even worse, to write it?

The basic answer comes, I think, from the hemlock drinker himself, Socrates, who enunciated the fundamental tenet of what was once called the life of the mind: "The unexamined life is not worth living." Anyone who values intellectualism — that is, anyone committed to being truly thoughtful — knows the truth of this, and knows that he or she is therefore already a critic.

Many years ago, during an undergraduate class in literature at the Bronx campus of Hunter College in New York, my alma mater, Professor Leonard Albert was trying to explain to us the meaning of a key concept: *critical distance,* that ability to step back from even the most engrossing work of art or emotionally embroiling situation in order to observe and assess it disinterestedly.

"There was a traveling Shakespearian troupe in the Old West," he recounted by way of example (perhaps, I now think, a purely fanciful one), "that came into

Dodge City for a performance of *Othello*. In the middle of the fourth act, a cowboy in the balcony got so upset that he stood up, pulled out his six-shooter, and killed the actor who was playing Iago." He paused for a moment, then added, "Now *that* man lacked critical distance."

I was reminded of this a quarter of a century later, when, while browsing through an issue of the *Village Voice*, I came to the advertisements for various psychiatrists, therapists, and New Age health practitioners. The headline on one ad caught my eye. "DO YOU SUFFER FROM CRITICAL DISTANCE?" it read, then went on (approximately) thus: "Do you experience moments of detachment from your feelings? Are you unwilling or unable to be up-close and personal every single minute of your waking life? Our one-on-one treatments and encounter groups can help you!" How about that, I mused . . . a capacity I've worked hard all my life to attain is now defined as a disease.

Obviously, in a culture that's historically demonstrated itself to be anti-intellectual, where the therapeutic model prevails and our relation to art is almost terminally contaminated with the deadly mix of gossip and intentionalism, the forces dominating that culture will do their level best to discredit critical thinking. Trivializing it by defining it as a neurosis seems a clever strategy, and will probably work with many. Resisting that tendency—maintaining the ability to think critically about anything, even one's most cherished beliefs—remains a genuine triumph, even if it goes unrecognized and unacclaimed.

The music critic Robert Commanday speaks of the "active listener or everyman critic," insisting that "properly, everybody should be one." He adds, "Considering the value of an experience is simply part of experiencing it and fixing it in the mind. . . . When the listener, no matter how imperfectly, acts on the need to establish the meaning, the value or just the nature of the music heard, . . . the circuit of the artistic experience is completed."[14]

And, lest you think that it's presumptuous to take as true the folk wisdom "everyone's a critic," consider what the film scholar P. Adams Sitney says: "Criticism is not a profession, it's a disposition of the soul at certain moments."[15] If we agree with him—and I do—then it follows that the people we identify as critics are simply those who have made this disposition into a calling, or at least a profession; the working critic is someone who chooses to live the examined life continually, and in the public eye.

When you leave the jazz club, the concert hall, the quadplex, the theater, the gallery or museum, concerned only with whether or not you enjoyed yourself, you have simply passed your time. But once you not only acknowledge your pleasures and displeasures but exercise that "disposition of the soul," you have stepped into the territory of critical thinking.[16]

Entering that terrain is risky business. The personal hazard is implied by something else that Sitney said: "Criticism, like biography, is the process of falling out of love with your subject."[17] Now, falling out of love (by which I take Sitney to mean relinquishing one's infatuations or unanalyzed emotional responses) can be sobering and painful. It certainly doesn't mean not loving anything; it means not loving blindly, but instead learning to truly see things for what they are — and then loving them, if one still chooses to, warts and all. As the photographer Robert Frank has said, "[C]riticism can come out of love."[18]

But to love someone or something is also to take the risk of hating it — or at least hating aspects of it. After all, hate is only the obverse of love, its flip side. The true opposite of love is not hatred but indifference. You can love something and hate it simultaneously, but you cannot do either and also be indifferent to the subject of your attention.

One does not need to establish critical distance in relation to something one finds affectless or irrelevant; only if one has been gripped by it does one have to find a way to disengage. No critic writes well or usefully about works or issues to which he or she is truly indifferent. Only that which evokes passion merits attention. Passion comes, of course, in two basic flavors. And while writing about work one loves is one of the most pleasurable aspects of a critic's work, I've come to the conclusion that such acts of appreciation are not the essence of the critic's task.

Critics in our time and culture wear many hats. Sometimes they're also reviewers, providing quick-take consumer-guide reactions to the available artistic "merchandise." Sometimes they take on the role of interviewer, biographer, historian, appreciator, theorist, eulogist. All of these are valuable functions; they fulfill necessary tasks. But, after twenty-eight years as a working critic, having tried my hand at all of the above, I must report that none of them is at the core of what I do. The fundamental truth is that I and my colleagues in criticism — at least those of us who do our jobs right — are in the destruction business.

Many people, including many of those same colleagues, are fond of disguising this difficult truth from others and even hiding it from themselves by evoking the notion of something they call "constructive criticism." To me, that's an oxymoron; there ain't no such animal. Man Ray was right: "All criticism is destructive, most of all self-criticism."[19]

The root of the word *criticism* is the word *crisis*. As Roland Barthes reminds us, "To criticize means to call into crisis."[20] The job of the critic is *calling into crisis* the subject of the critique. My own metaphor for this is the metallurgical process known as *stress analysis*. Calling something into crisis, subjecting it to stress analysis, not only exposes its structure but accentuates and aggravates its flaws.

Stress analysis exacts a toll: The thing under scrutiny frequently shatters or collapses — or else, seeing it for what it truly is, with all its inadequacies and weaknesses laid bare, we "fall out of love with it."

Why on earth would anyone want to chance that? I can think of two reasons. The first, simply, is curiosity: to understand how the thing was made, what ideas and decisions went into it, how the sum of those holds up under pressure. The second is growth: to learn from those flaws so that one can build a better one next time. (Keep in mind here the Chinese ideogram for *crisis,* whose components are *danger* and *opportunity.*)

But building a better one next time is not the task of the critic. Nor is it incumbent upon him or her to instruct the artist on how to go about doing so. The critic's chore ends when the destruction is complete, when the stress analysis test is over. The rest — including the cleaning up — is left to others.[21]

Another way of thinking about this is to recognize that the critic functions as a *radical,* in the original meaning of the word — which comes from the Latin word for root, *radix.* The radical is one who insists on examining things from the roots up. Such a diagnostician is not likely to be popular among true-believer types, whose blind faiths insulate them from self-doubt and justify all deeds. Critics who take their obligations seriously plant themselves as roadblocks on the highways of groupthink, obstacles in the path of mindless majority rule. They are not unlike the "free radicals" about which I've read in contemporary biophysics, molecules containing unpaired atoms. In a stable, healthy biosystem — a well body, for example — it seems the free radical can attract atoms from other molecules, upsetting the organism's ecological balance and causing illness. Interestingly, though, in a sick body the immune system actually produces free radicals to combat infection from bacteria and viruses.

If we take this as a metaphor, we might propose that the critic-as-free-radical destabilizes his or her sphere of influence by pulling individuals away from consensus, from the easy conformism embedded in that epitome of *argumentum ad populum,* the locution "as we all know." Does this do a service to his or her culture, or an injury? Obviously, the answer depends on whether one believes one's own culture to be healthy or sick.

My view is that, however nostalgic we may be for a past in which things remained stable and static for long periods of time (or so we like to imagine), we live in an age of flux in which stasis proves fatal, for, as Bob Dylan wrote years ago, "He not busy being born is busy dying." In such an environment, the very presence of the magnetic tug of the free radical, the persistent nay-saying of the critic, keeps us healthy by forcing us to remain always aware of the full range of perspectival options, the availability — and utility — of different points of view, the unlikelihood that we are absolutely right about anything.

Yet there, in a nutshell, is why critics are unpopular. It's their job to be fault-finders, spoilers and contrarians: to break spells, ruin moods, poop parties, rain on parades, disrupt consensus, point out the emperor's nakedness, resist seduction, and speak truth to power. Power rarely likes to hear the truth. In fact, since truth makes a habit of unpleasantness, most of us, powerful or not, are loath to hear it with any frequency. Critics, when they set about their fundamental task, are generally the bearers of bad tidings, and the inclination to kill the messenger runs deep in the human psyche.

Obviously, one does not engage in these actions and emotions lightheartedly. They spring from intellectual passion, and, when effective, they evoke the passions of others. As a critic, you must be willing to stand by your words or be prepared to eat them. Because criticism in its most highly realized manifestation — as commentary in the agora — demands recognition as a public act.

There may be artists who genuinely make art "for themselves," whom I would define as amateurs by virtue of that choice. (More on that anon.) There are certainly professional artists who for various reasons — painful shyness, for example, or a distaste for the dominant trends of their time — have kept their work largely to themselves: Emily Dickinson and Franz Kafka are instances. But I guarantee you that there are no naïf, "outsider" or undiscovered critics, no folks posting critical commentaries on billboards in their front gardens, no trunksful of great unpublished critical essays moldering in someone's attic. To function as a critic is to publish, so as to engage in a public dialogue.

And that means to risk stress analysis yourself, to be constantly calling yourself into crisis and putting yourself in the way of finding yourself in that state. For if you publish, you will be read — by your fellow critics, by artists, by others in the field and by the general public. And if you're read, you will be disputed, sometimes even reviled. Peculiarly, critics not only expect that, they usually delight in it. I have yet to meet a single critic worth his or her salt who isn't surprised and disappointed when people widely or entirely agree with them (or merely remain silent), and who doesn't turn gleeful when sparks start to fly. Malcontents and troublemakers, the lot of us.

However, you can't upset those not yet conceived — or at least they're not prone to writing argumentative, denunciatory letters to the editor. So critics work for the audience of their own time, not for readers to come. The bonus value of doing so is that one may thereby sometimes contribute to the establishment and continuity of a critical tradition. The function this serves for the future, for history, for the ongoing life of a medium, the literary critic Hugh Kenner described in these words:

> There is no substitute for critical tradition: a continuum of understanding, early commenced. . . . Precisely because William Blake's contemporaries did not know what to make of him, we do not know either, though critic after critic appeases our sense of obligation to his genius by reinventing him. . . . In the 1920s, on the other hand, *something* was immediately made of *Ulysses* and *The Waste Land,* and our comfort with both works after 50 years, including our ease at allowing for their age, seems derivable from the fact that they have never been ignored [emphasis in the original].[22]

Becoming part of such a "continuum of understanding" is all the reward from the future a critic could ask.

That's what's in it for the critic. This brings me to several additional questions: Why should the public read criticism? And why should artists pay any attention to it?

In answer to the first, John Perrault has said, "There is a need to read about art as well as to look at it. The timid read art criticism to have their opinions and their investments confirmed; the brave to have them challenged."[23] In fact, a regrettably large number of people are so timid that they cannot even formulate independent opinions in the first place, and instead treat criticism as a source of ready-made substitutes for ideas and opinions of their own, doing what was once called "copping an attitude." This is perhaps the worst use to which criticism can be put by its readers; unfortunately, it's one that no critic can protect against.

Conversely, as Perrault suggests, the best reason to read critics is to call your own responses and opinions into crisis. Criticism can be said to begin at the point where we set aside or move beyond our simplest reactive patterns, unsatisfied with mere declarations of taste. Nothing closes off a discussion of a work of art so completely as the assertion, "I like it." For, as we so commonly aver, you can't argue with taste; criticism, on the other hand, is for arguing with. And one of the main stimuli for some of our most heated and productive arguments about art is the curious fact that many images important to us do not appeal to our "taste." I do not consider the taste patterns of critics to be of paramount importance. Certainly I don't assume that my own interest anyone but me. More significant by far are our lines of reasoning, the methods by which we approach the works that draw our attention, the variety of ways in which we ask the four questions that define intellectual activity: *Why? Why not? What if?*

Suppose I'm wrong? It's for those experiments in inquiry that we still read long-dead critics, writing about works long exhausted and forgotten.

For the audience, then, the critic functions as a stimulus to involvement and a sounding board off which the audience can bounce its own reactions to the works. After all, the excitement of becoming a member of what the late Minor White referred to as "the educated audience" goes beyond the pleasure of one's initial direct experience of the work, and also past one's later reflective reconsideration of it. Art, if it matters, is also a manifestation of our culture, our time. Criticism, John Berger suggests, "is always a form of intervention: intervention between the work of art and its public."[24] Actively engaging with the critical dialogue that emerges around a medium is a way of using art as a positioning device, a means for exploring yourself in relation to the field of ideas in your own day, of finding out what your culture has gotten up to and where you stand within it.

Moreover, the critic serves the audience as living proof that one can say no: no to specific works or entire bodies of work, no to one or another tendency in art, no to the spin put on the work by this or that functionary, no to the biases of institutional emphasis and exclusion. In a globalized art economy increasingly modeled after and intertwined with multinational capital, whose art-related products and presentations thereof spring less and less organically from within the cultural environments in which they appear, such exemplification of and permission for individual nay-saying has an empowering effect, to which I'll return shortly.

As for artists—well, I'd hardly presume to tell artists that they *should* read critics, especially critics of their own work. But I'm more than willing to suggest why they *might*.

Artists of course share membership in the audience for art, though they approach the field as performers in it; presumably, criticism of work other than their own has a usefulness to artists not unrelated to its function for other members of that audience.

Whether appreciative or caustic, commentary on their own work can carry a potent emotional charge for artists. There is, after all, a profound connection between what we do and who we are. Jesus reportedly said, "The tree is known by his fruit." To the extent that our deeds, our actions in the world, have an integral relationship to our central sense of identity, we feel ourselves indistinguishable from the work that we do, the things that we make—and criticism of that work, those things, seems necessarily and inarguably criticism of us.

The critic has an obligation to walk a fine line in this regard, recognizing the artist's sense of oneness with and inseparability from his or her art without ever slipping into a critique of the private person, whose precise, authentic relation to the work the critic cannot (and should not) pretend to know. The correlation between an artist's personality and life and his or her creative output remains always slippery and inexact; delightful people sometimes make dreadful work, while genius may well appear in appalling characters.

It strikes me as less than useful to transform the critical arena into a killing ground on which to parade one's hostilities toward individuals (though it remains appropriate to view critical discourse as not only a marketplace of ideas but a battlefield on which they contend, sometimes to the death). The critic is properly restricted to addressing only the deeds, the works themselves, and the lives those live in the world, regardless of his or her response to the works' makers. Responsibly undertaken, that challenge validates Nietzsche's comparison of the critic to the mosquito who bites not because he wants to but because he must, who "desire[s] our blood, not our pain."[25]

In that light, artists certainly should feel free to pick and choose among those who respond to their work, and are entitled to dismiss or bypass entirely anyone whose reaction is clearly the product of personal animus. Beyond that, not all critics prove themselves equally substantive and useful. As Man Ray noted, "Taste and opinion cannot replace intelligence and knowledge."[26] Far too many critics function only as tastemongers and starmakers.[27] This does no service to anyone. John Berger points in the right direction, I think, when he writes, "I have come to see that the arranging of artists in a hierarchy of merit is an idle and essentially dilettante process. What matters are the needs which art answers."[28]

It is in the short- and long-term response of the audience that the artist will discover what the needs are—beyond private satisfaction—that his or her own work answers. As a rule, the artist can only guess at this.[29] Perhaps it would be ideal if the artist could interrogate the receivers, the audience, ourselves. This could be done; someone may well have already attempted such an experiment. The utterances of all those who've commented publicly on a particular work could be scanned and correlated for recurrent mentions of particular aspects, similarities of interpretation, and such. Polls could be taken of museum-goers, interviews recorded with owners of prints. Perhaps we would learn something of value by this.[30]

But the effort would be enormous (not to mention the expenditure). As things stand, the most efficient, accessible, and dependable source of that response (at least for artists who don't perform in front of live audiences) will be critics—those atypical members of the audience, willing to work at the difficult and thankless task of articulating their reactions and perceptions and putting them out on the table.

Those "needs which art answers" that John Berger speaks of are, of course, the needs not only of artists but of the culture in which they live. He appears to assume, as do I, that we are speaking of artists concerned not merely with self-expression but with communication — because criticism is irrelevant to self-expression. And most art-making up until the Renaissance in European culture, at least, and through the present day in many cultures, does not prioritize self-expression. Quite the opposite, in fact. From cave painting through Egyptian statuary and African sculpture to the rock concert and Mai Lin's Vietnam memorial, the concerns of the individual psyche of the maker have played second fiddle to the communal functions of art.

I consider self-expression an act or function whose effectiveness has only one judge — the person doing the expressing; as I have no training in psychoanalysis, it lies outside the parameters of my expertise. It's my opinion that the statement "You're not expressing yourself well" is semantic nonsense. If a relative dies and I opt to manifest my response by (a) wearing black for a year, (b) throwing a party and tying one on, or (c) going about as if nothing had happened, no one but I can tell whether I've expressed my reaction effectively.

Self-expression, then, is fundamentally solipsistic as a final goal; intentionally, it serves no one but the person doing the expressing. For that reason, as I pointed out previously, it is the primary concern of only those artists who work "for themselves" — that is, those who are thereby self-defined as amateurs.[31]

Here, by the way, my muse and I part company; she insists that serious artists, even those we would classify as professional, have no obligation to take their audiences into account, no conscious relation to the process of communication, only the imperative to answer the felt urge toward self-expression. By no means does she find herself alone in this belief; many artists in all media issue such disclaimers.[32] Curiously, however, quite a few of them (my muse among those) speak nonetheless about critical misinterpretation of their own work and the work of others, the audience's failure to "get it," and so on. If one can misinterpret work, then, presumably, one can interpret it correctly (or, at least, more correctly in some cases than in others). Which means it has identifiable content that allows for a range of more or less accurate reading by others. Like so many artists, my muse here wants both to have and to eat her cake, claiming indifference to the audience while at the same time aspiring to find one.

Professionalism *per se* does not guarantee work that is better or more devotedly made. There are good professional artists and bad ones, just as some amateur artists are better than others. Many amateur artists have made a piece or two of work that's of professional caliber, and some amateur artists are consistently superior to some professional ones. Yet the obdurate fact remains: In art, as in every other field of human activity, amateurs and professionals play before different audiences, in different leagues, by different rules, for different motives, and for different stakes.

From my standpoint, to place one's work into the public sphere, before the polity, is by definition a political act, and an active solicitation of response. Even if the origins of that work lie in the self-expressive impulses of the maker, one cannot take its presentation to others as anything but an effort to communicate. I consider that the defining act of the professional artist (and, for that very reason, I restrict my critical attention to work that appears in public).

In addressing work that's publicly presented, a critic has every right to assume that (unless informed otherwise by the maker) he or she engages with the work of a professional artist. The professional artist may begin with the urge toward self-expression but is eventually concerned with something beyond that: communication. That commitment to communication involves acknowledging the existence of the Other — embodied in some audience, whether actual or hypothetical, identifiable or imagined. This acknowledgment is signalled by accepting the imperative of a shared symbol system, the first requisite of communicative activity. (If I wish to convey to some Other that my relative's passing has caused me grief, I'd best employ the cultural rituals of mourning; drunken revels, however much they might salve my wounds, are not widely equated with tears.)

This does not mean that all communications must be reduced to the literal or simplistic; states of mind and feeling are among the transmissions we receive from artists. Nor does it mandate any artist's uncritical adoption of some extant symbol system lock, stock, and barrel; one of the functions of professional artistic activity is the generation of new symbols and the redefinition of older ones. But it does imply that the professional artist is producing not mnemonics for him/herself but communications, *messages* — intended to be received, open to interpretation, and subject to evaluation.

Unlike self-expression, the effectiveness of communication can be evaluated, and its substantiality and usefulness can be judged. Failure to communicate is a frequent phenomenon, due to either some flaw in the transmission process or the absence of a shared symbol system. If the audience laughs at the object with which you sought to make them gasp in fright, you the maker have probably failed to manipulate the symbolic structure effectively so as to evoke the psychoids of fear. The audience thus serves the artist not only as a target for the communication but as a tool for refining its delivery.

This suggests that the meanings of a particular work of art, however complex and ambiguous they might be, are to some extent specific and determinable — at least within their own culture in the era of their making. Certainly some artists believe this to be true. Let's go back to Picasso for a moment. Here's something else he proposed:

> [Paul] Valery used to say, "I write half the poem. The reader writes the other half." That's all right for him, maybe, but I don't want there to be three or four thousand possibilities of interpreting my canvas. *I want there to be only one.* . . . Otherwise a painting is just an old grab bag for everyone to reach into and *pull out what he himself has put in.* I want my paintings to be able to defend themselves, to resist the invader, just as though there were razor blades on all the surfaces so no one could touch them without cutting his hands. A painting isn't a market basket or a woman's handbag, full of combs, hairpins, lipstick, old love letters and keys to the garage" [emphasis in the original].[33]

Now it's true that no meaningful work of art is merely an empty vessel into which one is free to pour whatever emotions and ideas one happens to have on hand at the moment. The artist isn't obligated to lead us by the nose to his or her meanings. But—unless he or she is satisfied with any old response any of us might make, regardless of its appropriateness—it is the artist's job to point the audience toward some territory of interpretation, an arena in which possible meanings battle it out for dominance.

At the same time, there are always aspects of a work of which its maker is unaware. And, while an artist can certainly have conscious intentions in regard to the work, we must beware the intentionalist fallacy. "Between the intention and the act falls the shadow," wrote T. S. Eliot. Any work's actual effect is at least partly determined by the audience, as I. A. Richards has argued.[34] And, as communications theory assumes, there is always a difference between the message sent and the message received.

When an artist pays attention to it, the audience's response to his or her work functions as what the founder of cybernetics, Norbert Weiner, first defined as the "feedback loop."[35] In communication theory, the feedback loop is any device used to measure performance so as to narrow that gap between intention and effect. Certainly one of the useful functions audience response in general and criticism in particular can provide to the artist is its service as feedback, as *information.* Used as a gauge of the differences between the message sent and the message received, such information enables the artist to use past performance to improve future performance.

If we agree that art is a manifestation of the cultural *zeitgeist,* the "spirit of the times," then one role of the critic in society is to serve as one of the culture's feedback mechanisms. Performance evaluations, if honest and thorough, are often less than favorable, and no one is ever expected to like the bearer of bad tidings. But no culture (and no individual psyche) has ever remained healthy that acquired the habit of disregarding its feedback and killing its messengers. Culturally and individually, giving and receiving criticism can easily bring out the worst in us; yet it is the only sure path to the discovery of what our best might be.

With all of that said and done, I come at last to that bullet my muse demands I bite, the function of nay-saying as such, the moral necessity of it. Let me then get to it.

Whether or not it was ever so, what we call culture in our time — including art, of course — to a considerable extent has become something constructed by and/or under the direct supervision of power, and foisted prefab onto the populace. The international marketing system for art can serve as sufficient example for this top-down imposition of art on the general public. A great many critics play far too complicitous a role in that structure, when they should instead be redressing the imbalance of power therein, providing a countervailing resistance, operating in the public interest, articulating the legitimate concerns of the populace in this manufacturing of culture.

The opinions of the citizenry in this regard are rarely solicited by curators, museum directors, grants panelists, arts administrators, and the assorted other gatekeepers who serve as functionaries of this complex, extensive merchandising and indoctrination system. On the contrary, let the average citizen raise his or her voice in anything but blind, wholehearted worship of the entire contemporary enterprise of art and the howl of indignation and scorn becomes instantly deafening. (Witness the dismissal of the working class manifested in the supportive art-world testimony about and editorial commentary on the Richard Serra "Tilted Arc" controversy.) If thoughts could kill, as in Shirley Jackson's grim parable "The Lottery," then much of the Midwest would be scorched earth right now, torched by the disdain for its inhabitants concentrated in New York's SoHo and related art ghettos in Los Angeles, Chicago, and a few other cities.

A century ago, Robert Louis Stevenson noted that "enthusiasm about art is become a function of the average female being, which she performs with precision and a sort of haunting sprightliness, like an ingenious and well-regulated machine."[36] This condition — its symptoms most prominently visible among docent lecturers and press-release writers at museums — has spread widely during the intervening years, across genders and gender persuasions, so pervasively that even those who have not succumbed to it feel obligated to defer to its sufferers. As Harold Rosenberg pointed out in the early 1970s,

[I]t is inconceivable that any exhibition can be mounted that would cause people to guffaw or howl. What has vanished is not advanced art, as the Nazis planned, but the independent and unruly spectator — the inexpert citizen who laughs when a picture (as of two dressed-up men conducting a debate with a naked lady on the grass beside them) strikes him as funny and who is irritated when works are boring. The outstanding fact about art in the past fifteen years is the restoration of public piety toward works under official auspices; it extends to anything, from pre-Columbian pot-sherds to big-edition prints, that has entered the precincts of art history. While avant-garde art was pulling down the pillars of the Salon, art theory was already toiling to restore them.[37]

The situation has only gotten worse since Rosenberg penned that observa-tion — with the signal exceptions of such recent debates as the Serra case and the Mapplethorpe / Serrano / National Endowment for the Arts flap, which sug-gest that unruly spectatorship may be making a comeback. Though the orches-tration by the fundamentalist right of the latter uproar cannot go unconsidered, the fact remains that informed and knowledgeable opposition to government subsidy of these works prompts the same hysterical art-world defensiveness as does ignorant knee-jerk reaction. The necessity for uncritical support of the arts, which of course serves all those who toil in the urban vineyards of art marketing and presentation, has spread as an article of faith throughout the brainwashed audience for contemporary art.

So cowed has that audience become by high-financed art-world propaganda that many of them have taken to parading around wearing on their heads, their handbags, their chests and backs — in the form of buttons and T-shirts and stickers — one of the most idiotic slogans I've ever come across. It emerged in the early 1990s, during the NEA brouhaha just previously mentioned, and it reads, in its entirety, "Fear No Art."

The fatuousness of this notion steals the breath away. It implies, nonsen-sically, that all art is good (and, presumably, good for you!) — and, at the same time, that art as a phenomenon is powerless, incapable of doing you harm. All of these insinuations are lies.

Let me speak briefly, then, about what so few of my colleagues seem willing to mention, much less identify: bad art.

To begin with, let me distinguish between what I'll call bad art and what we might consider mere failed art. Please note that I'm not speaking here, under either rubric, of the derivative picture-postcard floral studies of your local cam-era club, the amiable beachscapes produced by the amateur watercolorists in your community, the well-made macramé and pottery in your neighborhood art fair, or any of the thousand varieties of similar ersatz generated by people sincerely, if ineptly, trying to locate and externalize their own creative impulses in professionally unambitious, basically harmless ways. Such work, grounded in a notion of art-making as primarily therapeutic, crafts-centered, and hobbyist, rarely solicits and even more rarely attracts serious critical attention, and hardly ever requires it, save when the occasional eccentric curator mounts a show of "thrift-store paintings."

So the terrain I'm outlining encloses work produced by serious, craft-competent, working professional artists seeking to have, or succeeding in having, their works entered as reference points into the field of ideas for art activity in their own time, and the critical discourse around those works and ideas.

Much of that art, inevitably, doesn't make the grade — that is, doesn't prove provocative, resonant, or durable for any audience, even the most knowledgeable, even one composed of astute fellow practitioners. This is failed art, a large quantity of which gets generated in the production system for the art of Western culture nowadays. (It seems unlikely that the same statistics applied during the Gothic period, for example, or in African art at any time.)

Except to the extent that our encounter with it can exhaust our capacity to attend to art that in some way succeeds, or can even preclude our coming across the latter, failed art is not to be feared (only dreaded, perhaps, by the overburdened working critic).[38] Indeed, contemplating it critically often proves instructive, for the lessons it offers that only failure teaches. Nonetheless, to quote my former colleague at the *New York Observer,* Hilton Kramer, "Failed art is no less a failure even when all the conditions of failure have been accounted for."[39] Such work must be dealt with ruthlessly, if only to clear the decks. Someone has to put the art that pulls up lame out of its misery, and the critic is the only one likely to do so in public and on the record. This may discourage its producers, which is well and good; in a culture that, unprecedentedly, now produces far more art than it can consume, those who can be discouraged should be.

Beyond such art — art that proves itself tendentious, overwrought, less than fully realized, imaginatively limited, excessively derivative, vapid, too facile, merely clever, etcetera — we must come to terms with art that's problematic on deeper levels and in more pernicious ways. I refer to art (and art-related activities, such as its institutional presentation, for example) that, regardless of the presence therein of manifest genius, critical analysis reveals as deceitful, hypocritical, bullying, venal, in service to totalitarian forces, pandering to our worst prejudices, vicious, even sometimes murderous in its impulses.

Does such art exist? In my opinion, yes; surely each of us can name some loathsome, reprehensible, vile masterpiece. I'd cite Griffith's *Birth of a Nation,*

Riefenstahl's *Triumph of the Will,* and anti-Semitic aspects of the writings of Pound, Eliot, and Céline as evidence. They bring to fruition or contain the seeds at least of something that, beyond the explanations of even the most serious and cogent psychoanalysis, I believe one must judge to be *bad*—morally, ethically, philosophically flawed, with some degree of severity. (I would go so far as to describe some such work as *evil*; but that term discomfits many nowadays, so for the purposes of this argument I substitute its milder version.)

If we agree that some art, past and present, fits that description, then pretending otherwise serves no useful purpose. Nor should we mistake the censuring of such work for censorship thereof, and flinch from the former in order not to appear to propose the latter, out of some misguided protective impulse. "[W]e do art no honor and no justice," wrote Jacques Barzun, "when we represent it as invariably humane, heroic and disinterested in its intentions, exclusively good in its effects, and thus not subject to reproach and accountability."[40]

Precisely because its creators used their considerable craft expertise, artistic abilities, and access to inspiration to render those ideas palatable by making their works credible and seductive, such art proves *fearsome*. Its opposition falls to the critic as an unavoidable responsibility.

Identifying it as such, and attaching that identification to it in the marketplace of ideas, becomes the obligation of all who recognize its insidiousness and its potency, for art in all media has demonstrated extraordinary powers of persuasion. (Why else, as my muse insistently points out, would every dictator in our century have made absolute control of art a key element of totalitarian strategy?) And, as the analysts and explicators of the applications of those ideas and those powers, critics either stand against them or assist in their dissemination. The regimes of our century have all had their house critics along with their pet artists, and dissident critics of art have joined dissident artists in concentration camps and gulags, have had their heads too thrust to the chopping block.

I do not mean to imply that the uncovering of evil—or, if you prefer, of the morally wrong—in works of art can be achieved unerringly, and that these determinations can (or should) stand undisputed. Nor do I suggest that only one standard for gauging good and evil (mine) exists or deserves priority. Of course those evaluations remain open to debate; but, for that to be true, the debate must be opened in the first place. I mean rather that, in the words of Heinz Lubasz, "moral problems are real, irreducible and vital even when they are insoluble,"[41] and critics of art must find the courage to grapple with them in the arena of public discourse about art.

Finally, I do not want to appear to promulgate the belief that the only fearsome art is that which I adjudicate (my own choice of adjective here) as evil. I have encountered other art that I've found terrifying, though for different reasons — for its shattering insight into our individual and collective psyches, for example. The visual art of Francis Bacon and Francisco Goya, the writings of Marilyn French and Carolyn Forché, the photographs of Robert Frank and Joel-Peter Witkin, have generated profound tectonic shifts in my life, permanently altered my ways of thinking, feeling, seeing. While ultimately their effect proved nourishing to me (or I found nourishment in them, not always the same thing), their initial effect on me was enormously disruptive.

Those works, and works by many other artists in all media, have persuaded total strangers to rethink their fundamental assumptions, challenge the received norms of their acculturation, overcome their inhibitions, and otherwise change their lives. Though those changes were not always expected, or welcome, we — myself among them — learned to accommodate ourselves to them, for they left us little choice. That too is power, great power, fearsome in its own way.

Whether or not we share similar tastes, there is work like that in my life, and I expect there's work like that in yours; if there weren't, I doubt that we'd bother looking for more of the same, and reading and writing about the process. Proposing that art at its most potent poses no genuine threat to anyone or anything resembles nothing so much as telling your houseguests that your growling dog is toothless and can do them no worse harm than pissing on their shoes. I have a higher respect for the impact of art on culture than that. Were I given to button-wearing, in fact, mine on this subject would read thus:

Fearsome Art!
(and more of it)

Some of this I know my muse wanted to hear: that I accepted fully my involvement in the destruction business, my role as professional scold, the critic's position as "the disciplinarian of the arts" whose "function is to FRY the artists in kettles of boiling oil." (Her words, those. You'd like her. Trust me.) She no doubt will not find all her reservations overcome by this last draft, however. I have revised it primarily to get it, and not her, off my back, where I expect her to stay, periodically thumping my shoulder. Still, I hope it will both mollify and chasten her.

Perhaps it is my nature to act more bloody-mindedly in practice than in theory. On the bench, I've demonstrated my willingness to impose life sentences, even without parole. Yet I believe in the possibility of redemption, so I hesitate, where my muse clearly does not, to mandate the death penalty. Do I see myself as more merciful than I appear to those whose work comes to stand before me, and those who read my decisions? Could be. Perhaps, even if I fill the role of "hanging judge," I just admire and model myself after those who maintain a certain dignity, and see to it that the ropes are properly adjusted, the defendant treated courteously. Some like their executioners blunt, callous, and brutal. That's not my style. A matter of taste, in the last analysis; nothing you can argue with.[42]

NOTES

1. "Contribution to the Critique of Hegel's Philosophy of Law" (1843–44); reprinted in *Karl Marx/Frederick Engels, Collected Works* (Moscow: Progress Publishers, 1975), p. 177.

2. From my notebooks, source unknown. An apology for the absence of full citations for the sources of some of the quotes in this essay. Some come from notebooks I kept at the outset of my work as a critic, which began shortly after I left graduate school, expecting never again to write a footnoted essay; others have been passed along to me by correspondents, colleagues, and students who failed to annotate their origin. I would welcome their identification, confirmation, and/or correction.

3. The only exception of which I'm aware was the *Village Voice,* whose editors—on the occasion of my forced departure from its pages—censored dozens of letters that were written in relation to my final column in those pages, and in expression of concern and indignation over the censorship that resulted in my resignation. See "Minor White: *Octave of Prayer* (I) and (II) in *Light Readings: A Photography Critic's Writings 1968–1978* (New York: Oxford University Press, 1979), pp. 140–49; (second edition, Albuquerque: University of New Mexico Press, 1998).

4. Dear X: I appreciate your taking the time to write to me. However, I have to say "Thanks, but no thanks." After twenty-eight years in the field, I remain astonished at the fact that no one in photography seems to understand the difference between appreciation and support. The former without the latter constitutes nothing more than lip service. One of my mottos is, "Lip service is better than no service at all," but the utility to me of lip service has diminished considerably over time.

I'm well aware that there are numerous folks out there reading me, putting my reviews of their projects on their vitae and including them in their press kits, photocopying my work and using it in classes, and so forth. And I wouldn't at all mind hearing from them, might even reply to their private letters to me from time to time, did they actually constitute a genuine base of support. Unfortunately, they don't.

If everyone who's ever written to me like you, or spoken to me privately in this vein—to tell me how much they enjoy my writing, how useful they and their students find it, how important to them was my support of their work (or their way of working, or of some cause in which they believe, or freedom of expression in general), etc.—had in return taken the trouble just *once* over the years to write a letter to the editor of any publication to which I contribute, in order to add their voices to the dialogue on any subject and indicate that they read me with respect and interest, my life as a professional critic and a working writer would have been and would now be radically different. (I'm sure the same holds true for many of my colleagues.) I wouldn't expect that from the casual or occasional reader of my work, but it seems not unreasonable to look for it from the core of my readership, my fellow toilers in the vineyard.

Since I see such public feedback and debate in just about every periodical I read devoted to other subjects—politics, music, art, literature—I'm forced to conclude that the sophisticated audience for photography is uniquely *irresponsible:* in the fundamental sense of the word, *unable to respond.* I've begun to speculate, darkly, that perhaps something in the very nature of the medium itself actually attracts the irresponsible and feeds that incapacity in them. Even enlightened self-interest appears insufficient to overcome this basic inertia. I find it noteworthy—perhaps you will as well—that not even any of those to whose defense I've rallied publicly over the years when they were under censorious or other attack have ever bothered to send an open letter to the publication involved expressing thanks for that support.

Surely it was not your intent—which I have no doubt was just the opposite—but, at this stage of my professional life, I find backstage go-get-'em-kid encouragement like yours actually disheartening, just further proof that I take all my public stands alone; and I would prefer that you spare me any more of it. I'd propose to you the following as an appropriate rule of thumb: Don't presume to take up to a single minute of any public commentator's time with unsolicited private correspondence—no matter how flattering—until you have taken a public stand, at least once, pro or con something that person has published or said in a public forum, or have otherwise actively involved yourself in the public discourse to which he or she devotes such energies.

If you have something to say about my work henceforth, favorable or otherwise, the pages of just about every publication for which I write are, as a matter of policy, open to your comments. Sincerely, /s/ A. D. Coleman

5. A. D. Coleman "Why I'm Saying No to This New Arbus Book," *New York Observer* 9, no. 37 (October 2, 1995): 25.

6. For an analysis of this publication's umbilical tie to Random House (not coincidentally, Malcolm's publisher), see Richard Kostelanetz's investigative 1974 essay, "The Leverages of Collaboration," reprinted in his recent collection, *Crimes of Culture: Three Decades of Citizen's Arrests* (New York: Autonomedia, 1995), pp. 89–106. Malcolm's comments appear in her review of the Arbus book, titled "Aristocrats," *New York Review of Books* 43, no. 2 (February 1, 1996): 7–8. It's reprinted in the second edition of her collection of essays, *Diana & Nikon: Essays on the Aesthetic of Photography* (New York: Aperture, 1997)

7. Mark Power wrote that remarkable statement in a response to my essay that he circulated privately. In the published version of his reaction, he modified it somewhat, to "the right of privacy pales beside the necessity of ensuring that great art sees the light of day." See Mark Power, "Wielding the Scalpel," *The Photo Review* 19, no. 2 (Spring 1996): 5, 7–11. As I write this, I remain the only person who found either version of that position sufficiently objectionable to warrant refutation in print. A commentary by Anthony Georgieff—taking a position quite similar to Power's—eventually appeared: "Dead Woman Seeing," *European Photography* 17, no. 2 (Fall 1996): 74.

8. Mark Power, "Wielding the Scalpel," p. 9.

9. For my full response to Power's diatribe, see "Diane Arbus: Untitled, Part II—The Responses," *The Photo Review* 19, no. 3 (Summer 1996): 9–12.

10. Philip Wylie, *Opus 21* (New York: Rinehart & Co., 1949), p. 198.

11. From my notebooks, source unknown.

12. From my notebooks, source unknown. Beckmann also said, ". . . words are too insignificant to define the problems of art." The latter is quoted in Stephan Lackner, *Max Beckmann: Memories of a Friendship* (Coral Gables, Florida: University of Miami Press, 1969), p. 50.

13. Franz Schulze, "Henry Moore at 80: 'an artist must remain a mystery to himself,'" *ARTnews* 77, no. 6 (Summer 1978): 68–73. "Art critics have taught me next to nothing," this statement, to be found on p. 68, begins.

14. "Everybody Should Be a Critic," *San Francisco Chronicle*, Review (September 12, 1982): 14.

15. In conversation with the author, summer 1985.

16. "When we say 'It was great,' we are actually saying 'I liked it.' And 'I liked it' (or its antithesis, 'I disliked it') may, depending on its context, become the first step in the critical act. In any case, it remains a very small one, since unless the question 'Why did I like it?' follows, an act of criticism has not been initiated. 'I like it,' when it stands alone, is only a grunt of approval and while one has every right to grunt, let us not mistake it for other than it is. 'Why did I like it?' demands development and will invariably lead to further questions about one's self as well as to those about the celluloid strip. Since these are the two ingredients of film, film criticism has

begun." Joy Gould Boyum, and Adrienne Scott, "The Critical Act or I Just Saw Barbarella: It Was Great," *Film as Film: Critical Responses to Film Art* (Boston: Allyn and Bacon, 1971), p. 9.

17. In conversation with the author, summer 1985.

18. Robert Frank, "A Statement," *U.S. Camera Annual 1958* (New York: U.S. Camera, 1957), p. 115.

19. Man Ray, "To Be Continued Unnoticed," exhibition portfolio, Copley Galleries, Beverly Hills, Cal., 1948. Reprinted in *Man Ray* (Los Angeles: Los Angeles County Museum of Art/Lytton Gallery, 1966), pp. 23–24.

20. Roland Barthes, *Le Plaisir du Texte* (Paris: Editions du Seuil, 1973), pp. 25–26.

21. Several years ago, when I was using this metaphor of stress analysis during a lecture on criticism, I was greeted after my talk by a man who told me that his profession actually *was* stress analysis. Well, I asked him, did he think my analogy was apropos? "You may not believe this," he replied with a grin, "but when we joke around at the lab, do you know what we call our work? *Art criticism.*"

22. Hugh Kenner, *The Pound Era* (Berkeley and Los Angeles: University of California Press, 1971), p. 415.

23. John Perrault, "Power Critics," *Village Voice* 28, no. 42 (October 18, 1983): 81.

24. John Berger, *Art and Revolution: Ernest Neizvestny and the Role of the Artist in the U.S.S.R.* (New York: Pantheon Books, 1969), p. 9.

25. "IN FAVOUR OF CRITICS — Insects sting, not from malice, but because they too want to live. It is the same with our critics — they desire our blood, not our pain." From "Human, All-Too-Human: Part I, Miscellaneous Maxims and Opinions," in *The Complete Works of Friedrich Nietzsche,* edited by Dr. Oscar Levy (New York: Gordon Press, 1974), vol. 2, p. 82.

26. Man Ray, from an artist's statement in a limited-edition portfolio of prints, *les voies lactées* (Turin: Il Fauno, 1974), n.p.

27. For more on this issue, see the essay "Interesting Conflicts" in my book *Tarnished Silver: After the Photo Boom* (New York: Midmarch Arts Press, 1996).

28. John Berger, *Art and Revolution.*

29. My muse argues with this, proposing that artists, inherently informed by their connection to what C. G. Jung called "the collective unconscious," intuitively and always correctly perceive these needs and automatically produce in response to it — that, virtually by definition, the needs they feel and those of the culture are identical. Though of the Jungian persuasion myself, and willing to accept my muse's formulation as it might apply to previous eras, I am not convinced by what strikes me as both grandiosity and oversimplification in its relation to our own quite different times. Specifically, I find problematic its equating of, say, the work of a medieval sculptor of cathedral gargoyles — or that of a Van Gogh, obsessed but critically disregarded in his own lifetime — with the output of a typical graduate of our current academic-art context who produces work in which no audience or market or circle of practitioners shows the slightest interest, intending primarily to persuade doubtful parents that the money spent on expensive art-school education was not wasted.

30. The recent experiments by the Russian expatriate team Komar and Melamid suggest that such experiments are not impossible.

31. I do not seek here to ennoble professionals by denigrating amateurs; instead, I hope only to reverse a peculiar tendency in the visual arts generally and photography circles in particular to treat amateur standing as something for which one should strive. Tracing its origins among visual artists goes beyond the scope of this essay; in photography, we can track it back at least to the posturing of Alfred Stieglitz, and some of his disputes with Edward Steichen, though even today the medium has its ardent advocates of perpetual amateurism, such as David Vestal. Interestingly, outside the visual arts no serious practitioner feels honored by description as an amateur: imagine Merce Cunningham taking pride in maintaining amateur status as a dancer and choreographer,

James Brown doing so as a musician, Meryl Streep as an actress, Richard Meier as an architect. The very notion is comical.

Nonetheless, these definitions should not be mistaken for value judgments. The substantive issue is the distinction between vocation and avocation, between one's job and one's hobby. One's hobby is always enjoyable; anytime it stops being fun, one can disengage from it. One's job is not necessarily fun — often, in fact, it is frustrating, boring, and genuinely unpleasant — but one performs it anyway. The amateur is free to perform whenever he/she feels like it; the professional puts in a full work week, regardless of mood or whim.

Financial success is not the gauge; Jackson Pollock was no less a professional painter when he was starving in a Greenwich Village loft than he was a decade later when his paintings were selling in the five figures. The point is that painting is what he did for a living, even if the living he made from it was lousy for quite a while; it was the epicenter of his life, and whatever else he did to generate income was done strictly to enable him to paint. When Pollock got out of bed to go to work, his workplace was in front of his canvas.

Artists take on all kinds of work to support themselves, of course, and — as recent polls have reiterated — few make enough to live on from their creative activity. Sometimes the borderlines between the professional artist, the part-time artist, and the amateur are blurred, to be sure.

These comments on this subject found an earlier manifestation in "Expression and Communication," my introduction to the exhibition catalogue for "Photographers Dialogue," curated by Steven Carothers and Gail Roberts (Boca Museum of Art, Boca Raton, Fla., October 19– November 26, 1989). That essay turned into a series of three pieces for *Darkroom Photography:* "Amateur Standing vs. Professional Stature" 12, no. 3 (March 1990); "Check Your Focus: Is Your Artistic Expression Directed Inwardly or Outwardly?" 12, no. 4 (April 1990); and "Vox Populi," 12, no. 5 (May 1990).

32. Andres Serrano, for one; see my report on a panel discussion in which he and I participated, in my book *Critical Focus: Photography in the International Image Community* (Munich: Nazraeli Press, 1995), pp. 38–40

33. Quoted without citation of source in Sol Worth, "Man Is Not a Bird," *Camera Lucida* 5 (1982): 32.

34. See, for example, Richards, *Practical Criticism: A Study of Literary Judgment* (New York: Harcourt, Brace & World, 1961, a reprint of the original 1929 edition). Elder Olson's comments on related matters in the concluding "Metacriticism" section of his *On Value Judgments in the Arts and Other Essays* (Chicago: University of Chicago Press, 1976) are also pertinent.

35. See Norbert Weiner, *The Human Use of Human Beings: Cybernetics and Society* (New York: Avon Books, 1967), pp. 36–39.

36. *Virginibus Pueresque* (1881).

37. "The Art World: The Big Show — Art and the Crowd," *The New Yorker* 49, no. 11 (May 5, 1973): 103.

38. For more on this issue, see "The Vanishing Borderline," elsewhere in this volume.

39. "Schnabel Go Home! MoMA's Latin Mess," *New York Observer* 7, no. 23 (June 14, 1993): 1, 23. Even a stopped clock, I remind you, is right twice a day.

40. From my notebooks, source unknown.

41. From my notebooks, source unknown.

42. This essay is based on the text of a lecture that was first delivered at Loyola College, Baltimore, Maryland, on December 7, 1989.

On Redaction

It's been said (and I can testify to the truth of this) that professional writers are those who find writing more difficult than the average person. I've a close colleague, a photographer, who finds photography more difficult than the average person. Because I value his penchant for close readings of texts, last year I burdened him with a collection of my essays from the past decade for analysis and comment. One of his responses was to demand clarification of a motif recurrent in several of the essays. I'll quote to you the relevant passages. The first is from "Silverplating the Dandelion," a review of a duotone-printed monograph and traveling exhibit valorizing a set of relentlessly banal snapshots by Father James Harold Flye, the mentor of James Agee:

> Photography is, in its relation to the casual camera user, an inordinately generous medium. Most anyone who exposes a goodly amount of film (or even a small amount, regularly, over a long period of time) ends up with a certain proportion of negatives which, appropriately rendered in print form, could provide images of at least passing interest.
>
> Many snapshots do not transcend the closed network of private reference points for which they're made. Yet if their subjects are clearly stated, and if the equipment employed in their making is not so "hopelessly sophisticated" (Minor White's wonderful phrase) that it confounds the user, then images which articulate the commonness — the mutuality — of some fundamental human experiences sometimes result. Virtually everyone who makes snapshots will have a few. Think of them as dandelions: nice, bright little things, easily propagated, hard to distinguish from each other, plentiful, growing everywhere. . . .
>
> Working . . . without commitment to craft or deep interest in the pro-

cess, Flye functioned like any casual snapshooter. And photography, in its generosity, rewarded him as it does most snapshooters — by not interfering with the laws of statistical probability. Like every "sporadic" photographer, Flye lucked into an occasional image of mild attractiveness. And — time and nostalgia operating as is their wont — four decades later some of those pictures have acquired a faintly enjoyable patina as relics of another era.

They do not, however, constitute a "body of work," an oeuvre. Erratic, technically inept, lacking any true hermeneutic underpinnings, addressing no photographic issue at length, they are only what they are — a random assortment of occasionally charming snapshots by a dilettante. In short, a small handful of dandelions.

. . . Any competent and well-educated young photographer should be able to take any readable negative and render therefrom a tonally attractive and visually structured print. Certainly any photographer with a grounding in current modes of photographic practice could go through anyone's negative file and find a selection which, strategically printed, might appear to be at least tangentially relevant to some of the serious work done in photography over the past half-century.[1]

The second passage is from "Slim Pickings in Hog Heaven," a critique of Garry Winogrand's book *Stock Photographs*:

Winogrand once said, "You see something happening and you bang away at it. Either you get what you saw or you get something else, and whichever is better you print." But statistical probability is on the side of the small-camera photographer who "bangs away at it" — this is a very generous medium insofar as accident is concerned, surely the most generous of all the visual arts in that regard. And working a livestock show and rodeo is — for a grab-shooter like Winogrand — hog heaven; in such territory, potential "art photographs" are as plentiful as flies. Anyone who exposes as much film under such circumstances as has Winogrand, only to come up with such slim pickings, is hardly dependent on (or even touched by) luck. . . . Editing and sequencing are the only means by which Winogrand could give meaningful shape to the amorphous by-product of his omnivorous image-mongering, but he has cheerfully abdicated any control over those procedures.[2]

There's what my colleague asked me to elaborate: What did I mean by referring to photography as "generous"? And, if the medium *was* generous, how was serious activity therein defined? This is a first stab at an answer.

As a medium of artistic production photography is unique in many ways. One of these is that, at least in many of its forms, the medium encourages large-scale production and even over-production. (Consider that you cannot see a single exposure on a roll of film without developing the entire roll. No graphic artist has to draw thirty-five additional sketches — or waste an otherwise blank pad of paper — in order to see the first sketch from any session.)

For most workers, the ratio of potential images (negatives) to actualized images (prints) is low, as is the ratio of images actualized minimally (as contact and/or work prints) to images approved by the maker for public presentation via exhibition, publication, or other vehicle.

The question of *redaction* — of "putting in shape for publication" — is therefore a crucial one. To use a distinction from general systems theory, redaction is what transforms a quantity of images from a *heap* to a *whole*. The ability to redact is a hallmark of artistic maturity. As the photographer Lonny Shavelson has said, "Photography is about editing. If you don't edit your own work, you're not a photographer."[3] But photography has a peculiar attraction for artists who are incapable of confronting the challenge of redaction. There are surely more mulch heaps of imagery unredacted by their makers in photography than in any other visual art medium. And the unredacted heap has a peculiar attraction to certain types of curatorial and critical temperaments.

Let us take a case in point. Suppose I were to tell you that you were about to have slightly over a third of a million 35mm black-and-white negatives — negatives whose maker had never even seen them, much less edited them — dropped in your lap, to do with as you will. Would you consider that a blessing or a curse?

Some consider such bequests a bounty. Here is a passage from a Museum of Modern Art press release:

> When the photographer Garry Winogrand died at the age of fifty-five in 1984 he left more than 2,500 rolls of film — much of his last three years of shooting — that had been exposed but not processed. Because of a $14,000 grant from Springs Industries to the Museum of Modern Art, this film has now been developed. Walter Elisha, chairman and chief executive officer of Springs Industries, said: "Springs' previous commitments to photography have supported existing work of known quality. In this case we felt it was important, in light of Winogrand's prior record, to rescue this last of his work for study and evaluation. We felt the photography community would not want to risk losing what Garry Winogrand's last work might say to all of us."
>
> John Szarkowski, director of the Department of Photography of the Museum of Modern Art, stated, "Some of the film that Winogrand left undeveloped was presumably close to the point of deterioration. If those pictures were to be preserved, it was essential to develop the film without

much further delay. Winogrand was, in his first years as a photographer, an exceptionally prolific worker. In his last years his shooting became voracious — perhaps five rolls a day, seven days a week. We will soon be able to see whether this last work added something of consequence to his extremely influential earlier achievement."

. . . In addition to the film developed posthumously, approximately 7,000 additional rolls were developed by Winogrand late in his life, but not proofed. Winogrand's associate, Tom Consilvio, who during the past decade produced most of Winogrand's finished prints, was entrusted . . . with the job of developing (by inspection) the film that the photographer left unprocessed.

John Szarkowski said that "the Museum will mount a retrospective exhibition of Winogrand's photography, with an accompanying publication, after completing the very large job of studying the contribution of this extraordinarily fecund and original artist."[4]

Given 342,000 negatives (that's Winogrand's 9,500 rolls at 36 exposures each), it would be editorially possible to make dozens, perhaps even hundreds of radically different photographers out of this magpie's nest of negatives. Certainly it will be possible for Szarkowski and his co-workers to concoct any of a dozen Winogrands therefrom. Will it be a Winogrand who took off in dramatically new directions, or one who reverted to the concerns of his younger days, or one who hewed to his "mature" style, or one who tunnelled deeper into one specific area of concern? Why, that's what we'll call "curator's choice" — one of the privileges of playing Maxwell Perkins to Winogrand's Thomas Wolfe. (Legendarily, Perkins, Wolfe's famous editor, hacked self-contained chunks out of Wolfe's endless, undifferentiated manuscript production.)

What, then, are we to do with such midden heaps? Told about this Winogrand material, the same colleague whose query instigated these ruminations had a simple answer: "Pitch 'em out." A less drastic solution would be to paper the walls with randomly selected contact sheets. But in the case of Winogrand, I tend to concur with my colleague. How seriously are we to take the droppings of a gluttonous voyeur who spent the last seven years of his life producing a third of a million negatives without bothering to look at any of them, much less analyze them critically? This was not a photographer; this was a *shooter,* afflicted with a textbook case of terminal distraction, the quintessence if not the prototype of the dreaded "Hand with Five Fingers" you may have seen in Nikon camera ads on TV.[5]

Is it accident that Szarkowski has been the most corporately sponsored curator in the history of photography? Or that his protegé, Winogrand, was surely one of the medium's most corporately sponsored workers as both a commercial hack and a gallery artist? Or that both shared a commitment to a model of photography that venerates the single image over the various extended forms, the unresolved mulch heap of the posthumous negative file over the thoughtfully redacted body of work?

There is a connection here. The power structure has something to gain by the discreditation of the sustained narrative that is embedded in a carefully redacted oeuvre, by a disregard for the authorial autonomy of a work's maker, by the promulgation of the fragmented and incoherent, by what Richard Kirstel has called "reverence for the intensity of the glimpse."[6]

The power structure profits from our distraction. If we can be seduced into voluntarily interrupting our concentration frequently — say, 342,000 times in seven years — how much careful attention will we be able to pay to anything, especially the actions, patterns, and systems of that structure itself? Preoccupy us with a steady flood of data and we will lose our ability to organize it into information — and never have time to digest it into the coherent structure of narrative, which is the first step toward understanding. Yield the prerogative of redaction to management — whether management takes the form of picture editor, curator, critic, or historian — and you fundamentally disenfranchise labor, as Walter Benjamin argued so eloquently in his essay "Author as Producer."[7]

Szarkowski is particularly prone to curatorial situations that enable him to arrogate the power of redaction to himself; thus he can serve as a paradigm of this curatorial tendency. Consider his relation to the work of Winogrand, as demonstrated above, alongside his relation to the work of Diane Arbus (whose own stringent redaction was posthumously violated by her MoMA retrospective), E. J. Bellocq, Eugène Atget — and, most recently, Josef Albers.

A particular scent distinguishes the curator who lusts after the unredacted. You had a whiff of it in the press release I just cited. Perhaps you can sniff it in the following passage, describing Szarkowski's first encounter with a group of imagistically tedious and technically mediocre photographic prints that Albers had never exhibited, but instead had squirrelled away in his workroom:

> Shortly after finding the treasure trove of photographs, I [Nicholas Fox Weber, executive director of the Joseph Albers Foundation] informed John Szarkowski of what we had. Baited by the idea of portraits of Klee and Kandinsky, as well as by the studies of breaking waves and trees in winter and other such work, Mr. Szarkowski made the journey to New Haven. It took little time for his scholarly demeanor to be softened by a broad smile. "These are not just a painter's photographs," he explained. "They are the works of a first-rate photographer." It was occasion for a martini at lunch, "to celebrate a major achievement and a great body of work."[8]

There you have it—the spoor of the sensibility whose impulse is to *own* whatever work it can—to be in a position to define and aggrandize it with no contradiction from either the maker or the work itself.

But Szarkowski is hardly alone in this predilection. One can see it in Julia Scully and those others who worked on the Mike Disfarmer "Heber Springs Portraits" project, and those who have tried to make the Staten Island hobbyist Alice Austen into a seminal documentarian. One can surely find it in the writings of Michael Lesy (most problematically, in his case, in the section on the amateur Angelo Rizzuto in his book *Visible Light*);[9] Lesy's redeeming quality is that he both recognizes and acknowledges this inclination, thus making it a deliberate aspect of his work. At its most macabre, one can witness it in the machinations of that gaggle of ghoulish exegetes who, feeding off understandable parental grief over a suicided adolescent, have taken a not-untypical accumulation of student work and converted it into an ideological cottage industry: the putatively crypto-feminist "oeuvre" of Francesca Woodman. This is one of the few instances I know of where the cradle and the grave have been robbed simultaneously.[10]

What am I suggesting here? Should all anonymous photographs be automatically discarded? Should all unredacted work by identified photographers be destroyed, or left unexamined? Obviously not.

What I propose is that a commitment to taking photography seriously—whether one is a photographer, critic, curator, historian, archivist, or simple looker at pictures—begins with the recognition that the terms *body of work* and / or oeuvre in photography are to be reserved for those segments of a maker's output that have been *prepared for public presentation by the maker him/herself, or at least under his/her supervision*. (Please note that they need not have *achieved* public presentation; an unpublished book dummy is nonetheless a redacted body of work.) Those redacted segments constitute the whole of a photographer's body of work; the rest—no matter how much it may attract us—is merely part of the heap.

How are we to determine that portion of a photographer's output that might constitute a *body of work*? By scholarship, simple scholarship. Any image published, exhibited, or sold under the maker's name during his or her lifetime must be considered a part of the oeuvre; so, too, should be any images that did not reach the public but were clearly intended to—because they exist as finished, approved, exhibition-quality prints, or are included in book dummies or magazine layouts, or because the photographer's papers and notes make it evident that public presentation of a particular image was intended, or at least hoped for. Furthermore, categorization and / or compartmentalization established or adhered to by the photographer (for example, distinctions between "personal work" and commercial, applied, commissioned, or otherwise bespoke imagery) are to be respected through scrupulous annotation and clear labeling.

We have no difficulty, for example, in determining the contents of the oeuvres of Edward Weston, Aaron Siskind, Berenice Abbott, and Imogen Cunningham. These are redacted bodies of work. We will never be able to identify as an oeuvre any portion of the recently published work of "Itinerant Photographer," who passed through Corpus Christi, Texas, in 1934.[11] And we have avoided for the past twenty-five years the necessary and relatively simple task of identifying the oeuvre of Diane Arbus.

At the time of her death, Arbus had exhibited and published very sparingly (aside from her so-called magazine work). No more than four or five dozen of her personal images had been validated by her for public presentation. That is what constitutes her oeuvre, that and nothing else (save for the "magazine work," if one is to consider her full career in photography). All those shows and publications are known; her contributions to them would be easy to identify. Why is it that no one — not even her biographer — has taken the trouble to do so? Could it be because, as a total oeuvre, sixty images is hardly enough to support a major international reputation? Would that explain why her work-print and negative files were rifled after her death, in search of images she'd never approved, to bulk up and thereby validate a major retrospective and monograph? That is appropriation with a vengeance, whose purpose can only be to leave the photographer entirely out of the picture.

Hand in hand with such scholarship, we should require annotation in all exhibitions and publications (and on all prints made and distributed after a photographer's death) distinguishing between images redacted by the photographer and those selected by others. This would permit scrutiny and even display of a photographer's "sketches" — even his/her contact sheets — without conflating them with those images that the photographer considered to be resolved, finished works. (Examples of the responsible handling of such material are the Lustrum Press book *Contact: Theory* and the Da Capo Press volume reproducing all of Walker Evans's Farm Security Administration images.) Certainly, if a negative has never been seen by a photographer — as is the case with much of the Winogrand material, some of the Arbus material (at least according to rumor), and much work by photojournalists and press photographers — that fact should be indicated. Finally, as previously mentioned, the photographer's own distinctions (if any) between various forms of work must be honored.

The lack of clear policy and standard practice in this area seriously muddies the water for scholarship, historiography, and criticism. Estates — and the ambitious entrepreneurs who serve them (including not only galleries and private dealers but often curators, critics, scholars, and historians) — have a vested interest in inflating the oeuvre; the larger it is, the more they have to hype and to vend. So long as the current lax practice is permitted to reign, it will be understandable that uninformed pundits like Susan Sontag will feel free to opine that — except when defined as "all photographs taken by the same photographer" — there is no such thing as a body of work in photography.[12]

Critics, scholars, historians must make these distinctions — and must protest, publicly, when they are not made by others. We must be ready to guard against this impulse in ourselves, and to identify and denounce such conflation of the heap with the whole, particularly when it involves the attribution of *intent* to any part of the heap. Intentionalism is always a fallacy, but nowhere more corrupting to critical thought than when, lacking any evidence, it is premised solely on the intuition of the image's reader. Here, if nowhere else, the line between the facile act of reading into photographs and the more arduous task of reading out of them must be drawn by any responsible critic.

It follows from this that photographers, and their estates, should give serious thought to placing restrictions on the publication and/or exhibition of unredacted material; such display, without scrupulous annotation, does a serious disservice to any artist's true oeuvre, and impeaches subsequent criticism and scholarship thereof.[13] It also follows, I think, that photographers themselves should be paying more attention to redaction, making clear — through preparation and annotation — what is discarded/unrealized.[14]

Until some minimal qualifications for entry are established — until we have identified guidelines for discriminating between a *body of work* and any old batch of photographs — there will be no true canon in photography to be taken seriously. There will only be what we have now: a monstrous, constantly growing heap, a veritable heap of heaps. If we truly aspire to make of it a whole, I have this to say to you, my friends and colleagues: Wishing will not make it so. The time for major amputation is upon us.[15]

NOTES

1. "Silverplating the Dandelion: The Canonization of Father Flye's Snapshots" was first published in *VIEWS: A New England Journal of Photography* 2, no. 2 (Winter 1981): 31–32. Reprinted in A. D. Coleman, *Tarnished Silver: After the Photo Boom* (New York: Midmarch Arts Press, 1996) pp. 88–93.

2. "Slim Pickings in Hog Heaven" was originally published in *Camera 35* 26, no. 8 (August 1981): 20–21, 80. Reprinted in A. D. Coleman, *Tarnished Silver,* pp. 94–98. I had the Winogrand quote slightly wrong; it goes, "You respond to something you see, 'bang away at it,' and either it happens or something else happens, and whichever is better you blow up." Quoted in Jonathan Brand, "[Critic's Choice:] The Most Sophisticated Seeing That Ever Came Out of a Zoo," *Popular Photography* 63, no. 6 (December 1968):139.

3. Lecture, New York University, fall 1986. Shavelson is hardly alone in his belief in this regard. Consider the following comment from photographer Thomas Roma:

"As a photographer, I understand just how crucial a role in photography editing plays. After pictures are taken, a photographer must make a series of critical decisions, starting with looking at contact sheets and choosing which images to make into 'proof prints.' (A proof print is a kind of rough draft of the final, finished photograph.) The next decisions are even more important: Which of the proof prints should be made into final prints, and thereby become part of one's body of work? The photographs must meet self-imposed standards. Most photographers agonize over these choices.

"The question is not simply whether a picture is 'good,' in some formal, technical sense, but, Does it mean what I need it to mean? Writers can edit sentences that may be well-crafted but that don't express an intended thought. But in photography, there are no revisions: A photograph is in or it's out, and the photographer must live with the consequences of his or her choices."

See his review, "Looking into the Face of Our Own Worst Fears Through Photographs," *The Chronicle of Higher Education* (October 31, 1997): B11. I'd disagree with his assumption that the making of a "final print" automatically qualifies an image for inclusion in the body of work, however.

4. Press release No. 17, February 1986, Museum of Modern Art, New York.

5. For my critique of the eventual MoMA production involving this material, see "At Modern, Winogrand 'Unedited,'" *New York Observer* 2, no. 28 (August 1, 1988): 10. Reprinted in A. D. Coleman, *Critical Focus: Photography in the International Image Community* (Munich: Nazraeli Press, 1995), pp. 8–10. The Nikon ad referred to was part of a late-1980s campaign.

6. In conversation with the author, variously.

7. Reprinted in Victor Burgin, *Thinking Photography* (London: Macmillan, 1982), pp. 15–31.

8. Nicholas Fox Weber, "Preface," *The Photographs of Josef Albers: A Selection from the Collection of the Josef Albers Foundation* (New York: American Federation of Arts, 1987), p. 10. As this example suggests, such terminal hyperbole tends to metastasize with frightening speed. Here's further evidence: by 1995, less than a decade later, photography had become "a lesser-known but fundamental aspect of Albers's creative output. . . . Far from being a hobby or a means for considering problems he would solve in other mediums, Albers's photographs speak with an authority found only in the most celebrated voices of twentieth-century photography." ("SURVEY OF JOSEF ALBERS'S WORK IN GLASS, PAINTING, AND PHOTOGRAPHY AT THE SOLOMON R. GUGGENHEIM MUSEUM," Press release #685, May 10, 1995, Guggenheim Museum, New York.)

9. Michael Lesy, *Visible Light: Four Creative Biographies* (New York: Times Books, 1985), pp. 3–36.

10. See the essays by Ann Gabhart, Rosalind Krauss and Abigail Solomon-Godeau in the catalogue *Francesca Woodman: Photographic Work* (Massachusetts and New York: Wellesley College Museum and Hunter College Art Gallery, 1986).

The generic quality of Woodman's juvenilia is readily apparent to anyone who taught photography on the college level between 1970 and the present. For one of many possible illustrations of parallel graduate-student inquiry into the issues of self-scrutiny and female identity predating Woodman's efforts in this vein, see Caren Sturmer's sequence, "The Scream," in the catalogue of the exhibit "Extended Realism" (Baltimore: University of Maryland Baltimore County Library, 1976). My comments thereon can be found in the catalogue essay for that group show.

The valorizing of Woodman's work and the enshrining of its unfortunate maker have obscured the larger sociological phenomenon of which it is merely one instance: the emergence, in the early 1970s, of this genre of work as a recurrent exploration among the women — mostly young, mostly white, mostly middle- and upper-class — who were part of the nascent "art photography" education system.

11. See Sybil Miller, *Itinerant Photographer, Corpus Christi, 1934* (Albuquerque: University of New Mexico Press, 1987).

12. *On Photography* (New York: Farrar, Straus & Giroux, 1977), p. 137. Sontag's entire discussion of this issue (pp. 131–38) is remarkable for its confusion.

13. This becomes even more crucial an issue now that the U.S. Supreme Court, in its wisdom, has declared that the privilege of privacy does not pertain to one's garbage; anything discarded in the trash, even if sealed in bags or cans, thereby enters the public domain. Thus paper shredders are now essential equipment in photographers' darkrooms and offices. See Uviller, H. Richard, "The 4th Amendment: Does It Protect Your Garbage?" *The Nation* 247, no. 9 (October 10, 1988): 302–4.

14. Brett Weston set a remarkable example when, on the occasion of his 80th birthday in late 1992, he burned all his negatives at his home in Carmel, California—a redactive act significant enough that it was covered by the Associated Press, among others. For a report on this bold gesture, see the *British Journal of Photography*, 139, no. 6853 (January 2, 1992): 6.

15. This is a slightly revised version of the text of a lecture delivered during the panel "Creating the Canon: Writing History," on Saturday, October 17, 1987, at the Ontario College of Art in Toronto, Canada, as part of the "Talking Pictures" conference sponsored by Toronto Image Works Ltd., *Photo Communiqué* magazine, and the Holocene Foundation.

Documentary, Photojournalism, and Press Photography Now

PRELUDE

The first chapter of the 1984 edition of Upton and Upton's now-standard introductory text, *Photography,* is titled "Photographers at Work." It comprises profiles of individual photographers who, it is claimed, represent specific "fields" of photography. To typify the field they label "Documentary Photography/Photojournalism," the authors chose Susan Meiselas, whose coverage of turmoil in Latin America has been published around the world. For the sake of argument, I'm going to assert that the Uptons made a terrible mistake: regardless of her own training and intentions, Susan Meiselas — her recent MacArthur Fellowship notwithstanding — is only occasionally allowed to be a documentarian, even less frequently a photojournalist. For the most part, in the way in which her work is publicly presented, what she is (*de facto,* though I think not at all by her own choice) is a press photographer. And, speaking more broadly, most of what's described as photojournalism isn't.

I. WORKING DEFINITIONS

In the communications environment of our time, the modes of still photography on which we most depend for reliable information about the social and political context in which we exist — those overlapping forms we loosely call "documentary," "photojournalism," and "press photography" — are very much in flux. All three have changed drastically in the last third of this century, as a result of complex interactions between such factors as the imperatives of practitioners, the editorial/distribution systems that deliver their work to the audience, the expectations and desires of that audience, and the emergent new technologies for visual communication. All three will continue to change, as network news shows supplant newspapers, as video supplants the still image, and as electronic imaging undermines the claim to credibility of all forms of digitized lens imagery.

Originally, the function of two of these forms — *documentary* and *photojournalism* — was informational and/or representational. It was the general purpose of those involved to *inform* — literally, *give form to* — what would otherwise be a welter of dissociated data; their intent was "to bring clearly before the mind" the events of their time — that being the primary definition of *representation*. This seems no longer to be the case, yet we continue to talk about them as if those terms still meant what they were taken to mean forty years ago. If we examine these changes and their causes, some new, more applicable understandings may emerge.

Pursuing this argument requires some definitions, which are sorely lacking in most discussions of this topic. Let me propose a few, provisionally — not to be taken as fixed or absolute, but rather as approximate dividing lines between categories that often overlap.

I don't think it's appropriate to define these forms in terms of the specific subject matter addressed, since that can range from the death of a child to the birth of a nation. There's no proscribing or prescribing the subjects about which we might desire informational/representational material. All we can safely say in this regard is that producers and consumers alike appear to operate on the assumption that such imagery is not primarily concerned with the private life or inner landscape of the photographer. Instead, it is taken for granted that such work addresses events external to the photographer, occurrences in what we refer to as the "real world."

Similarly, we can't define these forms usefully in terms of image-making techniques or imagistic styles. Documentary projects have employed 35mm cameras, while photojournalists and even press photographers have utilized large-format equipment at one time or another. Stylistically, these forms range from the fixed, confrontational stare of Lewis Hine to the gestural, furtive glimpses of Henri Cartier-Bresson.

Nevertheless, these forms do have characteristics, some of them structural, some conceptual, and some performative. For each of the three forms under discussion, I'm going to propose its relationship to several aspects that are central to informational/representational imagery in general. This should make some basic comparison possible.

Let me begin with *documentary photography*. Implied in this term (at least when used to describe activity beyond the perfunctory and/or applied[1]) is *extended form* — that is, a work composed of a sizeable number of images. I can think of no documentary project that consists of a single image; it is, in fact, arguable whether any single photograph can be identified with any certainty as "documentary" (or, to put it another way, whether there's any single photograph that can be readily determined to be *not* documentary on the basis of internal evidence alone).

Some relation to text is a given, even if it's only minimal, as in the identification of subject, date, and location; the text may, in fact, be extensive. Excepting the increasingly rare cases of governmentally and corporately sponsored endeavors,[2] editorial control over any text is assumed to be vested, at least in part, in the photographer, whether or not she or he is the actual author;[3] control over image selection and sequence — and, for that matter, initiation of the project itself — is also assumed to rest with the photographer. The photographer involved in such a project is responding primarily in terms of his/her own point of view — or what Richard Kirstel calls the *personal matrix of distortion*.[4]

There is no external time limit implicit in this form; some documentary projects (August Sander's study of German society, Edward Curtis's *The North American Indian*) have stretched over decades. For this reason, the documentary photographer is likely to have the opportunity to refine the project, not only through the analysis of the work-in-progress at various stages but even by the reshooting of unsatisfactory segments of the work.

The elaborate nature of such projects lends itself to subjects that are seen as enduring; for much the same reason, the final forms they assume tend to be durable: the book and the exhibition have to date functioned as the primary embodiments of documentary projects, though certain audio-visual formats (principally videotape and slide-sound) are serving this purpose with increasing frequency. Occasionally, documentary projects have magazines as their vehicles; few, if any, ever find their intended final form as newspaper presentations.

Photojournalism also implies extended form; its basic structure is the picture essay. Since, as its name implies, its primary vehicle is the journal, the magazine, or newspaper, there are size/length restrictions imposed by the editorial and graphic traditions of the periodical(s) sponsoring or presenting the work. As the name also implies, some relationship to text is inherent in this form — sometimes nothing more than bare-bones captioning, but often more extensive informational/editorial commentary. This may be provided by the photographers themselves — I think here of W. Eugene Smith, Margaret Bourke-White, Philip Jones Griffiths, David Douglas Duncan, and many more — or by a reporter collaborating with the photographer.

By the nature of the business (at least in its most common manifestations under virtually all political/economic systems), editorial control here is ultimately vested in the editorial/financial hierarchy of the journal, with the photojournalist presumably a trusted and semiautonomous extension thereof. Though essay themes may be initiated by the photojournalist, they must be approved by the editors prior to publication (sometimes also by the publishers), and are often assigned. Control of image selection, sequencing, and layout, as well as textual determinations, rests with management, though often in consultation with the producer(s) of the work. So, while the photojournalist may bring his/her own matrix of distortion to any particular project, it may well be contravened and even overpowered by the editor's and publisher's biases.

Some external time limit is the rule in photojournalism; only a few essays stretch over months in the production stage, and it's a rare one indeed that extends over an entire year. Some of the reason for this is economic; some has to do with the nature of the publications themselves. The photographer working in this mode will have some opportunities to assess and refine the work at intermediary stages, but the subjects addressed are often of such a topical and immediate nature that this will not be a dependable aspect of the working method.

The subjects acceptable to and/or assigned by editors of periodicals are likely to be not only topical but even transitory. Compared to the documentarian, the photojournalist's investment of time and energy in any essay is likely to be superficial. The final forms for such projects tend to be temporary and disposable — journals (which may mean magazines, newspapers, or both) with a short shelf life, or television news shows on rare occasion.[5] While some photojournalistic work does get preserved in book form, the book — by definition — is not the primary vehicle for such work. Nor, obviously, is the gallery or museum exhibition.[6]

This brings us to *press photography,* which we might define operationally as the provision of pictures to fill specific editorial needs. The press photographer is not engaged in a delimited project, in any sense, but is instead providing an ongoing service — the rapid production of specific images whose use is largely predetermined. Such use is largely oriented toward the single image; a three- or four-image cluster is as close as the press photographer is likely to come to extended form.

The image will almost undoubtedly be accompanied by text; indeed, its meaning will be almost entirely constructed by that text (the "grip and grin" is a classic case in point). The press photographer will have no control over that text, and usually no connection with it — not even contact with its author. Nor will she or he have much say, if any, about any other aspect of the image's utilization. Moreover, the human subject or subjects of the press photographer's work increasingly determine not only what the photographer will be allowed to see but the vantage point from which she or he will be allowed to observe it; the carefully orchestrated "photo opportunity" has become the norm.

The photographer's own matrix of distortion under these circumstances will likely be suppressed in favor of a posture of neutrality. With the inflection of the image so completely at the disposal of others, the manifestation of an individual point of view can only be erratic at best. This is exacerbated by the imposition of an absolute and extremely short time limit — one or two days' notice, in most such assignments. The chances of reshooting the image, or even thinking through the assignment in advance, are exceedingly slim.

Since the press photographer's relationship to his/her subjects is inevitably hurried, the images that result are likely to be stereotypical and ephemeral. Their most logical vehicle, thus, is the ephemeral publication, particularly the daily newspaper. Moreover, there are types and styles of images that editors are habituated to/looking for, and that are for various practical reasons more suitable than others to the layout patterns and reproduction quality of such publications. Experimental deviations from the predictable, no matter how successful, are rarely welcome.

Sometimes a selection of images may be compiled, by a periodical's picture editor, into a "picture story" containing images by several press photographers, but whatever statement such a sequence makes has more to do with the editor's attitudes than with the photographers' own.[7]

INTERLUDE

Perhaps my reasons for proposing that Susan Meiselas is a press photographer are becoming clearer. I should indicate, at this juncture, that I not only admire Meiselas's abilities as a photographer and respect her commitment, but am also sympathetic to her politics and purposes. What I am offering, therefore, is not an accusation but a lament.

Meiselas, given her druthers, seems intent on not only witnessing but bearing witness to some of the major social crises of our time. While she is capable of producing extraordinarily powerful single images, her preference is for working with extended forms in situations that provide her with maximum control over the accompanying text; she is well aware of the extent to which such text serves as what Roland Barthes called the "anchor" and "relay" for photographs, shaping the way in which the viewer comprehends the work. (A show at the New Museum for Contemporary Art in New York some years ago, "The Nicaragua Media Project," provided several powerful examples of the ways in which the meaning of one of her photographs could be shifted by a dozen or so words.)

For a number of years she spent most of her working time in Latin America, concentrating on the social transformation of what ex-president Ronald Reagan chose to call "America's backyard." What she produced during that time constitutes, in effect, a documentary archive of inestimable value for future students of this period. At the same time, because the events she addressed were so crucial, often dramatic, and fast-paced, she could have provided us with exactly the kind of first-hand account we needed: a coherent, carefully shaped report, an informed opinion from a thoughtful observer who had been on the scene long enough to get past first impressions and snap judgments.

That's what photojournalism is supposed to be. But Meiselas wasn't allowed to practice photojournalism in the mass media very often. She was able to produce several important documentary books — among them *Nicaragua,* a collection of her own images, and *El Salvador,* a collaborative effort involving some thirty photographers. But few newspapers or magazines in this country ran her images in sizeable groups, with text over which she had any control. Despite her abilities, despite her commitment, Meiselas's work was reduced by the mass media to the function of press photography — isolated single images, recontextualized by editors and caption writers who lived and worked thousands of miles distant from the situations she was trying so hard to bring to our attention.

Thus it was with a sense of considerable irony that I opened *Esquire* Magazine's "Golden Collector's Issue" of December 1984, celebrating "The Best of the New Generation: Men and Women Under Forty Who Are Changing America." Meiselas was among those so honored, not undeservingly.[8] But there is another compendium, in my head, in which she also belongs: Men and Women of All Ages Who Are Not Being Permitted to Change America. Among those commemorated therein are Meiselas and her entire generation of photojournalists, who are being relentlessly marginalized, turned into image-mongers, converted to press photographers by virtue of what happens to their images between the camera and the page.

That's what I mean when I say most photojournalism isn't.

II. RETHINKING THE PAST

Over the past several years, on several occasions and in locations as far-flung as San Francisco, Amherst, and Vienna, I've encountered a curious version of the history of the documentary tendency in photography. In summary, it goes something like this:

– Documentary was invented by Lewis Hine and Jacob Riis, the latter of whom loses all credit due to character flaws and wrong politics.

– It was carried forward by August Sander, who was stopped by the Nazis in Germany; the members of the Photo League in New York, stopped by the right wing at home; and the Farm Security Administration team, whose work was perverted by the patriotism and subsequent corporate allegiances of its organizing mastermind, Roy Stryker.

– The only remaining documentary work of any significance being done by 1945 was that of Paul Strand, who unfortunately achieved nothing more than he already had (except that he "got old").

– There are no significant lessons to be learned from the work of the photojournalists and documentarians who were presented in mass-circulation magazines and books — David Douglas Duncan, Margaret Bourke-White, Henri Cartier-Bresson, Dorothea Lange, all the others.

– W. Eugene Smith — arguably the most influential, certainly the most controversial, and to my mind the most seminal and richly problematic of those workers — is to be mentioned only in passing, and only in order to be dismissed. The standard method for this is to decontextualize his work (something he resisted actively during his lifetime). This is accomplished by showing only the single image "Tomoko Uemura in her bath" from Eugene and Aileen Smith's *Minamata,* analogizing it to a "Pietà," and insinuating that the analogy somehow invalidates both. (A significant subtext to this devaluation of Smith is the omission of any mention that *Minamata* was a multicultural collaborative work: a collaboration between a Japanese and a North American, between a man and a woman, between a husband and a wife. Since collaboration is a buzz-word among those who offer up this version of recent history, one can only assume that they find Smith guilty of what cartoonist Jules Feiffer once called "premature morality.")[9]

– Thus, according to this account, by 1955 or so the documentary mode had fallen into abuse and neglect, so much so that nothing of any note was achieved therein until — *mirabile dictu!* — it was "reinvented" in, of all places, San Diego, California, circa 1974.[10]

– Characteristically, in these accounts the work of these purported reinventors of documentary photography, and that of others accepted into their circle, is described as "politically effective" when, in fact, it has had no demonstrable political effect whatsoever. Those involved in producing these works — and generating the obligatory critical validations thereof — seem intent on deliberately confusing the term *political effec-*

tiveness with the term *ideological correctness.* One can understand their avoidance of the latter, with its totalitarian overtones, but that must be what they mean, since to speak of the political effectiveness of patently inconsequential work is to utter nonsense.

There are far too many flaws, errors, and gaps in this eccentric (and, in several cases, egocentric) history for me to correct here. Let me suggest, very briefly, what I think is missed or misunderstood about the documentary work of the late 1950s through the early 1970s.

As a result of policies that originated during World War II and were entrenched by the time that conflict ended, editorial control over text, captioning, and layout in mass magazines often restricted the freedom of writers and photographers to make their statements exactly as they wished.[11] Sometimes this led to accommodation, often to compromise. (There is a noteworthy difference between the two.)

This made book form the preferred vehicle for those involved in image-text work of a primarily informational or representational nature. More control and greater autonomy over text, picture selection, design, and other essential matters was available to those who worked in book form. What was lost in immediacy — books take longer to produce than magazine issues — was compensated for by editorial freedom.

The two decades between 1955 and 1975 were an extraordinarily fertile period for documentary and photojournalistic work, particularly in its exploration of book form as a vehicle. To name just a few of the key works produced during that era, there were Henri Cartier-Bresson and Jean-Paul Sartre's *From One China to the Other*; Robert Frank's *The Americans*; Marion Palfi's *Suffer, Little Children*; Philip Jones Griffiths's *Vietnam, Inc.*; Paul Fusco's *La Causa*; Michael Abramson's *Palante: Young Lords Party*; Jill Freedman's *Resurrection City*; Leonard Freed's *Black in White America* and *Made in Germany*; Herb Goro's *The Block*; Geoff Winningham's *Friday Night at the Coliseum*; W. Eugene and Aileen Smith's *Minamata*; Danny Lyon's *The Bikeriders* and *Conversations With The Dead*.[12] Additionally, it should be noted that numerous other long-term documentary projects — including those of Manuel Alvarez Bravo, Roy DeCarava, Billy Abernathy (Fundi), Marion Palfi, Milton Rogovin, Jerome Liebling, and Laura Gilpin — were under way during that time.[13]

The published works mentioned above were all produced and intended for a very broad general audience, which its makers assumed was the appropriate audience for social and political debate. These were not thought of by their makers as "artists' books" — precious, limited-edition, expensive, self-expressive artifacts aimed at an art-world audience. Commercially published books such as those listed above were significant precisely because their makers found ways to create works about topical social and political issues that could be widely disseminated to the general public at low prices through existing distribution systems.

The restrictions inherent in book form, however, have been amplified over the past fifteen years. Costs of paper, printing, warehousing, and shipping have skyrocketed; this has made publishers wary of projects whose topicality is too localized to guarantee extensive sales. With decisions as to what to publish made more cautiously, production time has increased.[14]

Therefore, book form is becoming a counter-productive system wherever rapid information dissemination is concerned. Also, the cultural attitude toward the book itself has begun to change. The book as an artifact is becoming archaized — and thus, as Marshall McLuhan and others have suggested, aestheticized — as a result. Sometimes the very traditionality of the book as a medium — its actual physicality, the gravity, weight, and permanence of it — still evokes its resonant cultural history as a repository of knowledge and/or a vehicle for investigative social criticism. That is, the ghosts of Victor Hugo and Emile Zola, of Frank Norris and Upton Sinclair still rise up from the pages of some new books.[15] Yet those who can see or sense those revenants are ever fewer, those who can recognize them fewer still.

The emergent new forms of information technology — the computer and the electronically encoded image — seem to be the logical successors to the mass-circulation magazine and the mass-market book. Microfiche, videodisc, computer-based desktop publishing, and various other innovations offer remarkable opportunities for image-text encoding, storage, retrieval, and dissemination. Yet there has been surprisingly little exploration of these new vehicles by documentary photographers and photojournalists, who appear to prefer squandering their energies in doomed efforts to twist fixed, static institutional structures into new forms that can accommodate their work, however uncomfortably.

This attitude has so permeated the field that in May of 1990, at a conference organized as part of the Photography Sesquicentennial Project in Philadelphia, Pennsylvania, picture editor and author Fred Ritchin — normally a sensible chap — complained bitterly and at length that museums were not *sponsoring* enough photojournalistic and documentary projects. Putting a finer point on it, Ritchin indicated that his concern was that, rather than endorsing, underwriting, and/or committing themselves to exhibit such projects while still in the planning or intermediary stages, museum curators were actually waiting until such ventures were completed and resolved before making their sponsorial decisions.[16]

One wonders what W. Eugene Smith or Sebastião Salgado would have made of this bizarre lament, which is roughly analogous to holding mortuaries responsible for providing seminars on holistic health practices. As it happens, Smith's and Salgado's images are structured so richly and printed so finely that they reward prolonged attention and "hold the wall" acceptably in the context of gallery or museum exhibitions, where they frequently appear. But, fundamentally, they're meant to serve purposes only marginally compatible with those of repositories and showcases for fine art, made instead to be seen in ink versions on the printed page—hardly an enterprise for which museum patronage is either likely or appropriate, at least before the work has been generated and lived its life in the world.[17]

The charmingly antiquated commitment to aestheticized forms of presentation—gallery/museum exhibits, artists' books, and the like—on the part of so many contemporary documentarians and even photojournalists, to which Ritchin's plaint gave such eloquent voice, necessarily restricts their work to a select and extremely limited audience. In effect, they commit themselves to preaching to the converted. Their insistence on remaining within the confines of conventional contemporary art activity leaves an enormous vacuum at the center of the emergent communications environment. That vacuum may well be filled by corporate forces which will surely recognize the importance of these new forms, if documentarians and photojournalists persist in staring into their rear-view mirrors. The time for radical workers to engage experimentally with these technologies is now, at their birth.

I don't believe that technologies solve problems. Humans solve problems. Technologies are only problem-solving tools, tools that can generate problems as well. There are dozens of new technologies operative in the culture and at the disposal of communicators today. How is it that our arguments over documentary photography and photojournalism are still centered around three nineteenth-century forms—magazines, books, and gallery/museum exhibits?[18]

III. PRETHINKING THE FUTURE

As with poetry, there are those who believe that photography "makes nothing happen," while others see in it the trumpet that calls to battle. Many current workers in the forms we loosely call *documentary* and *photojournalism*, I am sure, would place themselves in the latter camp; but the work they produce all too often provides ammunition to the former. Forty years ago—or a hundred and forty years ago, when photography was new—it was thought by photographers, not without some justification, that simply making images of the conditions and consequences of social ills and injustices could be sufficient to provoke change. That has been demonstrated to be a false assumption, at least in our time; such photography, by itself, clearly "makes nothing happen." This is not a limitation of photography, but rather of some of its practitioners.

I've tried here to suggest something about the nature of those limitations, which I see as conceptual instead of technical or practical. One central problem, I've proposed, is a semantic one: we fail persistently to discriminate between documentary/photojournalistic procedures and press photography. There is very little of the former being presented anywhere in the mass media today, even including the alternative press. Consequently, too often our working definition of these forms is derived unquestioningly from the debased version of them that currently pervades the mass media. Even our agreement with the politics and goals of many contemporary practitioners held up to us as models — Meiselas, for example — only muddies the waters further, since, regardless of their ideologies and purposes or our own, what happens to their work en route to its public destination is a perversion of photojournalism so extreme that to call it by that name is to allow what Ben Bagdikian terms "the media monopoly" to control not only our information but even our definitions. And, as Stokely Carmichael once said, "He who controls the definitions controls the structure of society."[19]

We do no service either to photography or to whatever causes we believe in by forgetting that it's vital to distinguish between the message intended and the message received — that is, between what a photojournalist sets out to do and what finally appears in print. We achieve nothing by leveling at press photography a misdirected critique that would only be appropriate for photojournalistic practice, if there were such a thing anymore.

This is not to say that there can no longer be a real photojournalism or a documentary mode. For such forms to reemerge as healthy, contributory components of social colloquy, those working within them must overcome their own ignorance of (or, in some cases, disdain for) the history of these forms. I've suggested that there are lessons to be derived from earlier stages in the evolution of these modes. One of these, surely, would concern controlling the essential relationship to text, a relationship virtually abandoned by most work presently parading under the name of photojournalism and even by much of what's called documentary. The pioneers of documentary/photojournalism recognized from the beginning the importance of integrating imagery with text — whether first-person testimony, historical background, quantitative/statistical material, or something other. It is the most effective means for contextualizing visual imagery, empowering its human subjects by giving them voice, drawing generalizations from the photographs' particulars. How, when, and why was that umbilical connection severed? What would be necessary to restore it?

Another such inquiry would concentrate on the symbiosis between earlier forms of documentary/photojournalism and the then-prevalent informational media, in order to derive understandings that could be applied to the new informational media of our time. Videodisc and/or CD-ROM diskettes, for instance, offer an ideal presentational format for large-scale documentary projects, or for anthologies of smaller projects grouped around a theme. (They are also media whose industries are starving for programming.) Microfiche — a postcard-sized format capable of encoding hundreds of images and/or pages of text — is an inexpensive technology that could function as the news magazine of the future. The same is true of the 3½-inch computer diskette. What would be the first steps toward creating the necessary linkages? What would be involved in developing an experimental prototype?

For the photographer committed to pursuing work in these modes, formal study and/or solid grounding in a number of specific disciplines would be enormously valuable: training in the crafts of writing, research, and graphic design, or in such relevant fields of study as anthropology, sociology, political science, economics, or psychology. This would go a long way toward correcting the situation bemoaned by critic Donna-Lee Phillips: "Because very little in the training of the typical photojournalist [or, I would add, the typical documentarian] addresses structural social, economic, or political issues, the photojournalist *under fire* must rely on intuition, instinct, conscience, and the lessons of experience to analyze and interpret quite complex events" [emphasis in the original].[20]

Such a commitment on the part of young photographers entering these fields would also be a first step toward solving a problem that has become endemic throughout them: the absence of anything remotely resembling a coherent, reasoned methodology. It's not that most documentary/photojournalistic work lacks analytical rigor; it's that there's no methodology at all. Everybody's winging it. Professed intentions aside, the majority of those working in these forms seem far more concerned with getting "good shots" or displaying their ideological correctness than they are with inquiring effectively into socioeconomic dilemmas.

There is a wide range of models from which principles, strategies, and tactics can be extracted for contemplation and testing in present-day practice. Our problem in that regard is hardly the shortage of exemplary work; to the shelfful I've already cited we could add the collaborations between John Berger and Jean Mohr, the installations of Hans Haacke, and dozens of others.

No, the problem, or part of it at any rate, is a schizoid self-image held by too many documentary/photojournalistic workers, which results in an internally contradictory, self-defeating agenda. On the one hand, they want (or believe that they want) to make something happen; on the other hand, they want to retain the social cachet of being recognized as artists. This leads them to identify themselves as an elite, whose work is intentionally directed toward appealing to an elite audience in the purviews of the elite: art galleries and museums, art magazines, "artists' books." They have turned their backs on the larger electorate and the available means of mass communication, vitiating whatever scope and impact their work might have had.

What I'm implying is that the conceptual rationale behind any documentary/photojournalistic endeavor — the way in which the project is (or isn't) thought through, from premise and purpose to choice of audience(s) and presentational vehicles — is the primary determinant of the effectiveness, or lack of same, that such a project can have. There is a considerable difference between being ideologically correct and being politically effective. There is also a distinction between both of those and the merely well-intended.

POSTLUDE

From this it follows logically that photographers working in these modes, as well as all of us who are the audience for their work, must let go of the ludicrous notion that any documentary/photojournalistic work can be either "objective" or "nonpolitical." I was bemused to read, in the *Esquire* profile of Meiselas cited earlier, the claim of one of her colleagues that "Susan is not political. Some people have put this label on her, which is a disservice and only shows their own weakness of perception."[21] Stuff and nonsense. This is a particularly foolish proposition in regard to Meiselas, whose empathy for populist movements and opposition to military regimes are patently obvious in her work. But that idea is specious in its relation to *all* acts of public communication; to quote Phillips again, "structuring information *is* ideological activity" [emphasis in the original].[22]

As W. Eugene Smith once wrote, "The first word I would remove from the folklore of journalism is the word objective."[23] Objectivity is not a state attainable by inevitably subjective humans. Neutrality is in itself a political stance, favoring as it does the status quo. Why have we permitted the wool of this mythology of objectivity/neutrality to be pulled over our eyes?[24] Why do we tolerate it even from the mouths of those who, more than any, should know better — the photographers themselves?

It's not inconceivable that our uncritical acceptance of this mythology explains the atrophy of documentary/photojournalistic practice in mass-media contexts. To have such conflicting, irreconcilable expectations placed upon them can only paralyze these forms' practitioners. The fault, I believe, lies with the audience no less than with the photographers and the middle management which controls their work.

That so little changes despite all the photographs made, published, and exhibited may be proof, it's true, that photography makes nothing happen after all. On the other hand, it might be attributable at least in part to the fact that, with some notable exceptions, generation after generation of photographers have rendered themselves (or have been rendered) impotent in relation to such issues. This disenfranchisement can take many subtle forms: succumbing to the lures of the fine print as fetish object and/or the "aesthetic appeal" of poverty and oppression; conversely, accepting the irrational notion that deliberately mediocre, visually uninteresting images are more "politically effective" than persuasive, potent ones; avoiding the demands of linear thought and thus the difficult inquiry into chains of events, causes and effects, all of which involve one in the rigors of sequential imagery and image-text relationships; indulging oneself in simplistic bleeding-heart empathy with victims, thus assuaging one's guilt without forcing oneself to undertake the more difficult challenge of developing solutions to their victimization; preaching to the converted; ignoring or scorning the very audience that must be engaged and persuaded if change is to come . . .

All of these self-defeating attitudes have become entangled with the tradition and practice of documentary/photojournalism. We need photographers willing to break the comfortable shackles of that cherished tradition, to rethink current practice from the ground up, without falling prey either to creeping paternalism or sarcastic patronization. The classic question of both criminal investigation and Marxism is, "Who profits?" That would be a good query with which to begin almost any documentary/photojournalistic inquiry. It would also be a good question for those working in these forms to turn on themselves; if what is produced in them only furthers the careers of those who produce it, it certainly will make nothing happen for those depicted, and thus will serve only to perpetuate their plight. Ironically, it is this self-inflicted impotence that assures future generations of photographers that they too will have the same subject matter to address, the same "tradition" to follow.[25]

NOTES

1. That is, I'm addressing myself to something beyond the claims adjuster's obligatory Polaroid of your crumpled fender, or the local studio's commissioned rendering of a shop window's display of fall fashions.

2. For example, the expeditionary/imperialistic projects sponsored by various Western governments during the nineteenth century, the Farm Security Administration and Standard Oil projects orchestrated by Roy Stryker, and the Seagram's "Courthouse" project directed by Richard Pare.

3. I'm using the singular as a stylistic convenience, but do not mean to exclude from this discussion collaborative projects by two or more photographers, examples of which abound: W. Eugene and Aileen Smith's *Minamata* (New York: Holt, Rinehart & Winston, 1975), the Exit Photography Group's *Survival Programmes in Britain's Inner Cities* (London: Open University Press, 1982). I also have in mind here those projects in which photographers turn the camera over

to others, as in Wendy Ewald's ongoing work with children of different cultures, or in which the power of image interpretation and contextualization is shared by the work's nominal subjects, as in Thomas Mueller's TAFOS Workshop in Lima, Peru.

4. This is a more precise version of what is loosely referred to as a photographer's "way of seeing."

5. So-called television news magazines such as *60 Minutes* are of course potential — and potentially effective — vehicles for still-photography photojournalism. Such programs often uses stills, though usually only when video footage is unavailable. Occasionally such a program will extract a brief segment from a photographic book or exhibition, but I know of no case in which a photojournalistic project has actually been sponsored by a television program.

6. A notable exception is that curious recent invention, the *A Day in the Life of* . . . concept for books and exhibitions. Immensely successful in terms of eventual sales and attendance, these ventures involve dropping dozens and even hundreds of photojournalists and press photographers into a selected country of which few of them are natives, instructing them to make photographs for one twenty-four-hour period, and extracting from their collective "take" something purporting to be a slice-of-life rendering of that country's quotidian essence. Intellectually, the idea is so wrong-headed and morally bankrupt as to be laughable in its naiveté. Practically speaking, what results are vast catalogues of stock shots.

7. The debate within the photography community and without over Edward Steichen's 1955 curatorial magnum opus, "The Family of Man," was in essence an argument over his assertion of a picture editor's prerogatives in regard to press photography, exercised in relationship to extracts from bodies of work understood to have their own autonomous integrity in the terrains of photojournalism, documentary, and fine art.

8. Gloria Emerson, "Susan Meiselas at War," *Esquire* 102, no. 6 (December 1984): 165–74.

9. For my most recent thoughts on Smith, see "The Psychoids of Oppression and a Faith in Healing: The Life and Work of W. Eugene Smith," in *Aperture* 119 (early summer 1990): 73–75.

10. Though its purported reinventors were variously friends, teachers, students, and colleagues of each other at the University of California, that fact is not considered essential knowledge, and goes unmentioned — as does the fact that several of the published and/or spoken versions of this history of recent documentary were authored by these reinventors themselves.

11. For an extensive analysis of the process by which this happened, see George H. Roeder, Jr., *The Censored War: American Visual Experience During World War Two* (New Haven: Yale University Press, 1992).

12. This list is only the tip of the iceberg insofar as books are concerned. Photojournalistic essays of major importance abounded during the same period — the work of Gordon Parks and W. Eugene Smith for *Life* would be only two examples.

13. A number of these photographers — Alvarez Bravo, Cartier-Bresson, DeCarava, Abernathy, and Palfi, certainly — are or were uncomfortable for various reasons with a discourse that situates their endeavors within the form called documentary. While respecting their disagreements with this rubric, I believe it's appropriate to consider their work relevant to this discussion.

14. For instance, David Douglas Duncan's *I Protest!* — a highly personal, editorializing image-text account of the crucial Khe Sanh battle in Vietnam in February of 1968 — was rushed into print in a special paperback edition that hit the stands *less than two months after the battle*. It's hard to imagine any American publisher undertaking such a project today.

15. Some recent examples, in my opinion, are Carole Gallagher's *American Ground Zero* (Cambridge: MIT Press, 1993) and Sebastiaõ Salgado's *Workers: An Archaeology of the Industrial Age* (New York: Aperture, 1993).

16. Ritchin spoke from the floor during a postpanel question-and-answer period. The panel, which I moderated, was titled "Changing of the Guard: Gatekeepers in an Era of Decentralization." It took place on Saturday, June 9, 1990, at the Penn Towers Hotel in Philadelphia.

17. I'd propose that, with very few exceptions, no creative work in any form should make its public debut in a museum. Some obvious exceptions would include work that's specifically crit-

ical/analytical of the host institution, such as Hans Haacke's controversial Whitney Museum project; work that's parodistic of museology in general, like Joan Fontcuberta and Pere Formiguera's "Fauna"; and work that's sponsored by institutions that are themselves innately parodistic, such as Los Angeles's Museum of Jurassic Technology. But that's another discussion.

18. Having said this, I must confess my own involvement as curator of "Testimonies: Photography and Social Issues," a large-scale traveling exhibit that made its debut at Houston FotoFest in early 1990. The show included substantial extracts from six projects by Herman Emmet, Eugene Richards, Linda Troeller, Lonny Shavelson, and the teams of Marilyn Anderson/Jonathan Garlock and Fran Antmann/Sebastian Rodriguez. Several of these projects have resolved as books in which I've had a hand.

19. From my notebooks, source unknown. I heard Carmichael say this in speeches in Berkeley and San Francisco, circa 1965–66, and it stuck with me in his distinctive locution. I haven't found an exact replication of it in his works in print, but the following—from Stokely Carmichael and Charles V. Hamilton, *Black Power: The Politics of Liberation in America* (New York: Random House, 1967)—comes close: ". . . we must first redefine ourselves. We shall have to struggle for the right to create our own terms through which to define ourselves and our relationship to the society, and to have these terms recognized. This is the first necessity of a free people, and the first right that any oppressor must suspend" (p. 34). "Today, the American educational system continues to reinforce the entrenched values of the society through the use of words" (p. 37).

20. From her essay, "Nothing Lies More Easily Than the Camera . . . ," *San Francisco Camerawork Quarterly* 11, no. 2 (Summer 1984): 11.

21. Emerson, *op. cit.*, p. 183. This was said by photojournalist Harry Mattison, thought to be the model for the Nick Nolte character in the movie *Under Fire*.

22. Phillips, *op. cit.*, p. 12.

23. From my notebooks, source unknown. But Smith issued frequent variants of this statement, such as, "The journalistic photographer can have no other than a personal approach; and it is impossible for him to be completely objective. Honest—yes. Objective—no." From "Photographic Journalism," *Photo Notes* (June 1948): 4–5; reprinted in *Photographers on Photography,* edited by Nathan Lyons (Englewood Cliffs, N.J.: Prentice-Hall, 1966), p. 103.

24. Eric Alterman lays the blame for this notion—which has no currency outside the U.S.— squarely at the feet of Adolph Ochs, who instituted a policy of presumed impartiality and nonpartisanship at the *New York Times* upon his purchase of that newspaper in 1896. See Alterman's book, *Sound and Fury: The Washington Punditocracy and the Collapse of American Politics* (New York: HarperCollins, 1992). Overcoming such staunch opponents as John Dewey, Walter Lippmann served as the foremost public promulgator of this concept in the 1920s and 1930s. Not coincidentally, I suspect, in that same period these ideas infiltrated photography's theory, discourse, and practice, finding their way in through Paul Strand's writing and teaching, the polemics of the "*Neue Sachlichkeit*" (New Objectivity) movement in Germany, and, eventually, the Group f.64 philosophy. A thorough study of the history of the idea of objectivity in photography might reveal a great deal.

25. This essay began its life as an assortment of marginal notes on the debate over documentary that emerged in the late 1970s. Portions of my argument were intended as interventions, meant to rupture the superficial seamlessness of the emergent "new" version of the history of documentary then being noised about, whose authors—Abigail Solomon-Godeau among them—were willfully and irresponsibly eliding and otherwise falsifying the record in order to present themselves and/or their icons as not only innovative but *sui generis*. This seemed particularly hypocritical, and I thought it appropriate to point that out. Among the stimuli to my corrective response was a lecture by Solomon-Godeau, delivered at the San Francisco Art Institute in the fall of 1982. This was a comparatively boilerplate version of the by-then notorious generic "reinvention of documentary" presentation, as synopsized briefly in this essay. During the question-and-answer period, I intruded some of the issues I've raised here—including the failure to define the term

political effectiveness and the decision to eliminate W. Eugene Smith's collaborator on the Minamata project, the Japanese-American Aileen Smith, from any discussion thereof. I got no satisfactory answers that night, and have had none since.

Some of those notes and questions were turned into a lecture first delivered during a symposium at Hampshire College, Amherst, Massachusetts, on March 3, 1984. In considerably different form, other passages first appeared in "In the Fields," *Photo Metro* 2, no. 5 (February 1983): 10, and a series of essays for *Lens' On Campus* in which I initially worked these ideas through: "Information, Please!" vol. 7, no. 1 (February 1985): 8–9; "Most Photojournalism Isn't," vol. 7, no. 2 (March 1985): 6–7; and "Who Profits?" vol. 7, no. 3 (April 1985): 10–11. Those, in turn, eventually resolved into something approximating the form taken here: "Documentary and Photojournalism Now: Notes and Questions"/"Bemerkunsen und Fragen Zur Dokumentarfotografie und Zum Fotojournalismus Heute," *Fotokritik* (Germany) 20 (December 1986): 12–21.

Then, in 1987, Solomon-Godeau chose to launch her own attack. In "Who Is Speaking Thus? Some Questions About Documentary Photography," an essay elaborating those recent documentary theories and praising works by Victor Burgin, Martha Rosler, Allan Sekula, and others — published originally in Lorne Falk and Barbara Fischer, eds., *The Event Horizon: Essays on Hope, Sexuality, Social Space and Media(tion)* (Toronto: Coach House Press, 1987), then reprinted in her own book, *Photography at the Dock: Essays on Photographic History, Institutions, and Practices* (Minneapolis: University of Minnesota Press, 1991), pp. 169–83 — she announced that "apologists for traditional forms of documentary might be loathe [*sic*] to recognize their work as such" (p. 182). In a footnote, she elaborated:

> At the same time that bastions of photographic orthodoxy would disqualify work such as Rosler's, Hatch's, Lonidier's, or Sekula's as documentary, the challenge posed by their critical interventions drive [*sic*] defenders of the faith such as A. D. Coleman into extraordinary reactions of hostility and redbaiting. Coleman, whose hero of documentary is Eugene Smith has, for example, written the following: 'the overall tenor of this reinvented documentary is unaffectionate [!], arch, ironic, hostile: hostile to the past, hostile to the present. I sense here the potential for the establishment of gulags of the spirit, aesthetic Stalinism.' . . . The very terms of such attacks, with their imputation of conspiracy and consistent equation of quantitative address (i.e., use of the mass media) with political effectiveness, should alert us to what is at stake in these different allegiances to documentary forms (p. 302).

The passage of mine quoted was one from the early formulation of this essay in *Lens' On Campus*, "Information, Please," a section discarded during the production of the 1985 version as not being crucial to the argument. (It's reprinted in my collection, *The Digital Evolution* [Tucson: Nazraeli Press, 1998].) Which doesn't mean I don't stand by it. I will leave it to the careful reader to determine whether I am — in this essay or elsewhere — an "apologist for traditional forms of documentary," a "bastion of photographic orthodoxy," or a "defender of [any] faith." I feel obliged to point out that, notwithstanding Solomon-Godeau's insinuation, I've never "disqualified work such as Rosler's, Hatch's, Lonidier's, or Sekula's as documentary"; I've merely questioned its motives, substance, and effectiveness. Bad poetry is poetry nonetheless.

Surprisingly, Solomon-Godeau's comment makes clear and explicit her own direct equation of Stalinism with communism. This strikes me as injudicious, even back in 1987; that's something I wouldn't have expected at that late date from anyone with leftist pretensions. I've never conflated the two; indeed, I find the proposal repugnant. Consequently, I do not consider my quoted statement to constitute "redbaiting." It wasn't even intended as a trap for die-hard Stalinists, though it appears to have worked as such in this case. And to read my brief foray into the sociology of knowledge — the passing comment that is now note 10 to this essay — as "imputation of conspiracy" is the very height of paranoia.

As Katha Pollitt has noted,

> [T]he biggest misconstruction . . . is that the "academic left," *aka* postmodernists
> and deconstructionists, is the left, even on campus. . . . How "the left" came to
> be identified as the pomo [postmodern] left would make an interesting Ph.D.
> thesis. . . . What results is a pseudo-politics, in which everything is claimed in the
> name of revolution and democracy and equality and anti-authoritarianism, and
> nothing is risked, nothing, except maybe a bit of harmless cross-dressing, is even
> expected to happen outside the classroom.
>
> How else explain how pomo leftists can talk constantly about the need to democ-
> ratize knowledge and write in a way that excludes all but the initiated few? ("Pomo-
> lotov Cocktail," *The Nation* 262, no. 23 (June 10, 1996): 9.

Solomon-Godeau's dismissal of what she describes as my "consistent equation of quantitative address (i.e., use of the mass media) with political effectiveness" should be understood
in that light. In fact, as I noted in the preface to my 1995 book *Critical Focus,* and as is obvious
from my own practice, I agree with Walter Benjamin that "the place where the word is most
debased — that is to say, the newspaper — becomes the very place where a rescue operation can be
mounted. . . . [T]he newspaper is, technically speaking, the writer's most important strategic
position." ("Author as Producer," in *Thinking Photography,* edited by Victor Burgin [London:
MacMillan Press Ltd.], p. 20.) I would extend Benjamin's insight to encompass the image as well
as the word; and I would add, as a further logical extension of his concept, radio, television, the
Internet, and other electronic forms of mass communication.

Furthermore, not only do I think Solomon-Godeau might benefit from pondering the
question of her title — "Who Is Speaking Thus?" — in its relation to her own style of discourse, but
she might do well to ask herself the question I posed in a 1980 essay, "Choice of Audience / Choice
of Voice":

To whom is my work addressed? To put it another way, who do you think you're talking to? By
this I mean quite specifically what audience do you as a critic desire and direct your work towards
conceptually? . . .

"The only option one does not have," I proposed, "is pretending that the question is
irrelevant. Brecht once cautioned writers who allowed themselves to be 'relieved of concern for
the destination of what [they have] written' with these words:"

> I . . . want to emphasize that "writing for someone" has been transformed into
> merely "writing." But the truth cannot merely be written; it must be written *for*
> *someone*, someone who can do something with it.

(Emphasis his. The Brecht quote comes from "Writing the Truth: Five Difficulties," translated by
Richard Winston, in *Art in Action: Twice a Year 1938–1948, 10th Anniversary Issue* [New York: Twice
A Year Press, 1948], p. 126. My essay is reprinted in my book *Tarnished Silver: After the Photo Boom*
[New York: Midmarch Arts Press, 1996] pp. 2–10.)

For whom, then, is Solomon-Godeau writing? The elitist, highly jargonized, often impene-
trable discourse she prefers and practices lends itself to parody, as has recently been demonstrated
by Prof. Alan Sokal of New York University, who managed to get "Transgressing the Boundaries:
Towards a Transformative Hermeneutics of Quantum Gravity," a brilliantly meaningless and
incomprehensible distillation of mannerist pomo gibberish — with all the mandatory sources
quoted and footnoted, of course — published in the cultural studies journal *Social Text,* to the
subsequent embarrassment of many and the righteous indignation of all. But I'm not sure such
efforts are necessary and don't intend to try anything similar myself. Ron Rosenbaum is right:
"Unintentional self-parody may turn out to be the most memorable, the most truly *defining* genre
of our time." ("The Edgy Enthusiast," *The New York Observer* 10, no. 24 [June 17, 1996]: 35.)

The Image in Question

> Yet it is not (it seems to me) by Painting that Photography touches art, but by Theater. . . . Photography is a kind of primitive theater, a kind of *Tableau Vivant,* a figuration of the motionless and made-up face beneath which we see the dead.
>
> *Roland Barthes[1]*

Indeed. Before me lies a newspaper story, full of the tawdry stuff of soap operas and Raymond Chandler novels, tattered lives summed up in a few lean paragraphs:

> Laguna Niguel, Calif., July 4 (AP) — A contractor going through a divorce and child custody suit appeared to be grief-stricken when sheriff's investigators showed him a photograph of his wife on a morgue slab, the authorities said Tuesday.
>
> The photograph convinced Frederick Penney, 57 years old, that his wife, Susan, was dead, although the picture had been posed, they said. He was later arrested for investigation of soliciting murder when he paid off a supposed hit man. . . .
>
> Deputies said Mrs. Penney, 35, cooperated in setting up her spouse after the authorities learned of a possible plot and spoke to her through her attorney. . . . [S]he was "very quiet, very cooperative" when asked to help, Sergeant [Timothy] Simon said.
>
> She went to the county morgue, where her hair was washed down and her face was tinted to make her look pale and gray. Investigators placed her on a morgue slab and covered most of her body with a blanket, Sergeant Simon said.
>
> ### A Photo-Perfect Ruse
>
> "The photo looked perfect, believe me," he said.
>
> Posing as a deputy coroner and backed up by . . . hidden cameras, another undercover investigator notified Mr. Penney of his wife's accidental "death" and showed him the photograph.
>
> Sergeant Simon said deputies could have made an arrest after the first installment was paid, "but we wanted to make it the best case possible."[2]

Is there some version of the conservative U.S. economists' "trickle-down" theory at work here? When, in 1976, I published an essay in which I attempted a first tracing of the photographic approach that I identified as *the directorial mode*,[3] the concept (though not new, and hardly original with me, except for its nomenclature; I was not making the news, only reporting it) was controversial, the position it represented in the community of serious photographers a minority one at best.

Now, twelve years later, it has achieved legitimacy within photography[4] and is everywhere in the art world; much of the so-called postmodernist enterprise vis-à-vis photography is unimaginable without it, for example. Moreover, if the bathetic, twisted tale synopsized above is any indication, a remarkably sophisticated version of it has seeped into vernacular usage as well.

The average camera user has always been directorially inclined. ("No, no, Emily, move over the other way, right next to Susan. John, you're the tallest, you get in back. Now, everyone *smile!*") In fact, it's only a small but vocal genus of the art-photography species (along with its historiographic symbiote) that resists this mode adamantly. Presently, however, for the very first time, the form I've called *directorial* is enjoying a vogue — with all the respectability and critical attention attendant thereon.[5]

What was I trying to pinpoint when I coined that name over a decade ago?

One way to answer is to indicate what I did *not* intend. Another critic, Douglas Crimp, for example, has proposed the phrase "*auteur* photography" as a substitute.[6] This evidences a profound misreading of what I meant by the term *directorial*. It also represents a deep misapprehension of the significance of the directorial approach within photographic practice, as well as an ignorance of the premises and purposes of *auteur* theory in film criticism.

Let us disentangle his muddle by starting with the latter issue. Criticism of all media is based on the assumption that the works under discussion are the product not of nature but of culture — that, unlike Topsy, they didn't "jes' grew," but instead evolved out of a set of choices made by the individuals involved in their production, individuals who can be considered accountable for their actions.

For obvious reasons, this is a particularly problematic assumption insofar as the scrutiny of any collective effort is concerned: the greater the degree of collaboration, the larger the number of collaborators, the harder it becomes to ascribe responsibility to anyone involved. "Who's in charge here?" is a question one can reasonably ask at any given moment during such events as a film, a play, a dance troupe's performance, or an orchestral concert.

Auteur theory in film criticism was an Alexandrian solution to the Gordian knot of film production, in which scriptwriter (and original story source, if the script were based on some pre-existent work), cinematographer, director, editor, performers, soundtrack composer, set and costume designer, and diverse others were inextricably entwined. Who, under those circumstances, was the "author" of the film (*auteur* being French for *author*)? *Auteur*ism's answer: The film ultimately was the "work" of its director — that is, it was the director who, at the crucial stages, "gave his/her consent"[7] to the final statement.

This bold stroke allowed film critics finally to discuss films as organic wholes whose successes and failures, in the last analysis, were not parcelled out among an assortment of quasi-autonomous functionaries in some fragmented (indeed, Balkanized) version of the film-making process. *Auteur* theory unified all these under the hegemony of the director — the *auteur* — making him/her accountable for all decisions, converting all other collaborators into a support system for the *auteur*'s controlling vision.

As an encompassing hypothesis, this idea embraced all styles of film-making, from the "documentary" through the "experimental" to the vastest Hollywood extravaganza. It applies no less to Sam Peckinpah than to Robert Flaherty, no more to Maya Deren than to Steven Spielberg.

For anyone familiar with the essay in which I identified and traced the morphology of the directorial mode, it will be obvious that the concept of *auteur*ism is not at all interchangeable with the directorial impulse. To reiterate what I sought to pinpoint:

> The substantial distinction . . . is between treating the external world as a given, to be altered only through photographic means (point of view, framing, printing, etc.) en route to the final image, or rather as raw material, to be itself manipulated as much as desired prior to the exposure of the negative.[8]

To propose the substitution of these two terms is thus to mix apples with oranges. There is no need for *auteur* theory in the critical analysis of still photography. Every photographer is an *auteur*. While there may be people who still believe that cameras take pictures, the understanding that the photographer is accountable for the images she or he makes has long been fundamental to any critical relationship to photography. Collaborations of the sort which pervade the film-making process are the exception in still photography, not the rule; the only ones to which *auteur* theory might fruitfully be applied are those between, say, commercial/fashion photographers and their clients/models/art directors, or press photographers and their editors — in which cases the *auteurs* are no longer the imagemakers, who are reduced to the still-photography equivalent of cinematographers, but rather those who wield the power of contextualization.[9]

Thus *auteur*ism as a concept, in and of itself, solves no problems for the criticism of photography — instead, it muddies the waters by introducing into the discourse a trendy, loaded, but ultimately inappropriate term. As an alternative to *directorial,* it is even more useless. As noted above, every autonomous photographer is an *auteur:* Robert Frank no less than Cindy Sherman,[10] Les Krims no more than Dorothea Lange.

The only significant connection between directorialism and *auteur*ism as concepts is that inherent in the directorial mode as an approach to praxis is the explicit assumption that the photographer — not the subject, not the medium, not the world at large — is the generative source of his/her work. This is a truth that is often forgotten (by viewers, even by practitioners themselves) in relation to work produced in other modes. Thus the increasing volume and influence of work in the directorial mode over the past decade and a half may well have helped lay to rest the lingering ghost of our culture's wishful fantasy of the photograph as a neutral, uninflected image that has *no* maker, *no "author."*

For the simple fact is this: There are no neutral photographs.

As Thomas Kuhn has pointed out, "any description must be partial."[11] By its nature, a photograph is a descriptive rather than a transcriptive artifact. As such, it reflects inevitably at least two sets of biases, two viewpoints, on which its existence in the world is predicated:

- Those of the inventors, designers, and manufacturers of the system — camera, lens, film, darkroom equipment, and chemistry — employed in the physical production of that particular image.
- Those of the photographer who controls the specific application of that system to the occasion of the image in question.

To assume that these biases merely inflect — or even *infect* — the photograph is to miss (almost entirely) the point. Which is: This conglomeration of biases, this stew of viewpoints — these *are* the photograph, these (in combination with its contents, the physical things represented) form its *content*. Every photograph, therefore, is a manifestation of these biases interacting with whatever was before the lens at the moment of exposure.

This is inescapable. Consequently, any response to a photograph — whether from an actively analytic critical attitude or a more passively absorptive, spectatorial mode — necessarily involves the viewer with the ostensibly invisible presence of the photographer as well as the more insidiously covert influence of the medium itself.

In short, we must think of every photograph as a form of collaboration between subject, photographer, and medium. The last of these operates subcutaneously — beneath the skin of the imagery; most commonly, it calls as little attention to itself as possible, seeking no credit for the final results, even if in fact it dictates them outright. The more immediate, observable transaction is between subject and photographer; it is in this dialogue — sometimes contestual and sometimes cooperative — that control of the final image is negotiated.

In that bargaining the photographer almost always has the upper hand. What I mean by this goes well beyond the fact that some subjects are extremely pliable, perhaps even helpless, insensate, inanimate. Any photographer worth his/her salt — that is, any photographer of professional caliber, in control of the craft, regardless of imagisitic bent — can make virtually anything "look good." Which means, of course, that she or he can make anything look "bad" — or look just about any way at all.

After all, that is the real work of photography: *making things look,* deciding how a thing is to appear in the image. For photographs do not "show how things look," since there is no one way that anything looks. Every thing has an infinitude of potential appearances, a multiplicity of aspects. *What a photograph shows us is how a particular thing could be seen, or could be made to look* — at a specific moment, in a specific context, by a specific photographer employing specific tools.[12]

The photographer, then, is an active partner (most often the dominant one) in the construction of any photographic version of the world.

But not every photographer works directorially.

I once described the microcosms generated by those who work in the directorial mode as "constructed realities,"[13] taking my cue from a famous statement made in the 1920s by playwright/director/theorist Bertolt Brecht:

> . . . [L]ess than at any time does a simple *reproduction of reality* tell us anything about reality. A photograph of the Krupp works or GEC yields almost nothing about these institutions. Reality proper has slipped into the functional. The reification of human relationships, the factory, let's say, no longer reveals these relationships. Therefore something has actually to be *constructed,* something artificial, something set up" [emphases in the original].[14]

The work of every photographer describes a unique, personalized world, a version of the universe shaped by that photographer's sensibility and intentions. In the imagery of those who choose to function directorially, this shaping is more aggressively done, thus more undeniable; the pretense that the photograph merely mirrors "the way things looked" gives way, as I've just suggested, to the forced realization that what the photograph encodes is a perspective, a viewpoint, an *opinion* — even, possibly, a *fiction*.

This is true even for the work of those photographers who choose to evoke the viewer's credulity by mimicking the "found," circumstantial, happenstance aspect of the casual snapshot, as does Ralph Eugene Meatyard and, to a lesser extent, Duane Michals. As Barthes has written, "[T]he photograph allows the photographer to *conceal elusively* the preparation to which he subjects the scene to be recorded," this preparation permitting the introduction of layers of meaning, connotations, "produced by a modification of the reality itself" [emphasis in the original].[15]

Once such other strategies as extended form (sequences, suites, photomontage or photocollage, image-text combinations), elaborate stage sets and/or costumes, highly stylized poses, and the like manifest themselves in the imagery, it becomes virtually impossible for the viewer to *believe in* the image as a slice of or report on reality. This frank acknowledgment of the photographer's control over the *mise-en-image* evokes a different viewer response altogether, the *suspension of disbelief* — making it clear that both photographer and viewer are operating, consensually, within what the late sociologist Erving Goffman called "the theatrical frame."[16]

Theater takes place in space; it requires a proscenium. Those who work within this mode are therefore less likely to be concerned with the photograph as a two-dimensional, graphic "composition." Their attention will more likely be pointed toward the photograph's capacity to serve as an effective visual illusion of three-dimensionality, a *spatial structure*. Yet this is not always the case. With his eccentric darkroom craft strategies, for instance, Joel-Peter Witkin produces objects that call attention to themselves as such by the internal evidence of their manufacture. Duane Michals's handwritten texts, though not embedded within the photographs themselves, remind us that the photographic print is a sheet of paper, not a sheet of glass.

Also typical of the directorial approach is the incorporation of dolls, masks, and other simulacra of the human into the scenarios. For many years relegated to mundane service in photography as sentimental signifiers of childish innocence, these artifacts were rescued in the late 1960s by image-makers who reinstated them as cultural icons, as *totems*. A direct lineage can be traced from the imagery of Richard Kirstel, Vilèm Kriz, and Michael Martone to that of David Levinthal, Ellen Brooks, and Laurie Simmons.

Some directorial photographers introduce other kinds of artifacts as protagonists in their dramas. Here directorialism reveals itself as — in part — an extension of the still-life tradition in painting, particularly the *vanitas* mode of the Dutch masters, with its deployment of symbolically charged objects in allegorical configurations. All still lifes that involve the photographer's arrangement of their contents are inherently directorial, even when the concern is a strictly formal one. But many current miners of this vein introduce objects intended to function on a metaphorical level as well. Sometimes, as in Arthur Tress's "Teapot Opera" sequence, the connotations implied by their appearance are specific and precise. In other cases, the photographs are occasions for the "chance meetings" so beloved of the Surrealists — as in Robert Fichter's world, where a kind of lunatic order prevails: everything inappropriate, everything neatly out of place.

The transformation of a *place* into a *space* — the creation of a photographic equivalent of the stage set — is another hallmark of the directorial impulse. Nowadays these efforts seem to become ever more elaborate; some of the environments and/or scenarios crafted by photographers involve extensive planning, then days of physical effort. (Consider, in this light, the work of Patrick Nagatani-Andreé Tracey, Sandy Skoglund, James Casebere, and Les Krims.) Perhaps, as the workings of the world become (as Brecht proposed) increasingly masked and remote, the operations needed to strip away the facade must become correspondingly intricate. At the same time, this approach still has its advocates of simplicity — Michals, Robert Cumming, and Ruth Thorne-Thomsen among them — arguing that an economy of means may yet suffice.

Also unique to the directorial mode — and extremely obvious in its difference from previous art-photographic practice — is the use of the human presence in predetermined, highly controlled fashion. None of these images are reports on spontaneous human behavior; none are observations of "found" human gestures or interactions. In all cases, the will of the subject has been surrendered to the dictates of the photographer, who *directs* his/her actors in the drama portrayed. This, too, has its roots in traditional photographic forms — think of the studio nudes of Ruth Bernhard and Edward Weston, or the formal portraits of Arnold Newman and Lotte Jacobi. Here, however, more clearly than in any other form, the people in the pictures have become the photographer's *dramatis personae,* the "cast of characters" for the *tableau vivant.* Eileen Cowin and Bernard Faucon (to name only two) employ humans not only as presences but as protagonists.

What the directorial photographer is involved in fundamentally, then, is the process of *evoking a performance* from a controlled configuration of props, stage sets, and/or actors for which she or he is fully responsible. Needless to say, some who work in this form are more skillful directors than others; among the best, too, there is a considerable range of strategies and tactics (some, for example, opt for a Stanislavskian conviction, while others pursue a Brechtian alienation).

Directorialism in photography has manifested itself in many ways over the years, from the multiple-negative montages of O. G. Rejlander and H. P. Robinson in the Victorian era to the interventions in the physical landscape of Mario Giacomelli from the 1950s onward.[17] The full-scale exploration and redefinition of this mode in our time signals its overdue acceptance as one of the central devices for creative inquiry into the world of appearances, and for the analysis of the medium of photography itself.

The directorial mode peremptorily challenges our long-cherished assumptions about the transparency of the photograph, its purported neutrality, its presumed objectivity; insistently undermining the credibility of the photograph, it *puts the image in question*. Since neutrality always favors the status quo, and the illusion of transparency serves the power structure rather than the disempowered, this mode has profound political and cultural implications.[18]

NOTES

1. *Camera Lucida: Reflections on Photography* (New York: Hill and Wang, 1981), pp. 31–32.

2. "Faked Morgue Photograph Helps Snare Suspect in Plot," *New York Times,* July 5, 1984, p. A8.

3. "The Directorial Mode: Notes Toward a Definition," *Artforum* 15, no. 1 (September 1976): 55–61. Reprinted in A. D. Coleman, *Light Readings: A Photography Critic's Writings, 1968–1978* (New York: Oxford University Press, 1979; University of New Mexico Press, 1998), pp. 246–57.

4. Indeed, in a recent editorial, Andreas Müller-Pohle proposed that "the currently dominate [*sic*] tendency is towards a *staging* of the picture as an answer to the aesthetic obsolescence of 'straight photography.'" ("Young European Photographers '86," in *European Photography* #29, vol. 8, no. 1 [January–March 1987]: 13.) This is an extremist stance with which I am not in agreement, though Müller-Pohle has argued eloquently for it elsewhere.

5. See, for example, the catalogue of an exhibition curated by Van Deren Coke, *Fabricated to Be Photographed* (San Francisco: San Francisco Museum of Modern Art, 1979), and Anne H. Hoy's *Fabrications: Staged, Altered, and Appropriated Photographs* (New York: Abbeville Press, 1987).

6. Douglas Crimp, "Appropriating Appropriation," in the exhibition catalogue *Image Scavengers: Photography* (Philadelphia: Institute of Contemporary Art, University of Pennsylvania, 1982), p. 34. Crimp seems to have swallowed whole Susan Sontag's assertion that "to be legitimate as an art, photography must cultivate the notion of the photographer as *auteur*. . . ." In *On Photography* (New York: Farrar, Straus and Giroux, 1977), p. 137.

7. This telling phrase I first heard from photographer Emmet Gowin.

8. Coleman, *Light Readings*, pp. 251–52.

9. Europeans often use the term *autonomous* to distinguish photography that's not bespoke from commissioned imagery or work for hire. It's a useful term, one that I hope may catch on in the U.S. But it's not an alternative to *directorial*, for it doesn't help us to distinguish between Mary Ellen Mark and Cindy Sherman.

10. Speaking of whom, critical inquiry into the seminal influence of the directorial/self-portraiture oeuvre of Bunny Yeager on Sherman's work is long overdue.

11. Thomas Kuhn, *The Structure of Scientific Revolutions* (Chicago: University of Chicago Press, 1970), p. 16.

12. One obvious implication of this is that Garry Winogrand's failure to conclude his famous tautological credo, "I photograph to find out how things look photographed," by adding the crucial words "by me," indicates a fundamental, profound, and apparently lifelong misunderstanding of the nature of the medium.

13. A. D. Coleman, *The Grotesque in Photography* (New York: Summit Books/Ridge Press, 1977), pp. 72–75.

14. Quoted in Walter Benjamin's 1927 essay, "A Short History of Photography," as translated by Stanley Mitchell, in *Screen* 13, no. 1 (Spring 1972): 24.

15. "The Photographic Message," 1961, translated by Stephen Heath; in Peninah R. Petruck, ed., *The Camera Viewed* (New York: E. P. Dutton, 1979), vol. 2, p. 193. It is worth noting that it is precisely such work that semiotic analysis has found most resistant to its methods; much of the thrust of Barthes's last work, *Camera Lucida*, consisted of an attempt to transcend the limitations of semiotics in order to grapple with the other aspects of photographs.

16. See Goffman, *Frame Analysis: An Essay on the Organization of Experience* (New York: Harper/Colophon, 1974), pp. 123–55.

17. Traces of this approach also can be found in the work of many photographers who might not be identified with it immediately; though they did not work directorially in the sense described above, W. Eugene Smith and Minor White clearly understood themselves to be utilizing the theatrical frame.

18. This essay originally appeared, in considerably different form, in the catalogue to the exhibit *True Stories and Photofictions* (Cardiff, Wales: The Ffotogallery, 1987). Portions of it first appeared in the essay "Collaborations Through the Lens: Photography and Performance Art," in f.stop Fitzgerald's book *Doc·u·men·tia* (New York/San Francisco/Los Angeles: Last Gasp/Post Contemporary Productions/Astro Artz, 1987), n.p.

Mutant Media

PHOTO/MONTAGE/COLLAGE

In our time, more than in any previous one, the degree to which visual images coexist, impinge upon, and breed with one another has been brought to consciousness.

Many factors have contributed to this awareness. One, of course, is its inevitability: whatever paucities afflict our lives, lack of imagery is not one of them. Most of us occupy environments that suffer from an image glut. (I speak broadly here, but would not exclude inhabitants of the so-called Third World, where film and television have made more inroads than bulldozers, or print.) That has been the consequence — necessarily neither logical nor predictable — of introducing into widespread cultural operation the photo-mechanical reproduction of still images and the kinetic/visual mass media.

Marshall McLuhan was fond of saying, concerning cultural attention to the effects of media, "Whoever discovered water, it wasn't a fish" — his point being that we take our environment for granted. Now, it could be argued that, as human beings are no less "natural" creatures than any others, an imagistically saturated environment *is* our natural habitat at a certain stage in our evolution; it simply took us a while to develop to the point where we could generate it for ourselves. Even if that were the case, though, clearly there was some transition, some metamorphosis — recent enough that some vestigial memory remains to signal us that we have undergone a noteworthy change.

At some point even the most unobservant among us must realize that the rising waters of imagery have already reached our chins. A century from now, if things continue on this present course, people may take this immersion as a given: the possibility of spending a day free from the intrusions of mass-manufactured imagery may then seem as far-fetched and mythological as our present-day folktale that people once drank water and ate foodstuffs uncontaminated by pesticides and other synthetic chemicals.

In our time, however, we have to live with the knowledge of this ongoing transformation. Because their work involves attunement to their own imagistic activities, visual artists are perhaps more immediately, keenly aware of these infringements. (In a sense, their production of images may be a device for achieving some semblance of control over the massive doses of imposed imagery.) But this uncomfortable knowledge is not exclusively privileged to them, nor restricted to a widened circle that includes academics and media critics; reference to it, even heated discussion of it, takes place everywhere: daytime TV, the pages of *People* magazine.

Combine this awareness with a fundamental insight we owe to psychoanalysis — that the unconscious generates endless combinations and permutations of whatever we feed to it — and it can come as no surprise that so much art in this century of mass media addresses directly the issues of received imagery and image hybridization. By this I don't mean the formalist, self-referential notion of "art about art," but something more urgent and more culturally introspective: an art about ourselves as members of an image-sodden species.

Nor should it startle us that a critical discourse centering around those concerns has emerged. Much of this discourse, that which is loosely gathered under the banner of semiotics, is an odd one — odd not so much in its jargonization (for it is irresistible to many critics to jargonize) as for the source of its jargon, the languages of the military and of high-tech medicine: appropriation, intervention, rupture, suture. . . . Borrowing those locutions, which were developed specifically to depersonalize the infliction of physical pain on individuals, is a curious critical tactic, apparently a mimetic attempt to anesthetize physical agony and keep emotional trauma at bay.

There are of course other, plainer ways of speaking to these issues, as critics such as John Berger have shown us.[1] Nonetheless, it is not coincidental that, in an age where so much of what we consume is force-fed to us, artists and critics have come to scrutinize and analyze their cultural diet. As Ezra Pound pointed out, "Artists are the antennae of their race." It is their job — and that of critics too, if I may be so bold — to taste the future for their culture, to see what nourishments and poisons it may hold.

That future promises to be inextricably bound up with the lens-based media: still photography, film, and video. Hardly accidental, then, that these technologies generate the bulk of the imagery that has pervaded our culture (reciprocity, as it were, for our culture's pervasion of photography). Yet an ever-increasing proportion of that imagery resembles only tangentially what we were until recently accustomed to referring to as *photographs:* self-contained, slice-of-life extractions from single moments in space and time. And many examples of it should not be thought of or described simply as photographs, in the literal sense of the word—either because that's not *what* they are, or because that's not *all* that they are.

Until relatively recently such works were misunderstood, disregarded, even despised, by the critical/historical establishment. However, the past two decades have seen a radically revisionist examination of the evolution of photographic picture-making, by critics, historians, and practitioners alike. One result has been the reconsideration and reclamation of all available techniques for the production of photographic images. Consequently, works that, twenty years ago, had to fight for the right to be considered as part of the continuum of artistic/photographic activity now seem classic examples of a tradition—indeed, a tradition that, given the increasing presence of digitized photography, is unquestionably on the verge of technological obsolescence.

Ironically, photography and the techniques of picture-making called *photomontage* and *photocollage* must take responsibility for that imminent archaism. Photography has proven that creative work could be done in a medium that involved machines and chemistry and was not dependent on manual mark-making. Photomontage and photocollage have demonstrated the potential inherent in certain strategies for the cross-breeding of the resulting images. And nowadays, as I've noted elsewhere, computers "make possible not only the encoding of images but the generation of virtually infinite permutations and variations thereof: not only everyone a photographer but everyone a picture editor, photocollagist, and photomonteur."[2]

Before proceeding further, it's necessary to acknowledge a problem of nomenclature. Simply put, there is no agreement in the field concerning the kinds of works to which the two terms *photomontage* and *photocollage* apply. Specifically, works produced by applying the cut-and-paste method widely known as *collage* to photographic prints or reproductions of photographs are with increasing frequency identified as *photomontages;*[3] and works produced by layering latent images over each other in a photographic negative or print, a process commonly taught and referred to nowadays as photomontage,[4] are given short shrift or omitted entirely from surveys and discussions of photomontage.[5]

We can perhaps lay the blame for this confusion at the door of the Berlin Dadaists, who originated the term *photomontage* just after World War I, for the purpose of differentiating their efforts from both Cubist collage and Surrealist photocollage. Gravitating to the polytechnic model for their endeavors, in opposition to the high-art model, they adopted a word, *montage,* that, in German, refers to the assembly line.[6] But the distinction they were seeking to establish was one of intent and effect, not one of craft; a Dada photomontage and a Surrealist photocollage share a commonality of facture.

Often used interchangeably by those who came after, and occasionally by the Dadaists themselves, these two terms have since become difficult to separate: even practitioners of the same method frequently define their process differently. (For example, John Heartfield called himself a *photomonteur, monteur* meaning engineer in German; Bertolt Brecht went so far as to claim that Heartfield had invented the form of photomontage; yet even Heartfield's brother and life-long collaborator, Wieland Herzfelde, acknowledges that *photocollage* is the more apt description of this work.[7])

The extent to which these terms have become problematically conflated is illustrated by the fact that in the spring of 1993 one could wander through the rooms housing the superb John Heartfield exhibit that opened at the Museum of Modern Art, wherein every work on view was dutifully labeled a *photomontage* (because that's what Heartfield called them, though he generated all of them by cutting and pasting together bits of found and/or commissioned photographs with added text),[8] then step into the adjacent supplementary exhibit, "Selections from the Collection: Dada and Surrealism," and find a work there by Heartfield's Polish disciple, Mieczyslaw Berman, sharing approximately the same politics and the same agit-prop purpose, produced by exactly the same technique, but identified as a "photocollage."

As these exhibits made clear, curators continue to have their difficulties with all this. Small wonder: To say that theorists and historians offer nothing resembling a consensus is to understate the case. Famously, Sergei Tretyakov, in his 1936 essay on Heartfield, proposed that physically a photomontage could incorporate elements that were nonphotographic, but that it had to "express not simply the fact which it shows, but also the social tendency expressed by the fact"[9] — i.e., that its status as photomontage was content-determined, and that content was in turn ideologically determined. In short, Tretyakov asserted that attributing photomontage status to a collage involving photographs was a (favorable) political value judgment.[10]

Herewith a sampling of subsequent attempts to grapple with the situation. Some scholars accept the term *photomontage* as identifying a genre of collage:

– In their massive reference work, *The Visual Arts: A History,* Hugh Honour and John Fleming refer to the Berlin Dadaists' invention of "a type of *collage* called photomontage" [emphasis in the original].[11]

– In a section of his book *Art and Photography* headed "Collage: Photomontage," Aaron Scharf opines that "Max Ernst shares with John Heartfield the distinction of having elevated this *collage technique* to a highly articulate level" [emphasis mine].[12]

Some insist that they are two separate forms:

– William Rubin asserts that "the most significant contribution of the Berlin group was the elaboration of the so-called photomontage, actually a photo-collage, since the image was not montaged in the darkroom."[13]

– Naomi Rosenblum follows suit, maintaining a distinction between the two, but defining montage narrowly as "the restructuring and combining of negatives in the enlarger."[14]

– And, in his essay for the catalogue of the Heartfield retrospective mentioned above, Klaus Honnef identifies H. P. Robinson and O. G. Rejlander as the "real fathers" of "genuine photomontage."[15]

Some deploy the term *photomontage* to subsume all combinatorial practices involving photographic imagery:

– Robert Sobieszek does just that in his 1978 essay "Composite Imagery and the Origins of Photomontage."[16]

– Dawn Ades, in her book *Photomontage,* which has become a standard reference on the subject, notes, "My practice in compiling this book has been to include works 'when the imagery is predominantly photographic, whether collaged or rephotographed, rather than according to the technique.'"[17] She credits the phrase she quotes to an undated letter from Aaron Scharf, but provides no context for it. She includes virtually every kind of work with photography beyond the traditional positive print from a single negative, including photograms and negative prints.

– Cynthia Wayne apparently follows their lead in the catalogue essay for the survey exhibit *Dreams, Lies, and Exaggerations: Photomontage in America.* In her definition of terms for this essay, Wayne proposes that photomontage be defined as "the composite or joining of photographs from disparate sources, brought together to create a single image"[18] — regardless of the work's content, style, or physical form. (Amusingly, Wayne feels obliged to plead her case for including works crafted by any technique other than collage — i.e., in-camera or darkroom-produced photomontages by Harry Callahan, Val Telberg and others — under the heading of photomontage!)[19]

Some employ the various terms whimsically and inconsistently:

– Rosalind Krauss, in her analysis of Surrealist practice regarding photography, treats as separate "stylistic options" three forms that she identifies as *combination printing, photomontage,* and *photo collage*; a few paragraphs later, however, she uses the term *montage/collage,* and then refers in quick succession to "the montages from the early 1920s by the dadaists" and to "dada photo collage."[20]

Some attempt to be all things to all men:

– Gordon Baldwin of the J. Paul Getty Museum, in his usually reliable handbook, *Looking at Photographs: A Guide to Technical Terms,* insists that collage "(from the French *coller,* to glue), is the combination on a common support of diverse fragments of various materials. These can be photographic or not, with or without specific image content. There is normally no attempt to conceal the edges of the parts, which may be roughly torn or smoothly cut, and there may be considerable handwork in pencil, pen or brush on the surface. The artistic result relies in part on juxtaposition and texture and often tends to the abstract.

"Montage (from the French *monter,* to mount)," he continues, "is the combination of diverse photographic images to produce a new work. The combination is often achieved by rephotographing the mounted elements or by multiple darkroom exposures. In the finished work, the actual physical edges become inconspicuous. The artistic result often tends to the surreal rather than the abstract." Baldwin illustrates this definition with a maquette for a poster by the Soviet artist Gustav G. Klucis (who considered himself to be a photomontagist). This piece, from the Getty's own collection, is pieced together from several different images and textual components. It bears on its surface a considerable amount of hand-lettering and other graphic alterations, is described in its caption as a "gelatin silver photomontage with applied paint."[21] Meanwhile, despite Baldwin's suggestion that montage can be achieved by "multiple darkroom exposures," separate definitions are given elsewhere in the book for "combination prints" and "double exposures."

Some muddy the waters with inappropriate comparisons:

– Beaumont Newhall, in the 1984 edition of his history, offers the bewildering proposition that "the pasting together or otherwise combining of separate and disparate pictures to form a new visual entity was one of the most striking contributions of the artists of the 1920s. Their work, *though not technically dissimilar to the 'combination prints' by H. P. Robinson, Rejlander, and other nineteenth-century photographers,* was utterly different in intent and result" [emphasis mine].[22]

And some, by not becoming part of the solution, position themselves as part of the problem:

– In *Montage and Modern Life,* a book addressed almost entirely to and illustrated almost exclusively by works produced via the collage process, Christopher Phillips writes, somewhat disingenuously, "One result of the mixed ancestry of photomontage has been a lasting confusion of terminology, with attempts to make general formal distinctions . . . yielding little in the way of helpful clarification."[23]

I could go on and on. What this muddle boils down to, patently, is that there is no consensus on the terminology to be used to identify several specific kinds of physical objects produced by significant alternative approaches to praxis. The cause of this confusion is that its sources are talking on several different levels of abstraction at the same time:

(1) The physical nature of the objects and their means of production; (2) the purpose of the work, especially its advocacy of particular political ideologies; and (3), as in the argument of Tretyakov, its success in ideological terms.[24]

That photocollage is not synonymous with photomontage, at least in terms of production methods, is evidenced by the fact that while photocollages are often described as photomontages, the reverse is rarely true; for instance, I've never heard anyone use *photocollage* to describe the work of Jerry N. Uelsmann. Thus it's obvious that critics, historians, and picture-makers alike recognize these two forms as substantively different in kind from a performative standpoint, whether or not they care to acknowledge it.

In my opinion, neither of these terms should be used as an umbrella to cover what are in fact two extremely divergent forms of photographic image-making. I believe it's useful and, in fact, instructive to distinguish between the two; and, at least within the confines of this essay, it's my intent to do so. In short, along with Rubin, Rosenblum, Honnef, and Herzfelde, I am arguing that what Honnef calls "authentic photomontage" is radically different from photocollage, and that their differences are not based on image content but on the process of facture.

The distinctions between photomontage and photocollage that I'm about to discuss do not pertain so clearly in the electronic-imaging environment, and those terms may cease to prove descriptively useful for such works in digital form; perhaps something like *image hybridization* will subsume and replace them both. However, the fact remains that what we've called photomontages and photocollages to date are specific types of physical objects whose production will not terminate simply because computers are available. Since the nature of those objects varies considerably, some attention to their divergent methods of facture is in order. Understanding how an artist worked — his or her relationship to tools, materials, and techniques — is essential to apprehending the full meaning of the resulting creative acts. As practices, both photomontage and photocollage can be traced back into the nineteenth century; their origins are in vernacular, commercial, and artistic Victorian-era photography. They emerged when William Henry Fox Talbot's invention of the negative-positive process brought with it the option not only of making multiple photographic prints on paper but also of interpretive intervention in the passage between exposure and print. This made possible the application to photographs of those techniques that came to be known as *photocollage* and *photomontage*.[25]

The French word *collage*, as Baldwin notes, means "gluing"; the craft process is that of pasting varied materials together. *Photocollage*, then, involves the cutting up and reassembling of parts of photographic prints or reproductions of photographs. In itself, this does not necessarily require any specific photographic activity.[26] All that is consistently photographic in such images is the origin of some of the component parts. Because many forms of such imagery can be generated without the use of a camera or a darkroom, it has attracted not only photographers but visual artists from outside the parameters of photography. Indeed, it is the form of photographic image-making that has been most accessible to photographers and nonphotographers alike.

The Dadaists Hannah Höch, Raoul Hausmann, George Grosz, and Heartfield all laid claim to the "invention" of photocollage and/or photomontage. Since they all acknowledged their prior encounter with vernacular, naïf, and commercially produced photocollages and photomontages, the claim was obviously meant to assert that their efforts brought this technique into the vocabulary of the avant-garde. Barbara Kruger, Doug and Mike Starn, John Baldessari, and Romare Bearden are only a few diverse examples of artists from the U.S. who've explored this technique in the latter half of this century.

Some of those who work in this form — Heartfield and Kruger, for instance — conceive of the original collage as a matrix from which to derive photographic copy prints with a unified surface, or even as a basis for the generation of photomechanical reproductions: posters, newspaper and magazine illustrations, book covers. Others, like Bearden and the Starn brothers, conceive of the original collage as the finished work.[27] In both the latter cases, as in others, the collages may also incorporate nonphotographic elements (paint, colored paper, cellophane tape, objects, texts, and so forth). As Man Ray once wrote, "A certain amount of contempt for the material employed to express an idea is indispensable to the purest realization of this idea."[28] Suffice it to say that photocollage — requiring as it does some version of that "contempt for materials" — is not a medium for purists.

Though photocollage concerns itself with elements of the photographic, its patchwork end results tend to be objects that cannot be literally described as photographs. Moreover, even when rephotographed and printed on light-sensitive materials (as Bearden did with his first efforts), internal evidence — the seams joining the various components, for example — generally remain apparent, undermining any illusion of photographic integrality.[29] For those reasons, photocollage does not seriously challenge the recordative function of the photograph; as a form, it simply employs fragments of lens imagery for patently different purposes.

In the visual arts, the term *montage* — French for "assembling, putting together" — was first applied to film editing. In essence, with each splice the film editor decides when to merge and how to blend two separate moments of vision, and how to rationalize their linkage. The term is as variously defined in cinema-studies discourse as it is in art and photography, and the debate thereon is even more extensive and bewildering. (The Soviet film director Sergei M. Eisenstein, one of filmic montage's prime theorists, once proposed discriminations among no fewer than five different varieties.[30] More recently, Gene Youngblood has argued for what he calls "montage as collage," based on the idea of "a mosaic simultaneity."[31] It would take a bolder or more foolhardy soul than I to essay a map of the territory in which their positions function as landmarks.)

In all cases, however, the nature of film and the perceptual phenomenon known as *the persistence of vision* ensure that, even if briefly, the viewer's memory of moment A will be *overlaid* on moment B.[32] For that reason, transferred from the kinetic medium of cinema to the static medium of photography, the term can have a precise meaning. It's my argument that, strictly speaking, *photomontage* is the superimposition of one latent image on another so that the two are blended and coexist within the emulsion of a single negative and/or a single print. This can be achieved in such a way that both are simultaneously present and visible — that, is, that they overlap and show through each other, as in the work of Heinz Hajek-Halke and Edmund Teske — or done so that all the diverse image components appear integral to the depicted scene, an effect mastered most consistently by Uelsmann.

Accomplishing this requires photographic methods. One of these is "double" or multiple exposure, done while the negative is still in the camera; Harry Callahan, Duane Michals, and numerous others have utilized this technique. There are also montage processes applicable in the darkroom, among them multiple printing (exposing the printing paper to part or all of several negatives in succession) and what's known as combination printing or the "sandwiching" of negatives (printing two or more superimposed negatives simultaneously). These are the techniques in which such practitioners as Telberg, Uelsmann, Maurice Tabard, and Barbara Morgan have specialized. In such cases, both the image components and the techniques involved are purely photographic in nature.

Photomontage tends to be produced on photographic paper and to look — at least at first glance — like unmanipulated imagery; as an oeuvre such as Uelsmann's demonstrates, even when the combinatorial nature of the finished work is recognized it may offer little or no indication of where one component ends and another begins. Those who employ it as an imagistic strategy demonstrably lack devotion to any realistic imperative connected to photography, though they are no less clearly aware of the omnipresence of that attitude in our cultural relation to the medium. Thus they deliberately propose a radical alternative to the naturalism that has been the stock-in-trade of photography since its inception. Photomontage provides unsettling evidence that, paradoxically, although the camera must always address something in front of the lens, some photographs portray events that never happened. Even when (as is often the case with Uelsmann and others) the viewer is confronted with deceptively seamless images that at first and even second glance may be perceived as literal documents, the antirealism of what is depicted manifests itself rapidly, if not immediately. Only someone extremely unsophisticated in relation to lens imagery could fail to realize, during the course of his or her first encounter with a body of such work, that these are not documents of any single moment of external "reality." Their purpose, patently, is not to delude the viewer into the permanent conviction that that's how things really looked. Instead, they set the viewer up for a delayed perceptual double-take.

By thus contradicting the viewer's assumptions concerning the predictability and literalness of the photograph, they redirect attention to the specific image itself; the viewer is asked not to believe but rather, in a theatrical sense, to suspend disbelief. This heightens awareness of the imagery's artificiality and evokes a different set of questions in regard to its purpose.

Because this process inherently contradicts the "window on the world" assumptions that Western culture imposed on photography from its birth, dispute has always swirled around this practice. The process of photomontage first attracted widespread attention in the mid-nineteenth century through the directorial, literary work of Henry Peach Robinson and O. G. Rejlander, whose techniques and results were the subject of heated and even violent debate among photographers and critics. Meanwhile, however, documentarians utilized it for such purposes as the insertion of clouds into landscape pictures. Vernacular photography — postcard imagery and studio portraiture in particular — popularized photomontage. The pictorialist movement of the late nineteenth and early twentieth century accepted it; works by Alvin Langdon Coburn, Alfred Stieglitz, and Edward Steichen bear witness to that embrace. In the 1920s it became a staple of modernist practice in Europe, even entering the photographic curriculum devised for the Bauhaus by Laszlo Moholy-Nagy, who called it "simultaneous seeing by means of transparent superimposition."[33] But modernists in this country — led by Edward Weston and Paul Strand — repudiated it.

Photomontage never fell out of favor abroad; but in the post–World War II U.S. photo scene, the "purist" approach advocated by Strand, Weston, Ansel Adams, and the West Coast school on one hand and photojournalists and more autonomous small-camera photographers on the other was dominant. In one way or another, they mostly preached and practiced what Adams called "previsualization" — the full realization of the image at the moment of exposure; by their lights, any subsequent tampering with the data on the negative was anathema.[34] And the photo-historical establishment here, sharing their biases, virtually banished photomontage from the U.S. "creative photography" scene.[35] It was widely employed, however, in a variety of applied and commercial venues: book and magazine illustration and advertising, in particular.

Yet even when photomontage has fallen into disfavor, it has refused to die. Around the middle of this century — before Uelsmann and others of his generation began exploring this constellation of practices — such North American experimenters as Morgan, Teske, Telberg, and Clarence John Laughlin were pursuing them. However, they had to learn to survive in the cracks, enduring collegial opprobrium,[36] finding outlets for their work that were uncontrolled by the establishment, and cobbling together their own versions of their lineage and field of ideas. (For instance, until recently Telberg was better known among filmmakers and writers, due especially to his long-term collaboration with the writer Anaïs Nin; he is only now being brought into the ranks of significant contemporary photographers, though I can recall Uelsmann acknowledging his influence decades ago.[37])

One might argue plausibly that photomontage can be considered a form of "pure" photography, but no one would sensibly propose it — or photocollage — as falling within the tradition of realism. Regardless of approach, images in this form declare themselves to be non- and even anti-realistic. They are descriptions of inner states rather than external phenomena. This is true even of those images whose makers' concerns are patently sociopolitical—those of Heartfield and, sometimes, Morgan, for example. (Perhaps this explains why Sigmund Freud, who surely would have encountered examples of both forms, consistently chose what I'm defining as photomontage as an analogue to the condensation of experience in dreams;[38] implicit in his selection is an assumption of the psychological difference in impact of the two forms.)

Certainly photomontages are not "documents" in any sense of the word. At best, they provide only a facsimile of plausible visual evidence; instead, they persuade us to their cause (if they do) through metaphor—metaphor reliant on the logic of dreams as much as, if not more than, on the logic of rhetoric.

The impulse toward both of the forms under discussion should come as no surprise to anyone even moderately familiar with photography's history, and certainly not to anyone who works at making photographs on a regular basis. An awareness of the layering of the world, a sensitivity to the different levels of visual perception available at any given moment, is a natural consequence of learning to see photographically. Thus we might say that a montage/collage sensibility is inherent to what the photographer Walter Chappell calls "camera vision."[39]

Recall, if you will, the famous Walker Evans photograph which shows rows of standard head shots under a sheet of glass on which the word *Studio* is lettered. Or another of Evans's best-known works, "Truro, Massachusetts," from 1931, a close-up study of a torn movie poster with bits of other posters showing through its rents. What are these if not ready-made collages?

In fact, that last-named image anticipates the method of selection and appropriation employed by Jacques Villeglé and other practitioners of a form of art activity that emerged in France in the late 1940s called "*affichisme*." The term doesn't translate well; "posterism" would be a literal version, but a more accurate if more cumbersome rendition would be "art made from that which is affixed in public places." Briefly, what Villeglé and other members of the group known variously as *Affichistes* and *Nouveaux Realistes* did was to cut and tear away sections from the layers of posters plastered up one on top of another in urban spaces, and then present these accidental collages in the new context of the fine-art venue. (Villeglé, who was in New York for a retrospective show of these works at the Zabriskie Gallery in the fall of 1989, was delighted to be shown [by this author] the Evans image from Truro, with which he was not familiar—and which preceded by almost two decades his invention of "*affichisme*" in 1949. In the fall of 1993, an exhibit contrasting Villeglé's works with photographs of billboards and posters by Evans, Brassaï, Harry Callahan, Aaron Siskind, Berenice Abbott, and others was mounted at Stephen Cohen in Los Angeles.)

Part concrete poetry, part urban archaeology, part Duchampian found objects, the *Affichistes'* bits of cultural detritus are palimpsests of sorts, with sequential deposits of communication silted atop one another. Much of the imagery that appears in them is photographic; yet, as I'm suggesting, there is an even closer connection to the medium of photography in their method. It's not coincidental that such intermingled fragments from the cultural midden heap have long fascinated photographers — Evans being only one among many — who have employed them as subject matter for most of this century. (Richard Misrach's "Desert Cantos: The Playboys," comprising large-scale color photographs of the pages of several issues of the men's magazine that were used for target practice by anonymous shooters in the Southwest, is a recent example of this collagist concern.)

As for montage, just think of the many images by Eugène Atget in which what is seen through a window and what is reflected in its glass are blended in the negative. Isn't this a "found" photomontage? Surely the same is true of parallel works by Louis Faurer, Berenice Abbott, Lee Friedlander, and many others. I'm inclined to go even further, to propose that pulling an incident from the far background into coexistence on the picture plane with a foreground event constitutes montagist thinking, but that might be stretching the point — which I hope has been sufficiently made.

It's only a short step from these methods, none of them objectionable to photography's purists, to the acceptance of accidental in-camera double exposure, and a mere hop further to deliberately making multiple exposures on the same negative, as Coburn, Callahan, Carlotta Corpron, and countless others have been prone to do. Certainly the conceptual leap from there to negative sandwiches and combination printing is not a long one, and many in photography have chosen to taken it.

While the differences between photocollage and photomontage are crucial, what those image-makers who explore the two have in common is also worth pointing out. Regardless of which approach they embrace, they all alter or combine photographic imagery in ways that require a healthy irreverence for the documentary integrity of the original negative or the inviolability of the print. Yet while they may fragment or otherwise manipulate that imagery to a great extent, its photographic origin is obviously important to them. Thus, although their methods and intentions vary widely, it is apparent that they are all aware of and actively utilizing the peculiar psychological affect of the photographic image, whose facticity and temporality always refer us to its source in a specific time and place.

In the last analysis, their long-range intent is less to create an effective illusion of quotidian reality than to refer simultaneously to diverse aspects and moments of reality by combining portions of different photographic images, which encode the surface appearance of those aspects and moments. It is in the nature of photographs to particularize. But when thus fragmented, mixed, and reorganized, they can be made to generalize as well — to symbolize classes of things in addition to representing the single instance which is their subject. This is one strategy for indicating to the viewer that the appropriate territory of interpretation for such imagery is the poetic.

Notwithstanding a considerable degree of critical confusion over and even disdain for the forms called photomontage and photocollage, artists and photographers have for generations kept these forms alive and energized for their peers and those who have come after. By doing so, they helped to establish the present-day climate of acceptance in which the legitimacy of these forms is no longer seriously questioned. (It is revealing to note that the current generation of young picture-makers working in these forms — forms whose nature initially challenged academic notions of how "fine" art was to be made — are almost without exception academically trained, yet obviously take the viability of these approaches for granted.)

The persistence of these pioneering workers (and those of their countless colleagues — Dora Maar, Pierre Molinier, Tilo Keil, Wanda Wulz, James Van Der Zee, Claude Cahun, Wallace Berman, Nancy Burson, Robert Heinecken, Michael Martone, Ray Metzker, Robert Rauschenberg, so many more) in exploring these mutant media, despite the lack of any clear tradition or craft system, provides undeniable evidence that these forms are central to art in our time. The urge toward this hybridization, the dissolution of hierarchies within and distinctions between media, and the attack on the assumed inviolable realism of the photograph, have been first and foremost *creative impulses;* they originated with picture-makers.

What is called for now is a critical and theoretical approach to such work that recognizes the fundamental differences between these two techniques of picture-making yet also accepts their shared aspects — and that sees the investigations of them by artists and photographers as intertwined explorations along a continuum. The absence of a sense of embracing critical tradition, and the denial of common ground and a shared field of ideas, has been confusing and debilitating.

In short, it's time for a tentative unified-field theory of these mutant media to be developed and put into practice by critics and historians alike.

That is especially important at this juncture because photomontage and photocollage, it seems, have been all along a prophecy of the media environment in which lens culture finds itself presently situated. For we now live in a montage/collage context; not only has the montage/collage aesthetic permeated our visual environment, but we ourselves are involved in those activities constantly: we make an audio collage each time we search the channels on the car radio, generate an audio-visual collage whenever we graze the TV with remote in hand, set loose a media montage whenever we turn on the radio and TV, or the TV and the boom-box, simultaneously.

The historianship and criticism of nineteenth- and twentieth-century image-making are only beginning to catch up with these developments. To do so effectively will require those disciplines to address directly the impact of new image-making technologies on artistic production, as well as the complex interaction between "high" art, vernacular art, mass media, and culture — and the extent to which photography is deeply implicated in all of these. That this should take place is imperative — for it is only through such inquiry that we can evolve a comprehensive critical/historical overview of the hybrid imagery of the twentieth century and the forces that impelled its production. It is from the analysis of the hand-crafted, labor-intensive montages and collages of the past hundred years that we will derive the understandings needed to address their electronically generated descendants on the brink of their first swarming.[40]

NOTES

1. See John Berger, "The Political Uses of Photomontage" in *The Look of Things* (New York: The Viking Press, 1972), pp. 183–89.

2. See A. D. Coleman, "The Vanishing Borderline," *The Structurist* 25–26 (Winter 1986–87): 109–14, and elsewhere in this volume.

3. For example, in several late-1992 New York gallery shows by Martha Rosler.

4. Any basic instructional text in photography, when addressing the issue of photomontage, will describe in-camera double exposures and multiple or combination printing in the darkroom, not the use of paste-pot and scissors. E.g., Warren Bruce, *Photography* (Minneapolis/St. Paul: West Publishing, 1993): "[O. G. Rejlander and H. P. Robinson] used multiple printing techniques (*photomontage*) to achieve [their images]" (p. 285; emphasis in the original). And, further on, in a section on "Special Printing Techniques," there is the heading "Photomontage," followed by this definition:

> Photomontage is the combination of parts of images from two or more negatives into one print. The simplest photomontage is the negative sandwich, in which two negatives are placed one on top of the other in the negative carrier at the same time and printed.
>
> A more controllable method for photomontage is to print multiple images from different images on one sheet of printing paper (p. 323).

Warren provides some instruction in the technique as described, and illustrates this passage with an image by Jerry N. Uelsmann.

5. E.g., Matthew Teitelbaum, ed., *Montage and Modern Life* (Cambridge: MIT Press, 1992).

6. It seems highly unlikely, however, that given their interests and politics the Dadaists were unaware of the complex debates that were just then erupting over the meaning(s) and functions(s) of "montage" in film theory and practice, especially in France and the Soviet Union. Certainly that awareness was operative in the other direction: Sergei Eisenstein's first published essay, dating from 1923, addresses the "montage of attractions" as "fully analogous with the 'pictorial storehouse' employed by George Grosz, or the elements of photographic illustration [photo-montage] employed by Rodchenko." ("Montage of Attractions," in Eisenstein, *The Film Sense*, translated and edited by Jay Leyda [New York: Harcourt Brace & World, 1975], p. 231.) So there's reason to believe that the term's high profile in the discourse over cinema, seen as the quintessential art form of the new century, may have influenced its selection by the Dadaists.

7. Wieland Herzfelde, "Heartfield's Photomontages and Contemporary History," in John Heartfield, *Photomontages of the Nazi Period* (New York: Universe Books, 1977), pp. 17–18.

8. This terminology is maintained in the exhibition's accompanying catalogue, *John Heartfield* (New York: Harry N. Abrams, 1992). It seems likely that this project will aggravate and perhaps even institutionalize a confusion whose origins can to a considerable extent be laid at the door of this prolific Dadaist-turned-left-wing-satirist and polemicist.

9. Sergei Tretyakov, *John Heartfield: A Monograph* (Moscow, State Publishing House, 1936); reprinted in Heartfield, *Photomontages of the Nazi Period,* p. 26.

10. The basic uselessness of Tretyakov's "definition" — except as a yardstick for a work's adherence to whatever ideology is currently in the ascendant — seems self-evident: It is premised on a work's success, and it assumes that the "social tendency expressed by [a] fact" is specifiable and not open to various interpretations. If one sought to apply Tretyakov's rule, what would one call a work that sought to "express not simply the fact which it shows, but also the social tendency expressed by the fact," yet failed to do so? What if a work proposed a "social tendency expressed by [a] fact" with which the viewer/critic disagreed? In Tretyakov's terms, is a Fascist photomontage possible?

11. Third edition (New York: Harry N. Abrams, Inc., 1991), p. 684.

12. Aaron Scharf, *Art and Photography* (Baltimore: Penguin Books Inc., 1974), p. 284.

13. *Dada, Surrealism and Their Heritage* (New York: Museum of Modern Art, 1968), p. 42.

14. Naomi Rosenblum, *A World History of Photography* (New York: Abbeville Press, 1984), p. 565.

15. Klaus Honnef, "Symbolic Form as a Graphic Cognitive Principle: An Essay on Montage," *op. cit.,* p. 51.

16. "Composite Imagery and the Origins of Photomontage, Part I: The Naturalistic Strain," *Artforum* 17, no. 1 (September 1978): 58–65, and "Composite Imagery and the Origins of Photomontage, Part II: The Formalist Strain," *Artforum* 17, no. 2 (October 1978): 40–45.

17. Dawn Ades, *Photomontage*, revised and enlarged edition (London: Thames and Hudson, 1986), p. 17. Stephen Golding, in *Photomontage: A Step-by-Step Guide to Building Photographs* (Rockport, Mass.: Rockport Publishers, 1997), does her one better by cheerfully jumbling together collage, montage, and digital-imaging techniques.

18. *Dreams, Lies, and Exaggerations: Photomontage in America* (College Park, Md.: The Art Gallery, University of Maryland at College Park, 1991), p. 13.

19. Ibid.

20. "Photography in the Service of Surrealism," in Rosalind Krauss, and Jane Livingston, *L'Amour Fou* (New York: Abbeville Press, 1985), pp. 24–28. The most recent to conflate the two similarly is Graham Clark, in *The Photograph* (New York: Oxford University Press), pp. 197–200.

21. Malibu, California: J. Paul Getty Museum, 1991, p. 26.

22. Beaumont Newhall, *The History of Photography: From 1839 to the Present Day* (New York: Museum of Modern Art, 1982), p. 210. Except as a way of making clear his general disdain for all such imagery (i.e., as a form of the "they all look alike to me" locution), I cannot imagine how a reputable historian could suggest that Hannah Höch's collages were "not technically dissimilar to the 'combination prints' " of Robinson and Rejlander.

23. "Introduction" to Teitelbaum, *Montage and Modern Life*, p. 26.

24. This is not to suggest that, despite their art-world origins, either photomontage or photo-collage, as I'm about to define them, are in some way inherently "politically correct" and/or necessarily left-oriented. The recent revelation by Gerald Silk of Temple University that both forms were employed successfully by the Futurist Bruno Munari in his designs for the Italian Fascist magazine *L'Ala d'Italia* in the 1930s scotches that argument. (Lecture, College Art Association, Seattle, February 1993.)

25. There are in fact examples of daguerreotype photocollages and photomontages, the latter most notably in the genre of "spirit photography." An example of this form is in the collection of the J. Paul Getty Museum. But these are exceedingly rare.

26. For an account of Heartfield's working method, which was not unlike that of a contemporary art director at an illustrated magazine, see the lamentations of W. Reissman, one of a number of photographers he employed to produce photographic components for his maquettes that he imagined and sketched, as quoted in Ades, *Photomontage*, p. 49.

27. Although Bearden's first experiments in this form, which he called "photo-projections," involved rephotographing the finished collage and using the copy negative to make oversize black-and-white photographic enlargements for exhibition purposes.

28. Man Ray, "The Age of Light," in *Man Ray: Photographs* (New York: East River Press, 1975), p. xv. See my introduction in that volume for further discussion of Man Ray's relationship to photographic process.

29. There are of course exceptions, such as the work of Heartfield, Adál Maldonado and Allen A. Dutton.

30. "Methods of Montage," in Eisenstein, *Film Form: Essays in Film Theory*, edited and translated by Jay Leyda (New York: Harcourt, Brace & World, 1949), pp. 72–83. Eisenstein's text was written in 1929.

31. "Syncretism and Metamorphosis: Montage as Collage," in Youngblood, *Expanded Cinema* (New York: E. P. Dutton & Co., 1970), pp. 84–91.

32. See Eisenstein, "A Dialectic Approach to Film Form," in *Film Form*, pp. 49–50.

33. "A New Instrument of Vision" (1932), in Richard Kostelanetz, ed., *Moholy-Nagy* (New York: Praeger, 1970), p. 52.

34. The whys and wherefores of this curious reaction are considered at some length in Sally Stein's essay, " 'Good Fences Make Good Neighbors': American Resistance to Photomontage Between the Wars," in Teitelbaum, *Montage and Modern Life*, pp. 128–89. See also Cynthia Wayne, *Dreams, Lies, and Exaggerations*.

35. For an account of the effect of this purge on the appreciation of the work of the leading pictorialist photographer, writer, and teacher William Mortensen, see A. D. Coleman, "Disappearing Act," *Camera Arts* (January/February 1982): 30–38, 108, and "Conspicuous by His Absence: On the Mysterious Disappearance of William Mortensen," elsewhere in this volume. See also my essay "Beyond Recall: In the William Mortensen Archive," *William Mortensen: A Revival* (Tucson: Center for Creative Photography, 1998), pp. 81–95. This publication is a special issue, No. 33, of the CCP's journal, *The Archive*.

36. Virtually alone among her North American peers, Barbara Morgan managed to keep a foot in both camps without any loss of credibility as a photographer of a basically purist persuasion. Though long overshadowed by her more famous (and more subject-dominated) dance photographs, her photomontages—which move curiously between the politically programmatic

("Hearst Over The People," for example) and the more ambiguously private — were exhibited and published at the time of their making, without significantly affecting her reputation. But those of her peers already mentioned who pursued this approach at greater length were either ostracized or ignored by the photo-historical establishment.

37. Although (and, perhaps, because) there are few traces of the stylistic influence of others to be found in even his earliest work, Uelsmann has been admirably scrupulous, generous, and affectionate in paying homage to his precursors. To give another example, I can also remember the delight with which, in 1974, Edmund Teske read to me a recent letter from Uelsmann punningly proclaiming him one of Uelsmann's "occult heroes."

38. His preferred example was the facial composite technique of Francis Galton. See, for instance, "Distortion in Dreams," p. 172; "The Dream-Work: The Work of Condensation," p. 328; and "The Dream-Work: Secondary Revision," p. 532, in Sigmund Freud, *The Interpretation of Dreams*, trans. and ed. by James Strachey (New York: Avon Books, 1965).

39. See his credo, simply titled "Walter Chappell," in Nathan Lyons, Syl Labrot, and Walter Chappell, *Under the Sun: The Abstract Art of Camera Vision* (New York: Aperture, 1972), unpaginated.

40. This essay, which incorporates several passages on the subject from my 1977 critical survey, *The Grotesque in Photography* (New York: Ridge Press/Summit Books), originated as the catalogue essay for the 1988 survey exhibition "Montage" (New York: Hillwood Art Gallery, Long Island University, 1988). This marks its first publication in this much longer form.

The Vanishing Borderline

SKETCH FOR A MANIFESTO ON THE
''DEMOCRATIZATION'' OF ART[1]

It is generally agreed that the origins of what we now think of as artistic production are to be found in the anonymous artisanry of tribal society. In Western culture, with some exceptions (literature, principally), artwork — at least through
the medieval period — was the result of the unsung and traditionally unsigned
efforts of what Bernard Leach calls "the unknown craftsman,"[2] often collectively
generated.

If, in a dialectical model, this can be considered the thesis of art, then its
antithesis is the concept of artistic creation emergent from the Renaissance:
that the highest forms of art sprang from acts of solitary genius at comparatively
rare moments of inspiration; and, further, that such genius was the mark of a
distinct class of people who by it were appropriately separated from their fellow
citizens, isolated by their uniqueness, even (at the most romantic extreme of this
vision) necessarily at odds with the culture from which they were so severely
differentiated.

Out of this contradictory mix of history and myth there appears to be evolving
in our day a synthesis both surprising and problematic — surprising in that much
of its impetus comes from unpredicted sources, problematic because its most
likely consequences will provide little ammunition to either those who have
advocated the "democratization" of art or those who have rigorously opposed it.

One of the stimuli to which this new stage can be traced is the presence and
availability of unprecedented media of visual communication. J. David Bolter
has argued that sometimes a technology becomes what he calls a "defining technology," one that is "always available to serve as a metaphor, example, model, or
symbol."[3] There are numerous such technologies currently operative in Western

culture; the two with which this essay is primarily concerned are photography and the computer, in all their forms.

With great effort, against great resistance, certain approaches to or usages of photography have finally established themselves as constituting a field variously called art/creative/serious photography (an unfortunate collection of adjectives with which few are entirely comfortable). Though debate still rages over whether this or that mode of photography can appropriately be considered to be art, it's a rare person today who refuses to concede that some of the work done by photographers has both aspired to and met the working definitions of artistic endeavor.

By establishing on the shores of Western culture a beachhead for a form of expression and communication that was very much involved with science and technology, photography paved the way for acceptance of creative work in subsequent media with an equivalent involvement in the scientific/technological. Thus, although we do not yet have even a single exemplary oeuvre representing a standard for what is loosely referred to as "computer art," much less an articulated hermeneutics thereof, there seems to be virtually no argument over the inevitable appearance of such a form.

The assumptions underlying this new attitude would not have seemed so self-evident even a century ago. Previously, the distinguishing characteristic of any work of art was considered to be the mark of the hand, evidenced in the physical form of unique, manually crafted objects. The medium of photography provoked an expansive rethinking of this assumption, since to accept a photograph as a work of art is to agree that what makes a medium viable for the production of art is, more broadly, its accessibility to idiosyncratic expression and its capacity for the metaphorical — the marks not of the hand but of the mind.

There appears to be a transcultural impulse to test new communications technologies for these qualities — that is, to experiment with their viability as vehicles for what might be described roughly as the concerns of the poet. Some media appear to be more suited to this than others (for example, to the best of my knowledge no artistic application of telegraphy has ever been demonstrated). Moreover, since media have different characteristics and biases, some make their actual and potential applications more easily accessible to larger numbers of people than do others.

Photography placed the capability for visual description and interpretation of the physical world in the hands of the public at large at the historical moment when direct observation of that world via lens instruments had become central to Western culture's epistemology.[4] Yet what was given with one hand was taken away with the other. Up until 1888 — that is, for the first half-century of the medium's existence — anyone who wanted to make photographs had to practice photography. If one worked with the direct-positive processes (such as the daguerreotype or the tintype) one developed one's exposed plates immediately. This was true also of the positive-negative processes that prevailed through the 1860s — the so-called wet-plate methods. Even the introduction of dry plates did not significantly reduce the photographer's involvement with the craft; it only provided some breathing room between exposure of the negative and production of the print. Short of hiring a personal assistant to handle darkroom chores, the person who wanted to make photographs had no choice but to become knowledgeable in all areas of the craft, to think his/her work through from exposure to print.

George Eastman changed all that, permanently, when he introduced the first Kodak camera in 1888. "You press the button, we do the rest," read the slogan under which it was advertised. The camera user received the loaded camera, ready to go; after 100 exposures the film, still in the camera, was shipped back to the company for processing and printing. Not only did this make it unnecessary for camera users to process their own film and make their own prints, it actually made that impossible, at least at first: The film for this camera initially was such that amateur processing was impracticable. Historians of photography are prone to celebrating this as a triumph. I'd suggest that, in fact, it was in another sense a setback of major proportions. This was a time when a continually widening segment of the public was acquiring craft expertise in the first democratically accessible visual communications system. The Kodak No. 1 — by appealing to people's capacity for laziness — allowed the "luxury" of foregoing any study of that craft. In separating the act of negative exposure from development and printing, Eastman's system effectively undermined the impulse to learn the process of photography, by rendering such knowledge unnecessary.

A year later, Kodak introduced a new film, on a plastic base, that gave amateurs the option of either developing and printing their own images or letting Kodak "do the rest." But the die had already been cast. By permitting camera users to remain ignorant of the processes they were employing, this approach to photography remystified the medium — made of it a prototypical "black box" — right at the juncture when its demystification was under way among the population at large.[5] Why do I consider this a setback? Because the camera is, on at least two levels, an instrument for the control of perception. Not only does the user employ it to tame and organize visual perception, but through its structure the originators of the camera and their descendants — those who design the cameras, films, and papers of our time — dictate how we will see.

The only truly effective way to come to an understanding of the degree to which "the medium is the message" in photography is to study the medium itself—that is, the process of production. Only in that fashion can one discover the medium's inherent biases—the kinds of ideas and information whose transmission it facilitates, the kinds that it inhibits or obstructs. Only through the direct experience of craft can one encounter first-hand the limitations, the controls, and the range of variables at the disposal of the practitioner.

Globally, there is now an enormous population of camera users, only a tiny fraction of whom actually practice photography. The two functions, initially integral to each other, have been severed in what I can only suggest is the photographic equivalent of pre-frontal lobotomy. Social historians of the far future will find it astonishing that—in a culture producing billions of photographs annually—much of the population still believed that cameras take pictures, that photographs don't lie, that seeing is believing. These are ideas of which photo students are effectively disabused by their second semester of coursework. They are ideas of which an entire culture could be disabused by a widespread emphasis on photography education.

Nonetheless, the situation I'm describing is rectifiable; even given the limitations noted above, photography made the power to produce recognizable images of particularized objects into common property. That there are those who choose not to exercise this power—or that there are those who, for reasons economic, educational, or physical, do not share access to it—does not contradict this; there is nothing inherent in the medium of photography itself that links it causally to such exclusions.

Writing, as a technology of communication, carried within itself the potential of social literacy—literacy shared by most, if not all, the members of a society. Not until the invention of the printing press, however, was this potential fulfilled. Similarly, photography embodies the potential for a culture-wide visual equivalent of literacy. The computer—which, among its other functions, combines these two forms—may represent the culmination of centuries of change in our culture's relationship between the senders and receivers of communication, including forms of communication that may be subsumed under the rubric of art.

The basic nature of the production/consumption cycle in art has changed drastically in the post–World War II period. Blame it on the G.I. Bill, the "baby boom," and then-current notions of progressive education and the good life, if you will. That change guarantees not only the instability of the art market but, more important (and more to my point), the redefinition of the concept of art.

To begin with, we now have the decentralization of art production, achieved through the spread of art education. It is a premise of virtually all progressive education theories that each person has a creative potential, the unlocking and fulfillment of which should be a goal of democratic societies. Art education is one of the presumed vehicles for this flowering; such training and encouragement, commenced as early as possible in the individual's life, is now widely considered to be a birthright. Such a stimulus — amplified by the increasing availability of technically accessible media of expression / communication such as photography, computers, and replicating devices like the Xerox — necessarily multiplies geometrically the amount of art being produced, the number of people producing it, and the economic class diversity of its producers.

This democratization (some — not I — would consider it a vulgarization[6]) of art has expanded both the knowledgeable and the less-informed audiences for art, which demand greater exposure to acknowledged "great" works of art through books, exhibitions, and other forms of presentation. (The blockbuster museum extravaganza, such as the "Treasures of Tutankhamen" or the Picasso retrospective of recent years, is a logical consequence of this development.) At the same time, this accelerates the inevitable cycles of appreciation and disregard to which all works of art are prone; no work of art, once established as significant, is likely to remain famous — *or, conversely, neglected* — for as long as it might have in the past.

This acceleration is a version of Andy Warhol's prophecy that in the future everyone will be famous for fifteen minutes. In a quite literal sense, art is consumed faster than ever before in Western culture. The decrease in the endurance, the staying power, of any given work of art in such circumstances, combined with the limited stockpile of acknowledged masterpieces and the appetites of an ever-widening audience, has created a vacuum. Into it rushes *new art*.

For reasons elucidated a few paragraphs earlier, an ample supply of new art exists; indeed, given the number of people now involved in art production, we may have reached the first occasion in the history of Western civilization when the supply of art actually exceeds the demand for it. There is no shortage of quite adequate and serviceable contemporary art: work that functions well as aesthetic merchandise, as interior and exterior decor, as subject for critical dialogue, and as jumping-off point for casual discussion.

Particularly novel in this context is the fact that the audience for this art and its producers are one and the same: the educated middle and upper classes, more and more members of which go beyond a spectatorial involvement with art to engage in its manufacture.[7] Since these are the classes previously disposed to invest in the artistic production of others, the situation ensures a destabilized art market. After all, a work of art has little intrinsic significance; the bulk of its importance, certainly including its financial value, has more to do with what the culture makes of it (both over time and at any given point) than with anything "eternal" or intrinsic to it.[8] So the demystification of romantic intangibles such as genius, passion, and taste that results from hands-on experience with artistic production leads to skepticism toward the process of cultural attribution by which "important works of art" are initially identified; similarly, a more broadly based education in art history — whether transmitted by schools, books, magazines, or television — creates a public with a more sophisticated understanding of the life a work of art leads in the world.

With the withering away of the artistic academy, the notion that high-art status requires certification simply disappears. The hierarchy of media of art production, and the borderline between art-makers and art consumers, vanishes. Walter Benjamin hinted at a parallel development in writing half a century ago, attributing it to the introduction of "letters to the editor" columns in the daily papers:

> . . . the distinction between author and public is about to lose its basic character. The difference becomes merely functional; . . . at any moment the reader is ready to turn into a writer. . . . [The] reader gains access to authorship. . . . Literary license is now founded on polytechnic rather than specialized training and thus becomes common property.[9]

There is an old American labor-union movement proverb: "Cream's gonna rise, unless you homogenize." I am suggesting that a combination of technological and cultural conditions is leading us toward such emulsification; in the words of Edward W. Waddell, "as the technological advances of our age erode traditional boundaries of community and social stratification, the likely consequence is that art, like the culture, will become more homogeneous."[10] Yet it's my belief that this will manifest itself not as a return to tribalism and anonymous artisanry, but as a new synthesis of attitudes and behaviors combining elements from both poles of the dialectic.

If photography makes the process of visual representation widely available, ,the computer makes the act of image manipulation into literal child's play. The combination of the two will inevitably transform visual communication, of which the visual arts are a subdivision. Kodak's disc system, currently on the market, already involves computer-encoded printing instructions and video display of individual images; other systems now on the drawing boards will incorporate the additional capacity to switch easily between still and kinetic image recording.

There is an ever-growing assortment of digital-camera systems, already in production or planned, aimed at the amateur market, designed for the production of vernacular imagery. In conjunction with simple home computers, they will make possible not only the encoding of images but the generation of virtually infinite permutations and variations thereof: not only everyone a photographer but everyone a picture editor, photocollagist, and photomonteur.

Equally important is the fact that this technology innately deemphasizes the physicality of art. What these systems offer, as a tangible final product, is a standardized, small-scale print-out on a sheet of paper, indistinguishable as a type of object from the print-out anyone else might generate. These print-outs can, of course, be used as matrices, transferred in various ways to other physical forms; no doubt they will be by some. But it is in the nature of such systems to focus attention on the differences between the images created with them, rather than on the distinctions between the objects that embody those images.

Furthermore, the primary display format for these images will be the video screen itself. If one can create, store, and call up at will an image — indeed, a wealth of images — on the monitor, why bother to derive a "hard copy" version of any unless and until a particular purpose for same is identified? These new systems permit image production without object production as a necessary concomitant. Thus they encourage a relationship to the work of art not as precious object but as dematerialized image and idea.

With such attitudes embedded in the technology — in effect, epistemologically bound to it — the user of these tools will absorb the epistemology through the experience of praxis. This process of internalization will no doubt begin in early childhood. The range of successful programs for empowering children as photographers is considerable;[11] parallel experiments with computers, such as Seymour Papert's,[12] are already under way.

According to Papert, the typical child's eventual relation to computing is holistic, leading to polymathic thinking — that is, a versatile, problem-solving approach to computer activity.[13] There is no reason to believe that this would not hold also for the computer artist. From an art-historical standpoint, the polymath (with his/her diversity of interests and abilities) is unlikely to become single-tracked long enough to develop virtuosity in any one form; rather, she or he will be more prone to a restless, synthetic, eclectic sensibility. At the pole opposite the virtuoso, one finds, typically, the seminal artist who, unconcerned with the polishing and perfecting of style, is more interested in seeding a multitude of ideas. Artists look to the virtuosi in their medium to set standards of performance; it is in the often rougher, less resolved work of the seminal figures that they find guideposts to the territories still to be explored.[14]

We might then predict that the new imaging technologies under discussion will tend to breed generations of polymathic artists who at their best may prove to be seminal and at their worst merely eclectic/derivative, but among whom virtuosity as we now understand it will be an even greater rarity than it has been to date, since the tools and materials of these media make it harder rather than easier to distinguish the master from the tyro. With artists less intent on the refining of masterworks than on the investigation of manifold aesthetic options, the number of new "masterpieces" will diminish, the number of computer-imaged "sketchbooks" will rise.

To many, this will appear to be the dreaded "decline of quality" about which we've heard so much (from such standard-bearers as José Ortega y Gasset, Aldous Huxley, Barbara Tuchman, and more), particularly since the sheer quantitative rise in the volume of artwork produced will make it ever harder for any single work or oeuvre to be noticed in the crowd, much less to sustain focused attention for any period of time. There will be much more mediocre work in circulation, the result of an inevitable leveling effect. More and more, the work achieving public circulation may be work produced primarily for the purpose of self-expression rather than communication; in a society permeated by the mind-set of the therapeutic model, art as therapy, as self-help, is on the ascendant.[15] Much work in this vein — perhaps most — will be tedious, like most premature autobiography; much will be half-digested, ineptly crafted, undistinguished, even bad. Wading through it is the price we will pay for our impulse to pursue whatever is meaningful in art to us.

Some despair at the very thought of this eventuality; I cannot help but share Charles Sackrey's hope that "everyone [will be] spending all their time writing bad poems rather than building good cars and electric appliances and highways and pineapple bombs."[16] We hear frequently, in this regard, that Nicaragua under the Sandinistas was a nation of poets — that everyone, from military leaders and diplomats to workers and foot soldiers, from the newly literate aged to the schoolchildren, was writing poetry.[17] Does anyone doubt that the bulk of this outpouring, no matter how heartfelt, could not compare to even the second-drawer work of such major Latin American figures as Neruda, Paz, Guillen? Does anyone believe, nonetheless, that Nicaraguan culture would have progressed faster if these fledglings had put aside their pens?

What we need, I think, is the generosity to grant to our own culture and people the poetic license we give so freely to those of the Third World. Manuel Alvarez Bravo, the dean of Mexican photographers, once wrote (on the specific subject of vernacular mural art), that what he called "Popular Art . . . the art of the People," was "the work of talent nourished by personal experience and by that of the community."[18] The art I'm prophesying will not be ill-served by such a description as Alvarez Bravo's — or, rather, by the revision of that description that would be mandated in a computer culture. The academy may atrophy, but the truly naïf artist is rapidly becoming a thing of the past; in an environment that presents programs about Picasso on national television and Van Gogh reproductions on coffee cups, there is no escape possible from the influence of "the experiences of other painters in other times and other cultures." And, though the community that nourishes the work and for which it is primarily intended may still be small and local, access to information (and art is, among other things, a type of information) in the electronic age is such that the audience for any work of art entering the database is certainly national, potentially global, conceivably inter-planetary. Under such circumstances, only a retrograde conservatism can validate nostalgia for clear demarcation between naïf and "high" art, uninformed region-alism, fixed critical standards, a permanently ensconced pantheon . . .

There are few in this culture uninfected by the viral strain of that conserva-tism, myself included. Excoriation or self-flagellation is a less than useful re-sponse to that revelation. My purpose here has been to point out the signs of an imminent, inexorable transition, so that — whether eagerly or reluctantly — we may begin to prepare for it. There is consolation as well as hope to be drawn from the words of choreographer-composer Pauline Oliveros:

> I feel it is important for people to make their own music, and to under-stand some of the processes involved in the making of music, so as to have media self-defense. . . . It does not matter that not all composers are great composers; it matters that this activity be encouraged among all the popu-lation, that we communicate with each other in non-destructive ways.[19]

NOTES

1. In reviewing a 1979 volume of my essays, *Light Readings*, for *Art in America* 67, no. 7 ("Fretting About Photos: Four Views," November 1979, p. 17; reprinted in his collection *Moon-light Blues: An Artist's Art Criticism* [Ann Arbor: UMI Research Press, 1986], pp. 245–53), Peter Plagens proposed that "if he could rid himself of residual lust for esthetic quality, [Coleman] might write the great manifesto of artistic democracy." I've been chewing on that thought for years now; this essay is the result. It was first published in a Canadian journal, *The Structurist* 25–26 (Winter 1986–87): 109–14.

2. Given the accumulating evidence that often, if not always, "Anonymous was a woman," we might do well to substitute the neologism *craftsperson*, if not the non-sexist *artisan*.

3. J. David Bolter, *Turing's Man: Western Culture in the Computer Age* (Chapel Hill: University of North Carolina Press, 1984), p. 11. For a more extensive citation of Bolter's argument, see "Lentil Soup," elsewhere in this volume.

4. A. D. Coleman, "Lentil Soup," *Et cetera: A Review of General Semantics* 42, no. 1 (Spring 1985): 19–31, and elsewhere in this volume.

5. The camera user's autonomy is recuperated only superficially by the advent of instant-print cameras such as the Polaroid SX-70.

6. E.g, Daniel Boorstin, *The Image: A Guide to Pseudo-Events in America* (New York: Athe-neum, 1962). See also Aldous Huxley's classic diatribe on this theme, in *Beyond the Mexique Bay: A Traveller's Journal* (London: Methuen, 1949), pp. 274–75.

7. A poll taken in 1985 by the National Research Center for the Arts under the auspices of Louis Harris and Associates indicated that despite a decrease in leisure time due to inflation, art

spectatorship was on the rise — and, further, that art production by the general populace was also increasing. For example, of those polled, 25 percent engaged in some form of creative writing; 47 per cent were involved with photography. (See Margaret Davies, "Americans and the Arts . . . A Recent Survey," *Art & Artists* [March/April 1985]: 4–5.) The infiltration into current "high art" activity of such "folk" forms as graffiti, break dancing, rock, and jazz merges the working class and even the underclass with the middle and upper classes as audience/performer, validating Louis Armstrong's observation: "All music is folk music. I never heard no horse sing no song."

8. This is a too-brief and certainly inadequate summation of what's come to be known as the *institutional theory of art*, which emerged from Arthur Danto's 1964 paper, "The Artworld" (*Journal of Philosophy* 61, no. 19 [October 15, 1964]: 571–84). For his subsequent elaboration of this idea, see Lars Aagard-Mogensen, ed., *Culture and Art: An Anthology* (Atlantic Highlands, N.J.: Humanities Press, 1976), pp. 9–20, and also the other papers in this collection. See also Howard Becker, *Art Worlds* (Berkeley and Los Angeles: University of California Press, 1982), and Peter Berger and Thomas Luckmann, *The Social Construction of Reality: A Treatise in the Sociology of Knowledge* (New York: Anchor Books/Doubleday & Co., 1967).

9. Walter Benjamin, "The Work of Art in the Age of Mechanical Reproduction," *Illuminations* (New York: Schocken Books, 1969), p. 232.

10. Edward W. Waddell, *Art Papers* 9, no. 3 (May/June 1985): 26.

11. There are many examples one could cite. Wendy Ewald's work with Appalachian and Latin American children, and the "Bushwick Project" organized by Builder Levy and others with New York City youngsters, are only two recent ones.

12. Seymour Papert, *Mindstorms: Children, Computers, and Powerful Ideas* (New York: Basic Books, 1980). According to the 1991 report of the U.S. Census Bureau, "46 percent of all American children [between the ages of 3 and 17] are using computers at school or at home," up from 30 percent in 1984. See "Periscope: Vital Statistics — Computerland," in *Newsweek* (April 8, 1991): 8.

13. Ibid., pp. 132–33.

14. Laszlo Moholy-Nagy was an excellent example of the seminal polymathic artist; the curriculum he outlined for the New Bauhaus in Chicago is a model for educating artists with those same qualities. See Richard Kostelanetz, "Moholy-Nagy: The Risk and Necessity of Artistic Adventurism," in Kostelanetz, ed., *Moholy-Nagy* (New York, Praeger, 1970), pp. 3–15.

15. Theodore Roszak, *Person/Planet* (New York: Anchor Press/Doubleday, 1978), pp. 86–91.

16. In a marvelous letter to the editor, "More 'Confessions,'" *New York Times Book Review* (April 27, 1980): 34; Sackrey identifies himself as the editor of *The Westbere Review*.

17. See, for example, Joe Klein's report, "Nicaragua at the Turning Point," *Rolling Stone* 458 (October 10, 1985): 37ff. Many of the Sandinista leaders, including Daniel Ortega, are published poets; perhaps the best-known of them is Minister of Culture Ernesto Cardenal. Vice-President Sergio Ramirez is an internationally acclaimed writer of short fiction. The inclusion of poetry workshops in the literacy campaign spearheaded by Rosario Murillo, leader of the Cultural Workers' Association and Ortega's wife, is well documented. For details, see *And Also Teach Them to Read*, by Sheryl Hirshon with Judy Butler (Westport, CT: Lawrence Hill & Co., 1983); "Nicaraguan Literacy Campaign," by Valerie Miller, in *Nicaragua in Revolution*, edited by Thomas Walker (New York: Praeger, 1982); and Miller's doctoral dissertation, "Nicaraguan Literacy Campaign: Education for Transformation" (University of Massachusetts, 1983).

18. Emily Edwards, *Painted Walls of Mexico: From Prehistoric Times Until Today* (Austin and London: University of Texas Press, 1968), p. 145. For a more extensive citation of Alvarez Bravo's comments, see this book's epilogue, "Items for an Agenda."

19. Quoted in John Rockwell, "The Musical Mediations of Pauline Oliveros," Arts and Leisure Section, *New York Times* (May 25, 1980): 20.

Conspicuous by His Absence

CONCERNING THE MYSTERIOUS DISAPPEARANCE
OF WILLIAM MORTENSEN

Let us begin with a context, and a time frame. It is January of 1934. We are in a conceptual terrain whose boundaries are defined by the readership and editorial staff of a magazine called *Camera Craft*. Published out of San Francisco, *Camera Craft* (hereinafter referred to as *CC*) is at this time the official organ of the Pacific International Photographers' Association, an organization whose aesthetic tendencies are what is generally understood to be "Pictorialist."[1]

CC's editorial torch has just recently changed hands. Departing is Sigismund Blumann; replacing him is George Allen Young. The reasons for this transition are not made clear within the pages of the magazine — no swan songs, no heralding trumpets. Yet, though there is no reason to suspect that a revolution has taken place, there's no avoiding a feeling of the changing of the guard, and no denying a sense that Blumann is — in the several meanings of the word — *relieved* by his own departure.

Something has been happening in West Coast photography of late. It is of obvious significance, and Blumann takes his editorial responsibilities seriously enough that he's not only given it space in the magazine[2] but has even spoken out in defense of its right to exist. Yet he has little sympathy for it as imagery; it goes against his taste patterns, which by now are firmly entrenched. He's tried to write about this internal schism in his column, "Under the Editor's Lamp," but it doesn't emerge too clearly. On the one hand, he is capable of generosity:

> This man [Edward Weston] has evolved a photographic art of his own. It
> is not greater, it is not less than the pictorialism which deals with other
> forms of beauty. He is a poet who tiring of songs to gods and fancies in
> stars and skies determines to make his epics of cosmic stars and the mate-

rial of which heavens are made. A Materialist who belies crass materialism by extracting the beauty, the poesy, out of realities.[3]

On the other hand, he can be driven to sarcasm by the same stimuli:

> . . . do not be discouraged when you see a photograph of a dissected cabbage or a distorted gourd, or the sexual organs of a flower, or a landscape as black as interstellar space. You may not understand it. Neither do the ultramodernists. They shun understanding. They merely feel. . . . There may be beauty and inspiration in the heart of a cabbage, in fact there is when it is properly pickled and cooked. There may be ecstacy [sic] in the stamen and pistils of a flower with the petals chopped off. Your coarse sensibilities may not respond to them but do not despair. . . .[4]

His ambivalence finds its fullest manifestation in a review of the work which provokes it. This essay is, perhaps consciously, Blumann's valedictory. Certainly it is a poignant confession by a man painfully aware that the world is passing him by. Its emotional and intellectual complexities reveal themselves best in the reading of the full text. But consider these excerpts:

> We went [to the f.64 Group exhibit] with a determined and preconceived intention of being amused and, if need be, adversely critical. We came away with several ideals badly bent and not a few opinions wholly destroyed. We were not amused, we could not criticize adversely. . . . Classic forms of beauty have been, to us, inalienable from the pursuit of art. The f.64 Group have shown that there is something to say in a 1933 way that still may react on the cultivated senses as expressive of the beautiful. . . . Sentimentalists that we are, we shall never forgive these fellows for shattering our pet traditions. On the other hand, we are grateful to them for chastening our over-sure spirit. The Group is creating a place for photographic freedom. They are in a position to do so for *not one of them but has made a place for himself in the hitherto accepted Salon field and not one of them but could make real pictures again if he wished. In fact we are certain that outside of the wholly legitimate showmanship that actuates and entertains their mood in this f.64 business, they are still making real pictures, surreptitiously if not openly* [emphasis mine]. For us the destruction of an older taste will be like unto a surgical operation. So thick-headed are our sort. . . . Now, right now, we will concede Weston's greatness in his field. We consider the field small. We estimate lowly the highest achievement in portraiture of Gourds and Peppers.[5]

Self-evidently, these are the words of a man who has no heart for refereeing the battle royal which is brewing. But his successor, George Allen Young, formerly the book review editor, takes on that task with gusto. First, he remodels the arena: volume 40, no. 9 (September 1933), wherein he assumes the editorship, is radically redesigned: a sparser, cleaner layout, more "modernistic" in tone, is established. Aside from this, there is only one hint of what is to come— a brief notice that one member of the f.64 Group, Ansel Adams, is offering in "his new gallery at 166 Geary St., San Francisco," a series of classes and "general lectures in which Mr. Adams will trace the development of photography with the idea of establishing an aesthetic rational [sic] as the basis for future progress. . . ."[6]

Yet shortly thereafter—and, unquestionably, at Young's instigation—the battle is joined. Within the next few issues of CC, Young introduces his readership to the two principal combatants. One of these is the aforementioned Ansel Adams, at that time a comparative unknown. The other, already a photographer of international reputation, is William Mortensen.

Who is William Mortensen? You might well ask. And, until quite recently, you could have searched all the standard histories of photography in vain for an answer.[7] William Mortensen (1897–1965) is—among many other things—one of photography's object lessons in how individuals become lost to history.

History—which is, after all, a highly subjective human systematization of coincidence, a Monday-morning-quarterbacking of chaos—often disposes of its protagonists arbitrarily and uncharitably. For centuries after his death Shakespeare was treated as a minor Elizabethan playwright. Charles Ives was, until quite recently, pigeonholed as an uninfluential eccentric. *Moby Dick* was for decades dismissed as an obscure novel about the whaling industry. There are cultural cycles of appreciation and disregard under which all creative works are subsumed.

There are also those creators who shun the spotlight, choosing to work reclusively; those who fail to find it, never gaining recognition during their lifetimes; and those—the true naïfs—who have no concern that fame or fortune might in any way be connected with their obsessive endeavors.

But one of the most curious aspects of the mysterious disappearance of William Mortensen is that he vanished not after his death, nor as a consequence of his own reticence or failure to find an audience. Rather, he disappeared from photographic history at the peak of his creative life and the height of his fame and influence, and certainly not by his own volition.

Even a cursory look at the man's career makes it clear that the photography historians of his time—among whom, in English, we must number primarily the husband-wife teams of Helmut and Alison Gernsheim and Beaumont and

Nancy Newhall—could not possibly have been unaware of Mortensen's photography, his writings, or his influence on the field. Born in Utah, Mortensen studied painting with George Bridgman, Robert Henri, and George Bellows at the Art Students League in New York City after World War I. In the early 1920s he moved to Hollywood and turned to photography, rapidly earning an international reputation as both a picture-maker and a writer. Between 1932 and 1955 he founded and ran the Mortensen School of Photography in Laguna Beach, California, where approximately three thousand students passed through his courses; his images were exhibited and reproduced widely, both here and abroad; and he published a total of twelve books, scores of magazine articles, and a steady stream of letters to the editors of various photography periodicals.

Those books included his magnum opus, *Monsters and Madonnas: A Book of Methods,* an oversize volume with excellent reproductions of many of his images accompanied by explanations of his aesthetic and his techniques. *The Command to Look,* a more compactly sized but not dissimilar monograph, went through several printings. There was also a series of smaller "how-to" treatises: *Projection Control, The Model, Pictorial Lighting, Flash in Modern Photography, Mortensen on the Negative,* and others. This series of instructional books was, from the standpoint of contemporary pictorialism, what Ansel Adams's volumes on craft were in relation to the so-called purist aesthetic: the invaluable codification and clear exposition of hermeneutic principles.[8]

Mortensen's books reached a large audience. Most of them were serialized first in *CC*; during the course of any such serialization the magazine almost invariably sold out its press run, as proudly apologetic notes from the editor indicate. The book versions sold equally well, usually going into multiple printings and/or revised editions. Many of the books were published under the imprint of the Camera Craft Publishing Co., and there is reason to believe that the financial survival of *CC* during this period was largely attributable to Mortensen's writings. This in turn suggests that the availability of *CC*'s editorial columns as a forum for the imagery and ideas of the f.64 Group also might have been due to Mortensen—that, in effect, he provided the staging ground on which their verbal and visual duels took place.

On the basis of these facts alone, Mortensen's place in the contemporary history of photography would seem to be assured, his right to that place secure and inarguable. When we add to that his eloquent, elegant, and indefatigable championing of the pictorialist stance—under the constant fire of such "purist" big guns as Adams, Weston, Willard Van Dyke, Roi Partridge, John Paul Edwards, and Nancy Newhall—in a controversial public debate that stretched over a decade, his absence from the history books reveals itself to be the consequence not of inadvertent oversight but of deliberate omission. As such, it is a serious breach of the responsibilities and ethics of historianship.

The frequently proferred justification for Mortensen's erasure is that purism was waxing and pictorialism on the wane during this period. That is true, but insufficient as an explanation — and considerably disingenuous as well. In fact, though nominally pledged to the impartiality of scholarship, both the Gernsheims and the Newhalls were highly biased in their approach to photography's history. They shared an intense attitudinal and aesthetic commitment to advocacy of the "straight/purist" stance; their distaste for any form of "manipulated" imagery was repeatedly made clear. The Newhalls, in addition, were already becoming entangled in elaborate personal and professional relationships with members of the f.64 Group, particularly Weston and Adams.[9] To their discredit, they allowed their prejudices and allegiances to overrule their obligations to the discipline of historianship.

Mortensen must have seen it coming. As an isolated occurrence, he might have been able to discount Ansel Adams's omission of his work — and, indeed, of all contemporary pictorialist work and most earlier pictorialist achievement — from "The Pageant of Photography," a large traveling exhibit that Adams curated in 1939–40. After all, "Purism" as such was relatively new as a movement, and its historical roots had never yet been traced in exhibition form. Also, Adams was a practitioner, and from practitioners of a medium one expects credos and grinding axes, not overviews and eclecticism.[10]

Adams's rationale for this exclusion of the pictorialists was dispassionate in tone.[11] However, Adams's antipathy to Mortensen ran deep, with an extremely personal undercurrent. Briefly put, he wanted him dead, and said as much on several occasions. In a recently unearthed, previously unpublished letter to Mortensen — apparently intended as part of their debate, but not printed at the time — Adams waxed positively vitriolic, concluding that "how soon photography achieves the position of a great social and aesthetic instrument of expression depends on how soon you and your co-workers of shallow vision negotiate oblivion."[12] In 1937, replying to a letter from Edward Weston in which Weston notes, "Got a beautiful negative of a fresh corpse," Adams in his autobiography proudly indicated that he wrote back, "It was swell to hear from you — and I look forward to the picture of the corpse. My only regret is that the identity of said corpse is not our Laguna Beach colleague [William Mortensen]. I am convinced there are several stages of decay."[13] Years later, he would describe Mortensen as "the anti-Christ."[14]

Indeed, Adams's vendetta pursued Mortensen even beyond the grave, and well into the terrain of outright censorship and blackmail. In correspondence with this author, Therese Thau Heyman, senior curator of prints and photographs at the Oakland Museum in California, confirmed that in December of 1980, Adams—then at the height of his fame and financial success—had demanded that a small Mortensen exhibit scheduled to run concurrently with Adams's traveling retrospective at the Oakland Museum be closed to the public during his opening; otherwise he would withdraw his own exhibit. "Ansel Adams had his own list of 'enemies,'" wrote Heyman, "and Mortensen was still there and not to be removed by time and his own very evident successes."[15]

But the handwriting was already on the wall by 1940. Mortensen's work and name—and the works and names of virtually all pictorialists—had already been conspicuous by their absence from the mammoth exhibit, "Photography 1839–1937," curated by Beaumont Newhall for the Museum of Modern Art in 1937. Mortensen was not even mentioned in the catalogue to that show,[16] nor in any of its subsequent versions as it developed into the infrastructure for Newhall's *History of Photography*. Mortensen's elimination from Adams's survey was part and parcel of this purist purge, therefore; and the announcement (also in 1940) of the foundation of the Museum of Modern Art's Department of Photography, with Newhall as its director and Adams as its consultant, made that purge the official policy of the contemporary art establishment. With the publication of Nancy Newhall's 1941 diatribe, "What is Pictorialism?"—a baby-with-the-bathwater dismissal of all pictorialist images, techniques, and theories—one hardly needed a weatherperson to know which way the wind blew.[17]

If I have not yet addressed Mortensen's imagery directly, it is not out of equivocation over its significance but rather out of ignorance.

I have seen, all told, perhaps one hundred and fifty of Mortensen's images. I've encountered no more than seventy-five in the form of original prints (many of these from a portfolio that sold, upon issuance, at the price of $10 for twenty-five signed prints!). The others I've experienced in the form of reproductions: fine ones from *Monsters and Madonnas*, mediocre halftones from *CC* and the technical book series, and slides. Given both his prolificity and his concern with the expressive quality of the original print as a crafted object, this slight acquaintance hardly qualifies as the basis for a balanced and thorough assessment of Mortensen's oeuvre. My impressions, at this point, run as follows:

The level of craft—that is, Mortensen's ability as a printmaker—was consistently high and frequently virtuosic. If one accepts the stylistic parameters, techniques, and materials which he elected to utilize (among them gum, brom-oil, and bromide prints; the use of paper negatives; combination printing, easel tilting; and the inclusion of hand-drawn elements in the final image), one must acknowledge that his mastery of these is self-evident. On the level of craft alone he was the model for his generation of pictorialists; and the current generation's pictorialists, who are busily reinventing these methods, could save themselves much time and trouble by looking to a man who quite literally wrote the book on this branch of photographic printmaking.

Mortensen worked exclusively in the directorial mode, staging the events he photographed (mostly in the studio), creating *tableaux vivants* that involved scenarios, actors, props, costumes, makeup, careful posing, and controlled lighting. Perhaps this came out of his early professional background—he began his career as a still photographer on Hollywood sets. (His credits include heading the still units for *King Kong* and Cecil B. DeMille's *King of Kings.*) Certainly it was his predilection, and he was aware of it as an issue for any photographer who works with human subjects. "The posing of a model," he once wrote, "involves delicate psychological problems. The status of the photographer is somewhat that of a stage director. . . ."[18]

Given a penchant for the staged event and a flair for the *mise-en-image,* joined to a romantic sensibility, it seems inevitable that his energies were concentrated on the creation of symbolist allegories. This in itself should not be too problematic for contemporary audiences; we have, after all, managed somehow to come to terms with such diverse romantics and symbolists as Minor White, W. Eugene Smith, and Duane Michals in our own day.

The images of Mortensen's that appear to be least accessible to today's audience—and to which I find I have most resistance—are those whose subject matter predates photography itself: those based on Greco-Roman myth and medieval history. I'm not sure why that should be so. Contemporaries of Mortensen's—not only in literature (Pound, Eliot, Joyce, O'Neill, Graves) but in dance (Graham), sculpture (Moore), and the other media—could use those same subjects as resonant, evocative reference points.

That may be because, for Mortensen's generation, education generally included an exposure to what were called "the classics." Thus, if only because they had cultural currency, those symbols still had potency. But that does not hold true for my generation, nor for the ones immediately preceding and following it. Perhaps it's that they were never formally transmitted to us as culturally essential parables and archetypes. Perhaps World War II forcibly imposed new myths of Europe over the old. Or perhaps the temporality of the photographic image, and our cultural commitment to it as recordative documentation, will simply not submit to such willful and flagrant anachronism.

In any case, these images of Mortensen's are the most difficult for me to integrate into my relationship with his work. His oeuvre comprises a consider-

Fig. 1. William Mortensen, *Lucii Ferraris,* ca. 1926.

able number of them. Among these I find the comedic ones least effective. But, along with his romanticism and his classicism, Mortensen has a Gothic mood: an obsession with the grotesque and, I suspect, a belief in evil as an actual presence in the world.

It is this turn of mind and eye that, for me, redeems much of his most classicist imagery: "Johan the Mad," "Lucii Ferraris" (Fig. 1), and "Death of Hypatia" (Fig. 2), for example, have no trouble standing by themselves as images, stripped of titular connotations. They are highly stylized, to be sure — declaredly and emphatically so, like all Mortensen's work. Here, however, the decadence of his visual style amplifies the grimness of his themes.

Madness, death, corruption, torture, and occultism are recurrent motifs in Mortensen's oeuvre, so much so that I'm led to believe his attraction to historical milieux stemmed more from those concerns than from any longing for the past. Those motifs persist even as his settings become more contemporary; thus the ominous "Caprice Vennois" shares with "The Kiss" an Art Deco angularity in composition that heightens the erotic suggestiveness of both.

When Mortensen addressed the attitudes and issues of his own time, his satire — no doubt because it was more pertinent — became more pointed and more effective. At the peak of the debate in *CC,* for example, he offered up a wonderfully sarcastic image, "The Quest of Pure Form" (Fig. 3), a visual spoof of the f.64 philosophy. (Apparently no print of this is known to exist, but a re-production accompanies Mortensen's acid rebuttal[19] of Roi Partridge's preten-tiously titled and inadequately argued credo, "What is Good Photography?"[20])

Several of Mortensen's images are blunt and enormously powerful political statements. "Human Relations 1932" (Fig. 4) and "Steel Stocks Advance" (Fig. 5) are excellent examples of his polemics. I believe they deserve to stand with the work of John Heartfield and Mieczyslaw Berman. Like Heartfield and Ber-man — though not as single-mindedly political as they — Mortensen was not afraid of making images whose frank purpose was persuasion. Indeed, the differ-ences between Mortensen's attitude toward the concept of propaganda and Adams's — as illustrated in the following quotes — seem paradigmatic of their conflict, and speak eloquently of the distance between their positions.

These two statements were made in 1934, shortly after the debate began. Coincidentally, both came in the April issue of *CC.* Appearing simultaneously in the magazine at that point were the contestants' opening arguments, in the form of two series of articles. Adams's were collectively entitled "An Exposition of My Photographic Technique," while Mortensen's were portions of "Venus and Vul-can: An Essay on Creative Pictorialism."

Adams's comments on the issue of "propaganda" come in a discussion of "The

Fig. 2. William Mortensen, *Death of Hypatia*, n.d.

Fig. 3. William Mortensen, *The Quest for Pure Form*, from *Camera Craft* 47, no. 2 (February 1940).

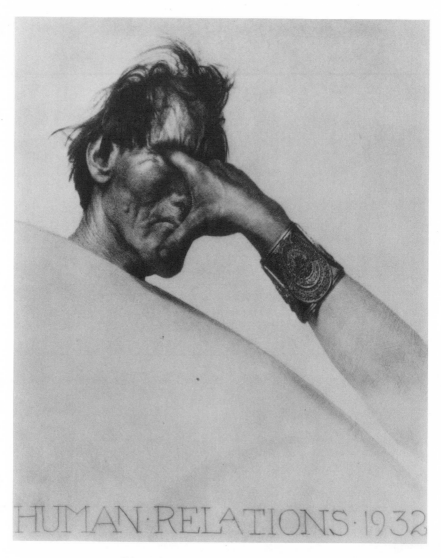

Fig. 4. William Mortensen, *Human Relations*, 1932.

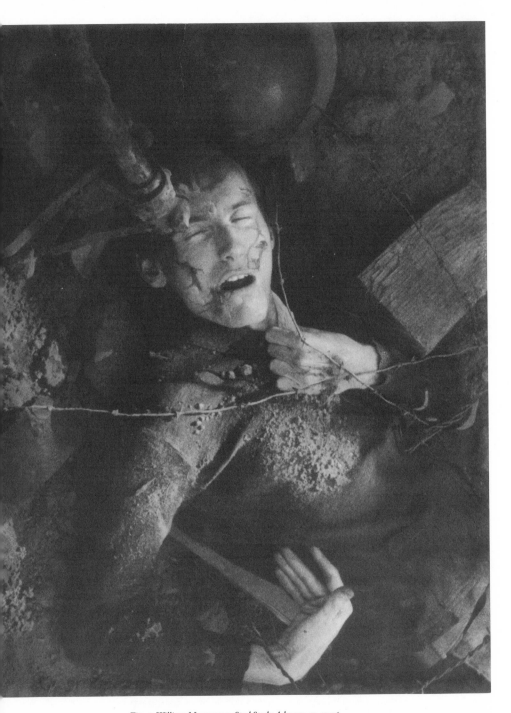

Fig. 5. William Mortensen, *Steel Stocks Advance,* ca. 1936.

Photo-Document." After predicting that this will be "one of the most important phases [sic] of photography," and particularly praising the work of Dorothea Lange, Adams cautions:

> One danger confronts the development of the photo-document—the danger of it becoming a tool of obvious propaganda. All art is delicate propaganda of some sort, but I do not feel that direct propaganda succeeds except in the injury to the aesthetic potentials. Perhaps one might say that the objective attitude admits delicate and suggestive propaganda which does not intrude on the aesthetic aspects, while the uncontrolled subjective attitude, without the vital check of taste, admits blatant and obvious propaganda. Comment is legitimate in art, but comment, motivated by reform or personal advantages, blends dubiously with aesthetic purpose. Art interprets; it cannot attempt prophecy, or motivate the social aspects of the world and still preserve its aesthetic integrity. In the social-constructive sense it is of immense value through subtle and significant comment on the contemporary scene.[21]

Mortensen—who, no less than Adams, appreciated the work of such "documentarians" as Lange and Atget[22]—responded in a different vein to this subject. In speaking of different kinds of "picture minds," he came to what he called "the didactic, propagandizing type," of which he wrote:

> Ideas, not sensations, are its basic materials, and the art-form is strictly subordinated to them. Two things mark the propagandist—the fact that he is obsessed by an opinion, and that he wishes to persuade you to a course of action. How shall he persuade you? Quiet speaking and subtle reasoning are of no avail. Paradoxically enough, propaganda, though dealing with ideas, must express itself in terms of action and emotion. Because of their direct sensory appeal, pictures are perhaps the most effective form that propaganda can take. Propaganda of this type impinges upon our minds at every waking hour . . . But provinces less limited than [advertising and political cartoons] are open to the propagandist. The whole human comedy is his. Joining with the sardonic amusement of the ironist or the moral indignation of the satirist, he may castigate human absurdities, obscenities, and brutalities, and seek the reform of humanity by revealing to it its own depravities. Goya's *Disasters of War* and *Caprichos* belong to this high type of propaganda. So do Daumier's drawings of the law courts. Pictures such as these are not purely "pictorial" in their appeal, and frequently carry a literary appendage in the form of an ironic title. But considerations of pictorial purity did not deter Daumier and Goya, nor will it discourage any modern propagandist with an idea worth expressing.[23]

Here we have the essences of the differences between the two men, and between the two photographic attitudes they embody. For Adams, propaganda — the active attempt to persuade — is close to sin, a taint tolerable only if "delicate and suggestive," requiring even then the presumably objective "vital check of taste" (whatever that might be). For Mortensen, propaganda is assumed to be forceful, and is merely another of the options open to the picture-maker. The purist posture is inhibitive and exclusionary; it narrows the range of choices. The pictorialist stance is embracive and inclusionary; it encourages enlargement of the vocabulary.

Which of these two positions has more relevance to the questions facing photographic image-makers today? Which of these two approaches to craft is more contemporaneous? Which of these two men made images more in touch with their own time — a time when this country was in a state of economic collapse, Hitler had come to power in Germany and World War II was imminent?

Adams — who, aside from the perfunctory images of the Manzanar internment camp for Japanese-Americans, never addressed what Oliver Wendell Holmes called "the actions and passions of his own time" — is usually thought of as the more "modern" of the two; whereas Mortensen, who often directed his imagery toward sociopolitical issues, has been largely dismissed as antiquated. Within a formalist frame, Adams can perhaps be thought of as the more contemporary; within a humanist frame, Mortensen might well emerge as "more in touch with his time."

But there are no easy answers to these questions. There may be no answers at all. Our individual tastes and sensibilities may pull us in one direction or another, but it would be foolish to dismiss either of these photographic philosophies as insignificant or inferior, since they represent one of the quintessential dichotomies of photographic theory and practice, and are most meaningful when considered dialectically, in relation to each other. For that reason alone it seems clear that the injustice done to the work and memory of William Mortensen has also been a profound disservice to all involved in the study of photography's history. To rectify this, we need the following:

> first, a definitive exhibit and monograph on Mortensen's imagery, to establish its scope, its volume, its issues, and its relevance to the field today;[24]
>
> second, a critical biography tracing the man's development as a photographer and connecting his work, his teachings, his life, and his times;
>
> third, a reassessment, by practitioners, of his principles of craft, to determine their pertinence to contemporary photographic image-making;

fourth, the republication of the complete purist-pictorialist debate from *Camera Craft,* accompanied by analyses and discussions of the theories and attitudes represented therein, reconsidered from a variety of standpoints;

fifth, the republication of all of Mortensen's tutorial texts.[25]

Without these, the history of photography in our century will assuredly be incomplete.[26] But worse than that, we will have lost a teacher who wrote, in 1934, that "photography, like any other art, is a form of communication. The artist is not blowing bubbles for his own gratification, but is speaking a language, is *telling somebody something.* Three corollaries are derived from this proposition.

> a. As a language, art fails unless it is clear and unequivocal in saying what it means.
>
> b. Ideas may be communicated, not things.
>
> c. Art expresses itself, as all languages do, in terms of symbols.[27]

And, perhaps even worse, we will have lost an open-minded thinker who, prophetically, urged photographers to "take unto themselves soapboxes and proclaim their opinions. Let verbal brickbats fly freely and sound body blows be given and taken. Perhaps the resultant tumult will serve to rouse the art of photography from its drowsy contemplation of its own umbilicus and persuade it to get up and go places. Perhaps the salons may be inspired to seek other meat than a monotonous succession of safe and sound banalities. Perhaps photographic degrees may come to be given on the basis of merit — and no other."[28]

It's been fifty years since William Mortensen was exiled from the history of his own medium. Isn't it time we welcomed this black sheep back?

POSTSCRIPT: HISTORY OF A FOOTNOTE

My awareness of the elimination of William Mortensen from the history of photography began in the late 1960s. Reading my predecessors and colleagues, I found frequent reference — usually brief and superficial — made to the "purist-pictorialist debates" of the 1930s and 1940s. But, while the "purists" were identified and quoted (often at length) as a matter of course, the "pictorialists" involved were never allowed to speak for themselves; invariably, their positions were synopsized and paraphrased. Even more significantly, they were never even named. The battlefield smelled of scorched earth; salt crystals crunched underfoot. I was intrigued.

The issue was not merely the accuracy or inaccuracy of the historical record in regard to a closed chapter. As a working critic, I found myself observing and discussing the emergence of a generation of photographers and artists who were busily resurrecting and/or reinventing the pictorialist approaches to praxis. If I could uncover no discussion of the accompanying theory, presumably they couldn't either, which meant that none of us had a dependable sense of lineage or precedent for what was being generated. This seemed unhealthy for all concerned.

So, somewhere around 1974, I hied myself to the annex of the New York Public Library on West 43rd Street, where back issues of old periodicals like *Camera Craft* are stored. The annex is one of those repositories whose dust motes are imbued with mysteriously soporific qualities. There I dug out, traced, read, and photocopied the entire published debate between Mortensen and his adversaries. It opened my eyes and kept me awake.

I didn't consider myself a scholar at that juncture, much less a historian. However, I'd always been a close reader of footnotes, having learned early on in my encounter with scholarship that they're often where the real action is. So, in an essay that I published in 1976 in which I made reference to Mortensen and this debate, I stated that Mortensen "was actually purged from the history of photography in what seems a deliberate attempt to break the [pictorialist] movement's back."[29] A footnote to this passage read as follows:

> From the first one in 1937 to the most recent of 1964, no edition of Beaumont Newhall's *The History of Photography: From 1839 to the Present Day* — the standard reference in the field — so much as mentions the name of William Mortensen. It will be instructive to see whether the forthcoming edition — a major revision supported by the Guggenheim Foundation — rectifies this omission.
>
> In fact, none of the books on the history of twentieth-century photography refers to Mortensen. If this could be considered even an oversight, the only questions it would raise would concern standards of scholarship. Since it cannot be construed as anything less than a conscious choice, however, the issue is not only competence but professional ethicality.[30]

The essay was well received, as was a book-length critical survey I published the following year in which I discussed Mortensen's work at somewhat greater length and reproduced a number of his images.[31] But when after a few years I could discern no effect traceable to these efforts on the field's attention to Mortensen, I began to feel an obligation to undertake the task of setting the record straight myself. So, upon being asked in 1978 to provide an essay on Edward

Steichen for a multiauthor critical anthology, I used the opportunity to pressure the project editor into commissioning a piece on Mortensen as well. Once he agreed, I dusted off my photocopies and notes and set to work.

The original version of this essay was drafted in 1978–79. But the anthology never appeared, because its putative publisher went broke. However, while that version of this essay was in the making I was contacted by Deborah Irmas, who informed me that a Mortensen retrospective exhibition, co-curated by herself and Suda House, was just then being assembled; supported in part by the National Endowment for the Arts, it would travel around the country, beginning in 1980.[32] I was particularly gratified that, in conversation and correspondence with me, as well as in subsequent public lectures, Irmas credited that footnote of mine from 1976 with sparking her initial interest in pursuing her investigation.[33]

My own argument's first public presentation came when, frustrated by my inability to find an editor willing to publish it, I used it as the text for a lecture under the auspices of the Friends of Photography at the Asilomar Conference Grounds, Pacific Grove, California, on July 12, 1981. This was an act of deliberate provocation: aside from the "master workshop" that I was teaching there, the occasion was a fully orchestrated Group f.64 hagiography, including a Beaumont Newhall workshop, pilgrimages to the sacred shrines at Point Lobos, and visits from Charis and Cole Weston.

Newhall, who was in attendance at the Asilomar presentation of this text, understandably took exception to much of it. In an animated dialogue between us that took place during the subsequent question-and-answer period (videotaped for posterity by the staff of the Friends), Newhall announced, unbidden, that he was well aware of my 1976 footnote. He went on to indicate that he found Mortensen's work to be "perverse," and that it was *his* history of photography and he could disinvite whomever he pleased. Then he noted that he was in the midst of the Guggenheim-funded revision of his history; therein, he stated with typical generosity, he was at last going to mention Mortensen — "but only to dismiss him!"[34]

Indeed, close reading of that edition discloses the following passage:

> The charter members [of Group f.64] formulated an aesthetic that in retrospect now appears dogmatic in its strict specifications: any photograph not sharply focused in every detail, not printed by contact on glossy black-and-white paper, not mounted on a white card, and betraying any handwork or avoidance of reality in choice of subject was "impure." It was a violent reaction to the weak, sentimental style then popular with pictorial photographers in California, as seen particularly in the anecdotal, highly sentimental, mildly erotic hand-colored prints of William Mortensen.[35]

Mortensen's work goes unillustrated in that volume, and none of his books are listed in Newhall's bibliography.

And since then, what? A version of the 1981 incarnation of my essay—revised, cut, and retitled without consultation with the author—subsequently appeared in *Camera Arts,* in early 1982.[36] More recently, Mortensen received shrift that's just as short and not much more sympathetic than Newhall's from Naomi Rosenblum's 1984 entry into the lists of single-volume histories of the medium.[37] A year before his death in 1993, Newhall would repeat almost verbatim that slightly inaccurate description (Mortensen did not hand-color all his prints), from the 1982 edition of his *History,* in his prefatory note to the catalogue for the "Seeing Straight" exhibit.[38] As for Helmut Gernsheim, the volume of his revised history covering the period in question has yet to be published.

As I write this, in the fall of 1993, none of the projects I proposed have been undertaken.[39] I suspect it will require a generation of historians of photography who are not emotionally committed to the purist approach to praxis to realize them; and it will take a full-scale reassessment of the international pictorialist movement from 1925 to 1950 to establish the true scope of Mortensen's influence on world photography.[40] But I would like to think that, however grudgingly, he's been allowed to return to the fold.[41]

NOTES

1. At the end of the period we are exploring—in April of 1942—*CC* will merge with, and be subsumed under the logo of, another publication, *American Photography.*

2. Edward Weston, "Photography—Not Pictorial," *CC* 37, no. 7 (July 1930): 313–20.

3. Sigismund Blumann, "Edward Weston in Three Paragraphs," *CC* 38, no. 1 (January 1931): 34.

4. Sigismund Blumann, "Art and the Camera," *CC* 39, no. 9 (September 1932): 390.

5. Sigismund Blumann, "The F.64 Group Exhibition," *CC* 40, no. 5 (May 1933): 199–200.

6. *CC* 40, no. 10 (October 1933): 437.

7. In fact, as of 1979 it was only in Arnold Gassan's blessedly unstandard and long since out-of-print *A Chronology of Photography* (Athens, Ohio: Handbook Co., 1972) that I was able to track down any direct reference to Mortensen. Gassan wrote, "*Camera Craft,* a west coast magazine, also supported this new aesthetic movement [f.64] in photography, and published a long dialogue of letters between Weston and William Mortensen, the last of the great manipulators of the pictorial tradition"(p. 95). And, further on: "The last protagonist of the gum print and manipulated image was the photographer William Mortensen, whose marvelous and horrible combination prints were published from the early 1930's late into the 1940's. A vivid dialogue between Mortensen and Weston was published at length in the editorial columns of *Camera Craft,* a magazine published in Los Angeles" (pp. 190–91). Unfortunately, there's quite a bit of factual inaccuracy even in these brief statements: the magazine was not based in Los Angeles, Weston was only one of the f.64 spokesmen, and the main body of the dialogue took the form of articles, not letters. (For more recent appearances by Mortensen in history texts, see the Postscript to this essay.)

8. The influence of Mortensen's approach to craft—including his impact on photographers who worked in other than pictorialist modes—has never been effectively traced. For example,

W. Eugene Smith certainly knew of Mortensen's printmaking strategies; four of Mortensen's instructional volumes on technique, plus copies of his two monographs, *Monsters and Madonnas* and *The Command to Look,* were in Smith's personal library when he donated his materials to the Center for Creative Photography in Tucson, Arizona. It seems entirely possible that Smith was affected by aspects of Mortensen's understanding of the relationship between negative and print, perhaps even by the look of Mortensen's prints themselves.

Nor was that influence restricted to photographers of Mortensen's generation and the generation afer that. Even a younger documentarian like Henry Gordillo has spoken of the impact of Mortensen's prints on his own way of seeing. See A. D. Coleman, "Outsider, Insider: Henry Gordillo," *Review: Latin American Arts and Literature* 38 (July–December 1987): 76.

9. See the interviews with Gernsheim and Newhall in Paul Hill and Thomas Cooper's *Dialogue with Photography* (New York: Farrar/Straus/Giroux, 1979). See also my essay, "Making History," *Camera 35* 24, no. 9 (September 1979): 14–15; reprinted in my book *Tarnished Silver: After the Photo Boom* (New York: Midmarch Arts Press, 1996), pp. 108–12.

10. The problematics of Group f.64-style "purism"—including the frequent contradictions between theory and praxis—are sketched nicely in Michel Oren's "On the 'Impurity' of Group f/64 Photography," *History of Photography* 15, no. 2 (Summer 1991): 119–27.

11. Ansel Adams, "The Pageant of Photography," *CC* 47, no. 9 (September 1940): 437–46.

12. The letter was first published in *Obscura* 1, no. 2 (November–December 1980): 17–21. Although that magazine dated it "ca. 1933," it is a direct response to articles published by Mortensen in *CC* in June and July of 1934; thus it was most likely written in August or September of 1934. It was subsequently reprinted in *Ansel Adams: An Autobiography* (New York: New York Graphic Society, 1985), pp. 113–15.

13. *Ansel Adams*, p. 244.

14. Ruth Teiser and Catherine Harround, *Conversations with Ansel Adams* (Berkeley, Calif.: The Bancroft Library), p. 181. Adams also used this term to describe Edward Steichen during the uproar surrounding Steichen's post–World War II supplanting of Beaumont Newhall at the helm of the Museum of Modern Art's Department of Photography. The implication that there was something Christ-like about practicing "straight" photography surely merits some analysis.

15. Letter to the author, June 5, 1984. Heyman subsequently organized the fine traveling exhibition "Seeing Straight: Group f.64 Revolution in Photography," whose catalogue texts touch briefly but accurately on the interaction between Group f.64 and Mortensen (Berkeley, Calif.: The Oakland Museum, 1992).

Typically, Adams dodged considerably in rendering his own account of this act. In the brief passage of his autobiography in which he discusses Mortensen specifically, he describes their exchange of opinions in *Camera Craft* as "one of the fiercest verbal battles in photographic history." He then goes on to say, presumably describing the Oakland Museum incident, "A few years ago I was not overjoyed to find an important museum showing a major retrospective of my work in their main gallery simultaneously with a Mortensen retrospective on an upper floor. Caveat emptor!" (Ibid., p. 112–13.) Indeed.

16. *Photography 1839–1937* (New York: Museum of Modern Art, 1937).

17. *CC* 42, no. 11 (November 1935): 653–63.

18. "Venus and Vulcan: An Essay on Creative Pictorialism, Part III: Selection and the Function of Control," *CC* 41, no. 5 (May 1934): 206–7.

19. "Come Now, Professor," *CC* 47, no. 2 (February 1940): 68–72.

20. *CC* 46, no. 11 (November 1939): 503–10*ff.*

21. *CC* 41, no. 4 (April 1934): 180.

22. "Notes on the Miniature Camera: Part III, Outdoor Portraiture," *CC* 42, no. 1 (January 1935): 3.

23. "Venus and Vulcan: An Essay on Creative Pictorialism, Part II: Sources and Uses of Material," *CC* 41, no. 4 (April 1934): 160–62.

24. Such a retrospective project, I'd propose, should include not only a presentation of Mortensen's own images expansive enough to encompass his oeuvre but also a survey of work by those who considered themselves his disciples, such as the Spanish master José Ortiz Echagüe.

25. As of this writing, none are listed as available in *Books in Print*.

26. I do not mean to imply by any means that Mortensen's inclusion alone would complete that history. His exclusion is emblematic of long-standing prejudice against those who've chosen to work directorially and/or to explore so-called alternative processes. The absence of blacks and the under-representation of women are among the other systemic biases that still demand corrective scholarship.

27. "Venus and Vulcan 5. A Manifesto and a Prophecy," *CC* 41, no. 6 (July 1934): 310–12.

28. Ibid., p. 310.

29. "The Directorial Mode: Notes Toward a Definition," *Artforum* 15, no. 1 (September 1976): 55–61. Reprinted in A. D. Coleman, *Light Readings: A Photography Critic's Writings, 1968–1978* (New York: Oxford University Press, 1979; University of New Mexico Press, 1998). For this footnote, see *Artforum*, p. 59 and/or *Light Readings*, p. 256.

30. Ibid., *Artforum*, p. 61; *Light Readings*, p. 256.

31. *The Grotesque in Photography* (New York: Ridge Press/Summit Books, 1977), pp. 149–50, 162–65.

32. Titled "The Photographic Magic of William Mortensen," this exhibit of some seventy-two prints—the same show to which Ansel Adams objected so vehemently, as indicated in note 15, above—toured for several years under the aegis of the Los Angeles Center for Photographic Studies. This project also included a small but handsomely produced catalogue of the exhibit. Further information about the making of this exhibit and its reception can be found in the issue of *Obscura* cited previously.

33. I would like to thank Ms. Irmas for sharing with me some of the imagery and information she uncovered in her researches, which included lengthy interviews with Mortensen's widow, Myrdith.

34. In conversation with me after the session broke up, Newhall told me that Adams's how-to books "owed a debt to Mortensen that had never been acknowledged," and suggested that I look into it. I put the thought aside until, in conversation with the researcher Matt Cook in Tucson, Arizona, November 1993, I learned that Adams's technical treatises, and the "zone system" in particular, drew heavily on several articles published in *U.S. Camera Annual* in the early 1940s, on the subjects of "Constant Quality Prints" and "Constant Quality Negatives." The author of those articles was one John L. Davenport—who, in turn, apparently learned much from Mortensen. In a letter to Mortensen dated November 16, 1935, that's in the archives at the Center for Creative Photography, Davenport, after asking Mortensen's advice on a number of technical questions regarding development and other issues, concludes by saying, "Congratulations on your book. [Either *Projection Control* or *Pictorial Lighting*, given the letter's date.] It will be a landmark in photography."

35. Beaumont Newhall, *The History of Photography: From 1839 to the Present Day* (New York: Museum of Modern Art, 1982), pp. 188–92.

36. A. D. Coleman, "Disappearing Act," *Camera Arts* (January/February 1982): 30–38, 108. A short but useful essay by Irmas accompanied this version of my own text.

37. Naomi Rosenblum, *A World History of Photography* (New York: Abbeville Press, 1984), p. 565. Rosenblum does include one illustration, a reproduction of "L'Amour" (p. 568).

38. *Op. cit.*, p. viii. Aside from that, the catalogue's text deals evenhandedly and accurately (though not extensively) with Mortensen.

39. However, the Center for Creative Photography—initially created at the instigation of Adams, as an archive fit to house his own work—has augmented its not inconsiderable holdings of Mortensen material with Deborah Irmas's donation of her own material on the subject. This includes virtually the entire Mortensen estate, which Irmas acquired from Mortensen's widow,

Myrdith. Research of the kind I've described is certainly now feasible. And Mortensen's oeuvre is thus preserved in an institution sparked by Adams; indeed, it sits in the same temperature- and humidity-controlled storeroom, breathing the same air. Wherever he may be, I suspect that Adams is "not overjoyed" by this clearly poetic justice.

40. I know of no such study now under way. But projects such as the anthology edited by Peter C. Bunnell, *A Photographic Vision: Pictorial Photography, 1889–1923* (Salt Lake City: Peregrine Smith, 1980) supply us with necessary background. And microstudies such as "California Pictorialism," a substantial survey (with accompanying catalogue) curated in 1977 for the San Francisco Museum of Modern Art by the late Margery Mann, are laying the groundwork for it. Meanwhile, an unpublished master's thesis by Edward Montgomery Clift, "The Manner of Mortensen: Aesthetic Communication and The Construction of Metaphysical Realities" (The Annenberg School for Communication, University of Pennsylvania, Philadelphia, 1992), explores the issues from a somewhat different perspective. Clift is a former student of this author.

41. This is this essay's first publication in its full intended form. Some necessary updating has been incorporated into both the body of the text and these footnotes. The reader interested in pursuing these matters further is advised to see also my essay "Beyond Recall: In the William Mortensen Archive," *William Mortensen: A Revival* (Tucson: Center for Creative Photography, 1998), pp. 81–95. This special issue of *The Archive*, the CCP's journal, contains considerable other significant Mortensen-related material.

Lentil Soup

A MEDITATION ON LENS CULTURE

For Theresa Weedy and Richard Kirstel, there at the beginning

Historians of photography have generally neglected the centrality to our culture of its ongoing relationship with the lens, particularly in their address to the prehistory of photography. That the Western world was deeply involved with lens-derived information and imagery for several centuries before the invention of photography as we know it goes largely undiscussed and even unmentioned in their chronicles. This essay is an attempt to begin rectifying that oversight. By examining the evolution of the lens, its impact on our culture, and its effect on abstract thought, I hope to establish a context in which the emergence and evolution of photography can be understood as a logical stage in humankind's ongoing involvement with the imperatives of visual communication.

It is my argument that during the sixteenth and seventeenth centuries the lens became what J. David Bolter calls a "defining technology," which he describes (and, simultaneously, illustrates) as follows:

> A defining technology develops links, metaphorical or otherwise, with a culture's science, philosophy, or literature; it is always available to serve as a metaphor, example, model, or symbol. A defining technology resembles a magnifying glass, which collects and focuses seemingly disparate ideas in a culture into one bright, sometimes piercing ray. Technology does not call forth major cultural changes by itself, but it does bring ideas into a new focus by explaining or exemplifying them in new ways to larger audiences.[1]

In addition to pointing out Bolter's use of the lens as his ow prime metaphor, I want to stress my agreement with his last sentence. I am not a technological determinist. As Lynn White, Jr., says, "a new device merely opens a door; it does not compel one to enter. The acceptance or rejection of an invention, or the extent to which its implications are realized if it is accepted, depends quite as much upon the condition of a society, and upon the imagination of its leaders, as upon the nature of the technological item itself."[2]

Most communication technologies are "invisible," in the sense that we as communicators are prone to paying attention to the content of our messages rather than to the media through which we transmit them. As an instrument of visual communication, the lens is unique in that, for all practical purposes, it is literally as well as metaphorically invisible. Made (most commonly) of glass, or some other transparent substance, it is not in itself *seen* during the process of image encoding, transmission, and decoding; rather, it is *seen through*.

Encouraged perhaps by its invisibility, we pay little attention to this technology—to its workings and its effects on our lives—even as we ingest massive amounts of its output on a daily basis, produced for our consumption by ourselves and others. (According to a Kodak press release, there were "more than eight billion color negative exposures—another record—made in the U.S. [in 1982]." Most of these were amateur-made; the total of all such "traditional exposures, including black-and-white film and color slides," was about *10½ billion*.[3]) On the whole, the members of this culture are demonstrably unconscious of the formal syntax of the visual language that informs them and which they themselves employ to communicate with each other.

There is always much to learn from what we take for granted; the problem, of course, lies in identifying those tacit assumptions. The French word for lens — *objectif* — is one indication of a continuing belief on the part of the majority of the population that lenses are objective, neutral artifacts. Certainly it is stating the obvious to say that most people who use cameras, telescopes, binoculars, and other lens instruments give no active thought to the lenses integral thereto. It is also eminently reasonable to suggest that, when looking at lens-derived imagery — film, video, and still photography — few of us consider the lenses involved in producing it. No news in this, surely.

Thus it should have been no surprise to me when a popular literary critic for the *Village Voice* (apparently intending to display his own knowledgeability, if not to suggest technical expertise) wrote in a 1983 review of a book of Civil War photographs that their makers were "intrepids, correspondents really, who lugged their awkward cameras across those wretched battlefields to report, *through an upside-down lens,* history in spasm."[4] (Emphasis mine.)

Yet it *was* startling to come across such a genuinely anachronistic ignorance of basics. Here was a highly literate, college-educated, middle-aged North Ameri-

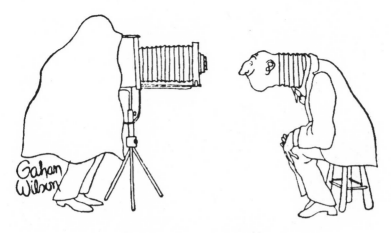

"I don't understand why I can't keep you in focus!"

can, unaware that there is no "right side up" to a lens.[5] This was startling because the Western world is, arguably, the most visually sophisticated culture in recorded history.

Most of that sophistication is comparatively recent, specifically attributable to photography: directly, through what camera vision[6] and photographs have taught us about the appearance of things, optics, and the phenomenon of visual perception; and indirectly, through the proliferation and repetition of imagery that photography makes possible. Though the theoretical grounding for most members of this culture is skimpy at best, the direct experience with lens systems and lens imagery is extensive. Thus, to borrow a concept from Noam Chomsky, the visual equivalent of *linguistic competence* in the language of lens imagery is now commonplace in Western society and, increasingly, to be found worldwide.

Consider, for instance, the two cartoons reproduced here. Not only were they both disseminated through photographically generated reproductions, but they are both *sight gags,* in more than one sense. They are meant to be apprehended visually (i.e., Gahan Wilson's caption is essentially gratuitous, and the humor of neither translates effectively into verbal form); and their subject matter — aside from the surreal improbability of Wilson's sitter and the sexist silliness of Rouson's sitcom[7] — is human vision and its relation to camera optics.

The implications of these two images are highly significant. Both appeared in widely distributed periodicals: Wilson's in *Playboy,* Rouson's in hundreds of

Boy and Girl

newspapers to which it was syndicated. The demographics of *Playboy*'s readership no doubt differ from those of Rouson's newspapers, but clearly both these cartoonists assumed that the optical principles which are operative in these two jokes could be easily recognized by the average person in a matter of seconds. Yet three hundred and fifty years ago there would have been few people in the world capable of interpreting these images in terms of the understandings of visual perception and lens optics implicit in them.

The perceptual revolution engendered by the lens and consolidated by photography, as epitomized in these two cartoons, has been profound, and so pervasive that we tend to take it for granted in large part. We do seem to be increasingly aware of the fact that over the past century and a half we in the West have become a *photographic culture,* aware too that a photographic culture is radically different in quality and in kind from a nonphotographic culture.[8]

But we do not seem to understand that photography was not thrust *sui generis* upon Western culture (as it has been, subsequently, on so many societies that were in no way prepared for it). Photography took root in already fertile and well-tilled soil: a *pre*photographic culture deeply involved with lens instruments, lens-derived information, optics, vision, and representation. Western European culture and its outposts, including the United States, developed into a photographic culture as a consequence of first becoming a *lens culture* — that is, a culture in which the lens was well-established as a defining technology. Optical principles and concepts, as well as attitudes and theories related to broader issues of information-gathering, observation, and verification, had been introduced to that culture via the lens, had become entrenched in the "scientific method," and had come to form the groundwork for a new epistemology, well before the invention of photography.

Historians date that invention somewhere between 1826 and 1839, the period in which the processes for "fixing" or making permanent a specific lens image were discovered. Yet the imagination of the general public in Western culture had been fired by the lens and its consequences for the previous two centuries, via the cameras obscura/lucida, the telescope, and the microscope. Although the precious-object aspect of the still photograph — first the daguerreotype, then the paper calotype — was certainly instrumental in attracting popular interest to photography, it is evident from the literature that the public's primary fascination was with the encoding of lens imagery in a permanent, retrievable physical form. (Had the public interest been in photography as, literally, *light drawing,* then the photogram — that early, elementary, accessible form of light drawing that requires neither camera nor lens — should have enjoyed a major vogue. It never did.)

It seems logical to propose, then, that the "invention of photography" in (for convenience's sake) 1839 was only one event, though a predictable one, in the morphology of the lens as a cultural tool for information management.

The first lens employed by human beings was that of the eye. In his book *The Intelligent Eye,* perceptual psychologist R. L. Gregory offers the provocative postulate that "eyes freed the nervous system from the tyranny of reflexes, leading to strategic planned behaviour and *ultimately to abstract thinking*" [emphasis mine].[9] His argument is that the perception of things at a distance, and their optical identification, made advance planning possible. Obviously the key here, in optical terms, is not mere retinal sensitivity but depth perception, which is made possible by the fovea, those "rods and cones" found only in the eye of primates and birds.

The eye, then, extends the reach of the hand, enabling us not only to flee and survive but to perceive, to imagine grasping, and to plan to grasp that which is beyond our immediate physical reach. Similarly, the artificial lens as a tool extends the reach of the eye. In an eccentric extrapolation from the work of the founder of general semantics, Count Alfred Korzybski, novelist and theorist William Burroughs suggested that we developed speech in order to achieve writing — i.e., that the concept of the written word is inherent in the spoken word, effectively preceding it, even if on an unconscious level.[10] Art historian

William Parker, apparently thinking along parallel lines, has insinuated that we evolved eyes in order to be able to photograph.[11] This is a deliberately extreme formulation containing a germ of truth: having evolved an eye, it was natural for a toolmaking creature to develop an instrument with which to enhance its scope. That tool is the lens, in all its diverse manifestations.

What is a *lens culture,* and when did we become one? It's my belief that we became a lens culture in the years 1550–53, and that we became formally committed to that new status some sixty years later — on the night of January 7, 1610. In order to make a supporting argument for such an ostensibly lunatic proposition, it will be necessary to establish a few reference points.

We could say that the evolution of the lens as a tool is implicit in the human eye itself, embedded as a potential even back in the dim recesses of biological evolution. But that's not what made us a lens culture. Nor was it the fascination with the phenomenon of vision, though awareness of and interest in the sense of sight goes back to such early theorists as Democritus and Euclid, centuries before the birth of Christ. Sight as a subject of contemplation and inquiry evoked the theoretical investigation of Ptolemy, followed centuries later by those luminaries of the Arabian Age of optics, Alkindi and his successor, Alhazen; and it has continued to be a primary concern of philosophy and theology through the work of St. Augustine, Roger Bacon, Descartes, and many other central figures in the cultural history of the West. As Bolter has suggested, what makes a tool into a defining aspect of the culture in which it functions is not merely its presence, but its integration into the conceptual assumptions of the culture and the derivation from it of understandings that become fundamental to the culture's world view.

More than two thousand years ago, an early form of lens had been developed: a spherical bottle filled with water, used as a fire-starting device, known as a *burning glass.* By the tenth century A.D., simple magnifiers had been produced; and, circa 1285, eyeglasses — or "spectacles," as they were then known — had been introduced in Italy. Though all of these had an impact on culture (eyeglasses, in particular, added decades to the useful life of people, serving as perhaps the first prosthetic device), they did not transform our understanding of the *world* in any essential way.

By the year 1500, visual images in multiples — produced by the woodblock printing technique — were circulating throughout Europe. It is not coincidental that this was the historic moment of the rise of mercantile capitalism, whose lifeblood is *information.* The photographer and theorist M. Richard Kirstel has proposed that, with the surge of manufacture and trading that followed the recession of the Black Death in 1398, the resolution of the Hundred Years' War in 1453, and the consolidation of alliances around the Hanseatic League through the various Wars of the Herring during the early sixteenth century, an information-based culture was established for the first time in history.[12] And visual information was becoming as invaluable as verbal or written information: books on such subjects as engineering, architecture, archaeology, astronomy, machinery and techniques of labor and production, anatomy, biology, and zoology — books illustrated with printed images — would flood Europe during the sixteenth century.

At this juncture, the system of representation known as Renaissance perspective had already been devised and was in use; this is an essentially arbitrary method for what William M. Ivins, Jr., called "the rationalization of sight"[13] — a means for ordering the depiction of objects and their relations in space. (By "arbitrary" I mean to indicate that other cultures have developed other systems; for example, in some the relative size of objects in pictorial descriptions is determined by their cultural significance rather than by either their actual size or their proximity to the picture plane.)

Thus, by the time Albrecht Durer's treatise on perspective was published in 1523, the fundamental understanding of the relation between seeing and picturing had been transformed and standardized, while a means for reproducing pictures cheaply and disseminating them widely had been introduced.

Between the years 1550 and 1553, several concepts and components came together to create the framework on which lens culture has been constructed. In 1550, Girolamo Cardano was the first to mount a lens in the light-admitting aperture of the camera obscura. This lens was made of "crown" or plate glass; it was of biconvex form (the shape of the lentil seed, from which the lens derives its name). There being at that time no known means for the chemical recording of camera obscura images, whether or not produced with the aid of a lens, such images were simply viewed on a screen, often a polished marble table-top.[14]

Three years later, in a treatise called the *Diaphana* (1553), Franciscus Maurolycus, an Italian professor of mathematics, became (in the words of one historian) "the first optician who thought of employing the theory of glass lenses to explain the action of the crystalline lens [of the eye],"[15] a hypothetical correlation later verified by Johannes Kepler.

At roughly the same time — circa 1550 — the compound lens was invented, possibly by the British mathematician Leonard Digges, though there is endless dispute over its actual originator, suggesting that the idea may have emerged simultaneously from several sources.[16]

I would propose that it is within this three-year period, from 1550 to 1553, that Europe became a *lens culture*. Though Cardano, Maurolycus, and (for convenience's sake) Digges were working independently of each other, their separate ideas combine, when viewed in retrospect, to form the necessary infrastructure of a lens culture:

– Cardano's lensing of the camera obscura allowed one for the first time to study the *lens image* without one's own eye being, in Simon Henry Gage's terms, "an integral part of the optical train"[17] — as it is, for example, in its relation to eyeglasses, magnifying glasses, microscopes, and telescopes. This crucial displacement provides us with critical distance in relation to visual perception: it permits us to see the imaging process itself — to contemplate that process, abstract ideas from it, and metacommunicate about it (*metacommunication* being *communication about communication*). As a device, Cardano's tool is the prototype of the contemporary photographic camera; I would go so far as to posit that the photograph — that is, the permanent version of that lens image — is implicit in Cardano's invention, an almost inevitable consequence of it, since the reproduction and dissemination of visual images was already a century and a half old.

– Maurolycus's analogizing of the eye to the lens provided, for the first time, a working model of the process of visual perception itself. Thus the culture could begin to study the act of visual perception through the use of that model — thereby beginning to understand the principles of perception, to think abstractly about the process, and to metacommunicate about it.

– The compound lens — which is, in essence, a system of two or more lenses in a (usually adjustable) fixed relation to each other — transcended by far the mere supplementation of human vision that spectacles represented. The compound lens embodied a radically different, far more aggressive relation to the cosmos, the microcosmos, and the process of the acquisition of knowledge through perceptual inquiry; it was the first optical tool that had as its sole function the *generation* of information. Digges was a telescopist, but the complex microscope was implicit within the compound lens — as was the assumption that the reach of the eye is potentially infinite.

In short, in that three-year span, using materials and ideas already at hand, Western culture created an interlocking set of instruments and paradigms that permits the endless reframing of humankind as perceiver, the world as perceived, and the lens image as both vehicle and repository for that transaction.

This made Europe (and its colonies in North America) a lens culture—though a prephotographic one, still lacking the means for permanent encoding of lens images, the invention of which would take almost three full centuries more. Then it should not be difficult to explain why I think our status as a lens culture was confirmed on a particular evening early in 1610. That was the occasion on which Galileo Galilei did something with a compound lens in a telescope which no one before him had done (or, if they had, had failed to report). What Galileo did seems ridiculously simple: He looked up at night. The evening on which he chose to do so is considered a turning point in intellectual history.[18]

It was Galileo's looking up into the night sky through a compound lens (and, more to the point, the meaning he ascribed to the information he acquired in that fashion) that transformed the world view of Western society, demolished Ptolemy's geocentric model of the solar system, and made of Galileo the patron saint (though hardly the father) of telescopy.

When Galileo saw what he saw—which included four "new" planets, the satellites of Jupiter among them, none of which had been accounted for in either Ptolemy's or Copernicus's visual models of the universe—he was confronted with a choice that symbolizes the differences between lens culture and prelens culture. He could believe his theology, which was based on a shaky interpretation of the evidence provided by the unaided eye; or he could believe the information that the lens had provided. Galileo took the latter path, embracing and amending the Copernican version of the universe. (Understandings of fixed-point perspective surely affected Galileo's interpretations of the lens-driven information he had acquired through these observations. Those rules governing the relations of objects in space had already revolutionized pictorial depiction and mathematics; they had been studied and absorbed by Galileo.[19])

This was the first time that our culture's fundamental beliefs were permanently reshaped on the basis of lens-derived understandings. Galileo's act reverberated for a century and more: the trauma and upheaval that followed give the measure of the gulf between lens culture and prelens culture. Deny people their fixed notion of heaven and all hell breaks loose. Yet though many, especially in the corridors of power in the institutions of church and state, could not accept the news that Galileo brought, there were others who were quick to see where it led and rejoiced at the doors it opened for the mind.

For example, within a few months of Galileo's publication of his findings under the title *Siderius Nuncius* (*The Starry Messenger*), the philosopher Tommaso Campanella realized fully the implications of this discovery. Campanella, then in jail for his unorthodox opinions, wrote to Galileo on January 13, 1611. In his letter, which praises the *Siderius,* Campanella "raises for the first time the question which was to tear the seventeenth century asunder: the question of a plurality of worlds and of the possible inhabitants of these [four] new planets."[20]

Campanella was not alone in recognizing the expansiveness of Galileo's revelation. Inspired by the *Siderius,* the German astronomer Johannes Kepler produced in 1611 his *Dioptrice,* a treatise that laid the groundwork for modern telescopic instruments.[21] He was also the first to discover that vision is due to an image focused upon the retina by the lens of the eye, which verified Maurolycus's hypothesis.[22]

Beyond these pragmatic extrapolations, however, Kepler proved himself a prophetic dreamer. His last work, published posthumously in 1634, was the *Somnium,* a romance of travel to the moon. It is often credited as the origin of modern science fiction—a form of lens-inspired theory that was to develop during the seventeenth century and continue through our own day.

Other theorists followed suit. In 1630, Christophorus Scheiner noted in his *Rosa Ursina sive Sol* the conceptual relativitism that the microscope encouraged, speaking of it as an instrument "by which a fly was made as large as an elephant and a flea to the size of a camel."[23] By 1663, the philosopher Henry Power had prophesied that as a result of the telescope and microscope men would come to consider themselves "but middle proportionals (as it were), 'twixt the greatest and smallest Bodies in Nature, which two Extremes lye equally beyond the reach of human sensation."[24]

The impact of the lens and its implications did not only affect scholars, scientists, and philosophers. It spread to artists and writers and, through all of these, to the population at large. As Marjorie Nicolson indicates, the telescope brought with it the shocking concept of the existence of a "plurality of worlds." Yet, she points out, "the seventeenth century, as it becomes conscious of indefinite space, became aware also that in the little world a new microcosm reflected the new macrocosm."[25] She suggests that there was in this a degree of comfort and reassurance, in part because the *microcosmic* aspect of the new model of the universe was not entirely unexpected:

> The proof of the actual existence of such an universe of minute life came as no surprise or shock to man; man's reason had anticipated it; his instruments offered proof of its existence. . . . [B]ecause the instrument was more easily used by the amateur and because the world of minutiae was more intelligible to him, [the microscope] had more "popular" appeal.[26] . . . Before the telescopic vision of the cosmos, even a brave man might shrink back, appalled at immensity, lonely before infinity. But the material of the microscopists was at once intelligible and flattering to man's sense of superiority.[27]

References to the microscope and telescope began to enter literature at this point; the lens and its effects were becoming cultural reference points. There is mention of these instruments in the writings of Samuel Pepys, Andrew Marvell, Samuel Butler, and many other writers, both major and minor. The microscope, for the reasons suggested above, was the first lens instrument to enjoy an actual vogue; it was a fad in England from the mid-seventeenth century all the way through the eighteenth. "[T]he microscope becomes the toy of ladies," writes Nicolson, "and the familiar theme of the 'learned lady' enlarges to include the 'scientific girl.'"[28] Thus the compound-lens instruments—particularly the microscope—were perhaps the first entry points into science and natural philosophy for women.

Though he certainly was not the inventor of the microscope, Anthony von Leeuwenhoek (1632–1723) did employ it in his discovery of bacteria, in 1676. In a telling passage, Nicolson argues for the tremendous shaping effect of this lens-derived understanding, along with Galileo's, on literature:

> As Milton in *Paradise Lost* [1668] produced a new kind of cosmic poetry, a drama of interstellar space, which could not have been written before the telescope opened to a generation of men a new vision of the universe, so *Gulliver's Travels* [1726] could not have been written before the period of microscopic observation, nor by a man who had not felt at once the fascination and repulsion of the Nature which that instrument displayed.[29]

Once again, as in Henry Power's metaphor of humans as "middle proportionals," a relativistic view of the human position in the natural order had been extrapolated from lens understandings, this time by Jonathan Swift.

At the end of the seventeenth century, heated debate arose in the sciences between those followers of the classical scientists, or "ancients," and the "moderns." The latter were Baconians, antihypothetical in their attitude, insistent on the primacy of observation, experiment, verification. "The telescope and the microscope came to be the most powerful weapons of the 'moderns,' and the arguments drawn from them proved more embarrassing to the supporters of the 'ancients' than any others which they were forced to answer."[30]

These debates were actively followed by the educated sector of the public—a sector which, it should be remembered, had enjoyed access for much of that century to compound-lens instruments, as well as to the concepts derived therefrom. Swift's *Battle of the Books* (1697), for example, was in part a refutation of the "modern" attitude, as manifested in William Wotton's *Reflections upon Ancient and Modern Learning*, the second edition of which was published also in 1697. According to Wotton, "the most important contribution of the new instruments is the coherence and intelligibility which they have shown to exist in the universe."[31] The telescope diminished humankind; the microscope revealed humankind's similarity to many other forms of life.

If, as I'm arguing, the lens is a central human invention, equivalent in importance to the bow and arrow, then some recording process for lens imagery was virtually inevitable once a full-fledged lens culture had emerged.

The preconditions for the invention of photography were twofold. One was the availability of the necessary materials, tools, and processes. With Johann Heinrich Schulze's discovery of 1727, that the tarnishing of silver could be employed as an image-making technique, these were all in place.

The second precondition was the imperative within a lens culture to develop the essential instrument that would make culture-wide metacommunication about lens imagery possible. That instrument was some permanent, reproducible form of lens-image encoding. The impulse toward such an instrument came from two sources: art and science.

It has been argued by some that photography was a direct consequence of the Industrial Age, unimaginable without it. For instance, Heinrich Schwarz reasons thus:

> The invention was not haphazard. . . . [P]hotography came into being as the logical outcome of its intellectual premises, the product of the needs and tendencies of the time, of an ethical and an artistic compulsion. The practically simultaneous, and at first independent, efforts towards it as an end bear witness that the time was ripe; and they refer the individual act of invention back to some motive power greater than the personal, to an impulse that was strictly determined by historical forces.
>
> In essence the discovery depended upon a changed social order, upon an aesthetic attitude of man to his environment which was new and based on scientific assumptions.[32]

The sociocultural context in which photography finally emerged has already been indicated to some extent. Among its salient features were: a mercantile-manufacturing economic system that placed a premium upon information, a growing and increasingly educated middle class accustomed to ideas derived from lens-based understandings, centuries of cultural experience with images reproduced in large multiples, and widespread contact with lenses and lens images. If this is the agar-agar in which photography grew, then the needs of artists and scientists were the spores.

The issue is not whether the lens influenced art, but rather to what extent and in what ways it did so. By 1558, eight years after Cardano added a lens to it, the camera obscura had gone beyond its function as a solar observatory to serve as a drawing-tool for artists, which is how it was defined in Giovanni Battista della Porta's *Magiae Naturalis* (1558).[33] In addition to such direct influence, there was the more pervasive conceptual impact. Nicolson has pointed out that "as in the period of the telescope one is aware—whether by coincidence or influence—of a new interest in perspective or for views, so in the period of the microscope there is found a delight in the depiction of the small and the exquisite."[34] Oswald Spengler may well have intuited the pervasive cultural impact of the lens when he wrote that "between the space-perspective of Western oil-painting and the conquest of space by railroad . . . are deep uniformities."[35] A fixed-point perspective, and the symbolic compression of space via the telescope, together constitute the link between the two.

Yet there is a more specific reason for the imperative of photography in the context of Western art during the late eighteenth and early nineteenth centuries. Philosophers, scientists, artists, and the educated sector of the citizenry had become accustomed to contemplating the physical world as seen through bits of glass. The ability to observe the world through the lens had come to fascinate the public, and microscopic observation, in particular, had profoundly affected the public attitude toward and respect for art. In a culture that placed progressively less emphasis on imagination and more on reason, the extraordinary complexity and delicacy of the world seen under the microscope led to a denigration of visual art as such. God was reconceived as the Divine Artist; compared to His handiwork, in even something so small as the shell of a snail, humanly produced works of art seemed necessarily cruder, less detailed, incomplete.

The thrust of art, then, began to turn toward that which was culturally approved: realism, description, what we now call the documentary attitude. God and/or Nature having been defined as the epitome of creativity,[36] the only proper function of art could be the observation and recording of that cosmic oeuvre. The cameras obscura and lucida (the latter invented in 1806 by William Hyde Wollaston) came into common use by artists, for exactly that reason. The urge to arrest their images would have been widespread, the frustration at the tedious manual method thereof endemic.[37]

In science, a parallel need was being felt. With the discarding of the "reasoned" science of the "ancients," the Baconian ideal of directly observed and verified fact became the watchword of "modern" science, with the lens as one of its primary tools. Yet the problem there (especially given the erratic quality of available lenses) was in the *verification* of observation—that is, independent corroboration of perception. Though not restricted to microscopy and the sciences built around it, this problem manifested itself there most emphatically. In the words of G. L'Estrange Turner:

> Without photographic emulsions a great part of modern science could not exist. . . . The scientist is indebted, therefore, to the great developmental driving force brought about by the popular appeal of photography during the Victorian period. This popularity also considerably widened the market for optical glass and lenses, which were made in the same factories as microscopes and telescopes.[38]

Thus we might say that when Joseph Nicéphore Nièpce (1765–1833) produced the first permanently encoded lens image in 1826, he himself was the instrument of a cultural urge that had been building steam for some three centuries. And when, in 1839, the daguerreotype process and the calotype (positive-negative process) were announced — invented, respectively, by an artist-showman and a gentleman scientist — lens culture had at last completed its first cycle. The capacity for rendering a lens image in static two-dimensional form in large multiples permitted the widespread cultural dissemination of such images, thus making them available for study and introducing them as a form of cultural currency, as reference points. Lens culture thereby had the means for time-binding its visual perceptions and understandings, making possible their transmission through time as well as across space.

It is important to understand that photography as we know it is one extension of lens-image consciousness. But it is no less important to realize that the spaceship is another. On November 16, 1974, the United States broadcast a message to the cosmos via the Arecibo radio telescope — the world's largest radio telescope, located in Puerto Rico. Transmitted in binary code, the message when reconstituted forms a series of images, the first of which (at the bottom) is an image of the telescope itself (Figs. 1 and 2). The reasoning? "Advanced civilizations may use radio telescopes to talk to one another," Carl Sagan writes in *Murmurs of Earth,* a book that documents these initiatives in intergalactic communication. "This picture shows that Earth is ready to enter the conversation."[39] As noted elsewhere in the book, "Thus, we described the state of advancement of our technology"[40] — first by depicting ourselves as a lens culture, then by portraying and demonstrating our most highly evolved version of lens instrumentation.[41] Perhaps we have been a lens culture long enough that we have become *lentocentric* — unable to conceive of a scientific, "advanced" culture that lacks the lens. Only the future can confirm or disabuse us of this conviction, but there's no denying that, consciously or not, we now all share it.[42]

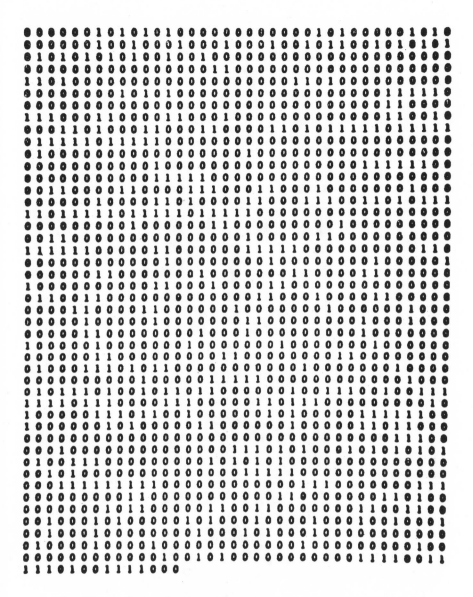

Fig. 1. Message in binary code transmitted November 16, 1974 by the Arecibo radio telescope.

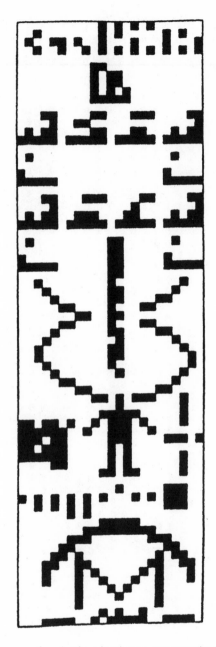

Fig. 2. Binary message from Arecibo radio telescope, reconstituted to form an image.

Thus, to bring this argument full circle, it would seem to be vital to our advancement as a culture that we come to understand the extent to which lenses shape, filter, and otherwise alter the data that passes through them — the extreme degree to which the lens itself *informs* our information. This influence, though radical in many cases, often manifests itself subtly. Yet even the most blatant distortions tend to be taken for granted, as a result of the enduring cultural confidence in the essential trustworthiness and impartiality of what is in fact a technology resonant with cultural bias and highly susceptible to manipulation. The very derivation of its name — from the Latin *lentil,* due to the resemblance of the double convex lens to the lentil seed — suggests the humble and the bland. The lens is neither, though many things may be said to have sprouted from it. Western society's daily diet now includes a hefty serving of "lentil soup" — that stock of lens imagery, perpetually simmering, that is also lens culture's primary export to the rest of the world.[43]

NOTES

1. J. David Bolter, *Turing's Man: Western Culture in the Computer Age* (Chapel Hill: University of North Carolina Press, 1984), p. 11.

2. Lynn White, Jr., *Medieval Technology and Social Change* (London: Oxford University Press, 1962), p. 28.

3. Eastman Kodak Co., press release CP18357NR (Rochester, NY, January 25, 1983), p. 1.

4. Eliot Fremont-Smith, "Making Book for Santa," *Village Voice* (December 20, 1983): 62.

5. After all, as far back as 1846 — less than a decade after the introduction of photography — Marx and Engels understood the principle involved. They wrote, "If in all ideology men and their circumstances appear upside-down as in a *camera obscura,* this phenomenon arises just as much from their historical life-process as the inversion of objects on the retina does from their physical life-process." *The German Ideology,* edited by C. J. Arthur (New York: International Publishers, 1984), p. 47.

6. The term — or, at least, the particular usage of it for these purposes — is Walter Chappell's. See his credo, simply titled "Walter Chappell," in Nathan Lyons, Syl Labrot, and Walter Chappell, *Under the Sun: The Abstract Art of Camera Vision* (New York: Aperture, 1972), unpaginated.

7. In that regard it is worth mentioning that while Rouson's boy has indisputably caught the bigger fish, the girl is demonstrably more visually astute.

8. William M. Ivins, Jr.: "From many points of view the histories of techniques, of art, of science and of thought, can be quite properly and cogently divided into their pre- and post-photographic periods." *Prints and Visual Communication* (London: Routledge & Kegan Paul Ltd., 1953; reprinted by Da Capo Press, New York, 1969), p. 116.

9. R. L. Gregory, *The Intelligent Eye* (New York: McGraw-Hill Book Co., 1970), pp. 12–13.

10. William Burroughs, *The Book of Breeething* (Berkeley, Calif.: Blue Wind Press: first edition, 1976; second edition, 1980), unpaginated.

11. Lecture, Society for Photographic Education National Conference, Asilomar, California, March 1978, unpublished.

12. In conversation with the author, January 1984.

13. William M. Ivins, Jr., *On the Rationalization of Sight* (New York: Da Capo Press, 1975).

14. See K. J. Habell, "Lens History," in *The Focal Encyclopedia of Photography* (New York: McGraw-Hill Book Co., 1971), p. 836.

15. Alfred N. Disney, Cyril F. Hill, and Wilfred E. Watson Baker, editors, *Origin and Development of the Microscope* (London: Royal Microscopical Society, 1928), p. 34.

16. Marjorie Nicolson, "The Telescope and Imagination," *Modern Philology* 32 (1935): 241–42.

17. Simon Henry Gage, *The Microscope*, 17th edition, revised (Ithaca, New York: Comstock Publishing Co., 1947), p. 554.

18. "We may perhaps date the beginning of modern thought from the night of January 7, 1610, when Galileo, by means of the instrument which he had developed with such labor [*sic*], actually perceived new planets and new worlds. . . . Galileo's *Siderius Nuncius* [of] 1610 [is] the most important single publication, it seems to me, of the seventeenth century, so far as its effects upon imagination is concerned." Nicolson, "Telescope," p. 235.

19. See Samuel Y. Edgerton, Jr.'s essays, "The Relations Between Representations in Art and Science: Galileo's Observations of the Moon—A Case Study," in Callebaut et al., *George Sarton Centennial* (Ghent, Belgium: Communications & Cognition, 1984), pp. 55–56; and "Galileo, Florentine 'Disegno,' and the 'Strange Spottednesse' of the Moon," *Art Journal* (Fall 1984): 225–32. Edgerton makes a persuasive case for the proposition that it was the high quality of Italian art education (which included perspectival study) that enabled Galileo to recognize the moon's "spots" as shadows on a sphere, whereas a contemporaneous British astronomer, unschooled in perspective, saw the phenomenon merely as inexplicable marks.

20. Nicolson, "Telescope," pp. 255–56.

21. Ibid., pp. 257–58.

22. Disney et al., *Origin and Development of the Microscope*, p. 64.

23. Gage, *The Microscope,* pp. 561–62.

24. Henry Power, *Experimental Philosophy in Three Books* (London: 1663–64). Cited in Marjorie Nicolson, "The Microscope and English Imagination," *Smith College Studies in Modern Languages* 16, no. 4 (July 1935): 10.

25. Nicolson, "Telescope," p. 234.

26. Nicolson, "Microscope," p. 2.

27. Ibid., p. 90.

28. Ibid., p. 3.

29. Ibid., p. 50.

30. Ibid., p. 61.

31. Ibid., p. 61.

32. Heinrich Schwarz, *David Octavius Hill* (New York: Viking Press, 1931), p. 3.

33. Helmut Gernsheim, in collaboration with Alison Gernsheim, *The History of Photography* (London: Oxford University Press, 1955), pp. 5–6.

34. Nicolson, "Microscope," p. 57. This was, of course, the age of the miniature in painting—a kind of object that the daguerreotype would quickly replace.

35. Oswald Spengler, *The Decline of the West* (New York: Alfred A. Knopf, 1939), p. 7.

36. Nicolson, "Microscope," pp. 62–66.

37. That frustration was the professed motive for the experiments of William Henry Fox Talbot, among others. See his "Brief Historical Sketch of the Invention of the Art," in *The Pencil of Nature* (London: Longman, Brown, Green, & Longmans, 1844), unpaginated.

38. Gerard L'Estrange Turner, "The History of Optical Instruments," in his *Essays on the History of the Microscope* (Oxford: Senecio Publishing Co., 1980), p. 20.

39. Carl Sagan, *Murmurs of Earth: The Voyager Interstellar Record* (New York: Random House, 1978), p. 119.

40. Ibid., p. 63.

41. The radio telescope is, in fact, what might be called a postlens optical instrument: it beams sound waves at its subject and reconstitutes them not as aural messages but as visual images, in a genuinely synaesthetic process. It is one manifestation of our entry into an era in which we may

obtain data in ways that do not involve lens instruments, but transform that data into images that read as if they were lens-derived — images of a kind to which we have now become habituated. For more on this subject, see Lisa Cartwright and Brian Goldfarb, "Radiography, Cinematography and the Decline of the Lens," *Zone* 6 (1992): 190–201.

42. It is my hope that this essay may stimulate further inquiry into the impact of lens-based communication systems — including, but hardly restricted to, photography — on non-European cultures. Correlation of such information with other sociocultural developments should prove fruitful, perhaps especially in cultures in which the lens was introduced forcibly. This would also make possible cross-cultural comparisons.

43. The initial research on which this essay is based, and an earlier version of it, were undertaken during the course of a seminar in Media Ecology conducted by Christine L. Nystrom and Neil Postman in the Department of Communication Arts and Sciences at New York University. It was first presented at the Media Ecology Conference held at Sacks Lodge, Saugerties, New York on October 27, 1984, and published in *Et cetera: A Review of General Semantics* 42, no. 1 (Spring 1985): 19–31. Extracts from this essay were subsequently used as the theme statement for a conference on the history of photography sponsored by the French government, "Les Multiples Inventions de la Photographie," Cerisy-la-Salle, France, September 1988. At that conference I presented a second paper on this subject, "Rationalism and the Lens," extending this argument further. See "Le Rationalisme et Les Lentilles," in the volume of proceedings, *Les Multiples Inventions de la Photographie* (Paris: Ministère de la Culture, de la Communication, des Grands Travaux et du Bicentenaire, 1989), pp. 31–38. A version of it in English subsequently appeared in *Impact of Science on Society* #154, vol. 39, no. 2 (1989): 101–12.

Fig. 1. Edward S. Curtis, "A Comanche," *The North American Indian,* vol. 19 (1930), plate 686.
Note that Curtis chose to leave his sitter's modern, European-style shirt clearly visible in this image, despite
the fact that the blanket draped across the man's shoulders could easily have been adjusted to hide it. Such
contrary evidence has been systematically suppressed in the current critique of Curtis's project.

Edward S. Curtis

THE PHOTOGRAPHER AS ETHNOLOGIST

> The cutting edge of social research through photography is . . . broad,
> varied, and ragged. There are many places for someone to pick it up and take
> another step forward. On the other hand, it owes immeasureable debts to a
> century-and-a-half's worth of photographers who were untrained as social
> scientists. These craftspeople and artists were fascinated by their equipment
> and what it could do, and there is a lot to be learned from looking closely at
> the photographic images they have already produced.
>
> *Jon Wagner[1]*

It seems the more we learn about Edward Sheriff Curtis, the more we find there
is to know; for every answer received, new questions arise. How is it that his
life's work, completed in 1930 only to be neglected for the next four decades, has
now become at once a reference point in popular culture, a marketable rarity,
a subject of scholarly and critical inquiry, and a source of seemingly endless
controversy?

As recently as 1970, it was none of these. At that time, the name of Edward S.
Curtis was so generally unfamiliar that it appeared in none of the standard
histories of photography.[2] His magnum opus, *The North American Indian,* had
slipped into an almost total obscurity. His writings were long out of print; his
images were never exhibited. Curtis had created a work so monumental that it
buried itself for forty years.

Today the situation is quite reversed. Dozens of books anthologizing Curtis's
images have been published, with more doubtless on the way. Some of these
have provided valuable biographical information and/or critical response; others have offered samples of the writings of Curtis and his assistants, extracted
from the project's texts. A filmed "docudrama" on his life (1868–1952) and
work has been completed and shown nationally. Curtis's original photographic
prints (in their several forms), and the fine gravure reproductions made therefrom, have been presented anew in scores — perhaps even hundreds — of museum and gallery exhibitions, not only across the United States and Canada but
around the world. No less an authority than John Szarkowski has opined (somewhat ungrammatically) that *The North American Indian* "might be the most
ambitious photographic book in the history of the medium, unless that prize
should be awarded to Eadweard Muybridge."[3] As a complete set, it now fetches

unprecedented six-figure prices ($396,000 being the record as of this writing[4]), while individual prints of his images have become collectors' items. There was even, for a time, a mail-order club selling new prints "hand-pulled from the authenticated antique Curtis copperplates." Without a doubt, we are in the midst of a Curtis renaissance.

The first phase of this rebirth, which began with an exhibit at the Pierpont Morgan Library in the fall of 1971, was a rediscovery of Curtis the photographer. Since his obituary in the *New York Times* in 1952 mentioned Curtis's photographic work only once, and then in passing, it is ironic that it should have been that facet of his endeavor which restored him to recognition. However, his photographs are among the most unusual aspects of his achievement; certainly they are the most accessible, so it is not surprising that they should have been the first to find renewed public attention.

The Morgan Library exhibit coincided with a surge of interest on the part of the general public in Native American cultures. The impulses underlying this have been suggested elsewhere;[5] reiteration of them is unnecessary here. For the purposes of this essay, what is significant about that *zeitgeist* is that, of all the photographers who had worked with Native Americans, it was Curtis on whom the attention quickly settled.

Simultaneously, and not coincidentally, the fields of anthropology and sociology were beginning to come to terms at long last with their increasing dependence on photography as an integral component of their procedures.[6] As a result, these disciplines were confronting for the first time the paradoxes inherent in "visual anthropology"—including the cultural biases of the technology and processes of photography, the equivocal nature of photographic information, and the impossibility of "objectively" generating or interpreting photographic imagery.[7]

At such a juncture, the very prominence of Curtis's imagery—its sudden omnipresence, its consequent availability as a ready reference point, perhaps especially its acceptance by an academically uncertified audience—made it a prime candidate for revisionist dissection. While such analysis is in no way unjustified, indeed must surely prove instructive, it's important to keep in mind that the real issue under discussion in that critique is the continuing failure of those disciplines to develop any rigorous methodology or encompassing theory for "doing visual anthropology," and its practitioners' consequent insecurities and anxieties in the face of professional pressure to evolve such structures of thought.

The work of Curtis, then, has provided the occasion for a reevaluation of all the "visual anthropology" produced about the Native (North) American tribes.

He is an odd choice of example: unschooled in ethnology, unsponsored by the anthropological establishment of his day, and never accepted as a paradigm in the field by his peers or his successors. Nonetheless, an example he has become. What follows is an attempt to describe his project as he conceived it; to indicate its relationship to ethnological practice in its own day; to respond in part to the current critique of it; and, finally, to compare it with the premises of the emergent methodology for "doing visual anthropology" in our own time.

> Visual anthropology makes possible a shift in focus from descriptive analysis of artifacts and behavioral process to the emotional overtones and fulfillments of culture.
>
> *John Collier*[8]

There have been hundreds of thousands — perhaps millions — of photographs made of Native American life, a large number of which have been preserved. Many were made by photographers no less gifted than Curtis. But most of those photographers, even if professional, stood as casual tourists in relation to the Native Americans. Their true subject was their alienation from and dominion over the cultures before their lenses; their images too often are little more than concretized gawkings. Ascribing no importance to the rhythms, rituals, and symbols of Native American life, they made no attempt to understand or describe these in their photographs. Consequently, their images testify to the gulf between immigrant and Native American cultures but provide little insight into the latter, conveying nothing of the feel, tone, and texture of the Native American world.[9]

Edward Curtis's project was unique for its time in that it was conceived as an attempt to bridge that gap between the two worlds. His purpose in making *The North American Indian* was to represent, as completely as possible, his vision of a network of cultures that was being inexorably destroyed — to do so in such a way as to render vividly what he believed to be the spirit of those cultures, thus helping to keep it alive. It was his goal to create a comprehensive survey of all the remaining indigenous tribes of North America — to explore, annotate, describe, and (when necessary) recreate every aspect he thought significant of prewhite Native American culture. This plan was both more coherent and, in its scope, more demanding than anything attempted up until then — or since.

This was no small challenge, offhandedly undertaken. Curtis was not just an entrepreneur, nor a mere adventurer with a camera. When, in 1906, the project that ultimately resolved as *The North American Indian* made its formal debut, its originator—who was then thirty-eight years old—had been photographing for more than twenty years and studying the Native Americans for a decade.

Curtis had several advantages over the photographers who'd preceded him in the nineteenth century. His equipment was somewhat less cumbersome and more versatile than theirs. He had more time for—or, to be accurate, devoted more time to—studying his subject in the field. He had access to some of the work of his predecessors, as well as to a far larger body of historical and ethnographic information about the Native Americans than did any previous photographer.

But there were difficulties against which these advantages were balanced. Unlike Jackson, O'Sullivan, and other earlier photographers, Curtis had to deal in many cases with even more severely acculturated Native American tribes and find ways to reconstruct the past from fragments. Also, while some Native Americans had overcome some of their religious objections to photography, those had been replaced, quite sensibly, with suspicion of the motives of the photographers who persisted in streaming through their world and invading their privacy. Gaining—or, rather, regaining—their willingness to cooperate must be seen as one of Curtis's major accomplishments; exposure to the range of his imagery makes it obvious how intrinsic that cooperation was to his purpose.

It is that sense of purpose, more than anything else, which differentiates Curtis from almost all other photographers of the Native Americans. Content with recording surfaces, others defined themselves implicitly as visual stenographers; Curtis, intent on rendering not only the surface but what he understood to be the substance, the very ethos of Native American life, became by virtue of that choice an interpreter of his subjects.

As Sol Worth has emphasized, "One should distinguish between the photograph as a record *about* culture and the photograph as a record *of* culture. . . . In the hands of well-trained observers, [photography] has become a tool for recording, not the truth of what is *out there*, but the truth of what is *in there*, in the anthropologist's mind [emphasis in the original]."[10] Curtis made images *about* Native American culture, where others made images *of* it; certainly he knew that what he was recording was, in Worth's phrase, "in there."

Curtis did not maintain this as a hidden agenda; nor was he unaware of his own haptic sensibility.[11] In his introduction to the very first volume of the project, he wrote, "while primarily a photographer, I do not see or think photographically; hence the story of Indian life will not be told in microscopic detail, but rather will be presented as a broad and luminous picture."

By the time Curtis embarked on the project that would consume twenty-five years of his life, break his health, and leave him impoverished, he had already developed three aspects of his medium that would be specifically valuable and pertinent to the task at hand. One of these was portraiture, the craft of particularization, at which he'd had long practice in his successful commercial studio. Formal portraiture in fact constitutes a considerable percentage of Curtis's imagery of the Native Americans; that segment of the project remains the most extensive archive of portraits of individual Native Americans produced by a single photographer up through the 1930s.

To suggest that such insistent individualizing is uncommon in anthropological photography would be to understate the case drastically. There is no substantial body of visual anthropology of which I'm aware that devotes so much attention to such transactional, one-on-one scrutiny as does Curtis's; after all, even up to the present day, virtually all such imagery has sought the generic rather than the idiosyncratic. (It is also worth noting that, while configurations of two or more Native Americans appear in a number of his images, Curtis as a rule eschewed the formal group portrait as such, always emphasizing the individual over the collective.)

Curtis's portraits are, quite simply, superb. Compositionally, they have a classic purity, simplicity, and strength that seem timeless. His use of natural light indoors, or inside a tent constructed with a special skylight—the conditions under which most of his portraits were made—was a determining factor in the look of those images; in combination with the slow speed of the films of his day, it mandated long exposures at wide apertures, with a shallow depth of field and a certain amount of blurring unavoidable. This required of him a technical virtuosity, and a patient self-control that his sitters had to share. One benefit of such a procedure was that it isolated each sitting within its own bubble of slow time; another was that it granted Curtis the fullest possible control over light as a sculptural tool. This allowed him to model each face he contemplated in such a way as to emphasize its bearer's identity and character, as well as to create an unusual sense of depth within a two-dimensional image.

In these portraits Curtis worked as a cartographer, reading each face as a map. He was sensitive to a wide range of delicate inflections of psychological and emotional nuance (see Frontispiece and Fig. 1). Consistently, he resisted the temptation to let artifacts distract him from the faces themselves; by and large, no matter how remarkable it may be in its own right, no artifact steals the scene from a human subject. Instead, such objects are generally de-emphasized by the device of selective focus. Rather than things, his subjects seem to wear the light itself, as though it were a garment, or a second skin.

Curtis also had an awareness of the scape, a feel for the emotional resonance of

Fig. 2. Edward S. Curtis, "A Haida Chief's Tomb at Yan," *The North American Indian,* vol. 11 (1916), plate 397.

the natural environment (Fig. 7). It was a form in which he had worked extensively, even winning awards and achieving the beginnings of a national reputation as a landscape photographer by 1900. This attunement to the physical surround amplified his flair for the directorial mode of photography and his genius for what must be called the *mise-en-image.* All of his tableaux were carefully planned; many were actually made during staged reenactments of important ceremonies or historic events. Yet they all have an ease, a sweep and movement astonishing for their day and still effective in ours.

Surely Curtis was constructing and operating within what sociologist Erving Goffman termed "the theatrical frame." His approach is narrative, his style almost cinematic.[12] Yet there is no stilted acting here, no awkwardly self-conscious posing, no sense ever that we are seeing anything but the natural flow of events. These images do not intend to reflect optical "reality"; they distill each scene,

Fig. 3. Edward S. Curtis, "Coming for the Bride," *The North American Indian,* vol. 10 (1915), plate 337.

bring it alive, and draw the viewer in (Fig. 3). At times they seem like dream-scapes, so closely do they match fantasies of life in the Old West before European incursions. Strictly speaking, there is as much dramaturgy as there is anthropol-ogy in this segment of Curtis's oeuvre (Fig. 8). But he was directing the original cast in something akin to its farewell performance; theatrical events of that sort generate a resonance all their own.

Until Curtis, no photographer of the Native Americans had explored these approaches so thoroughly.[13] Perhaps that was because they were simply pho-tographers, and for them the Native Americans were no less exotic a visual phenomenon than, say, the geysers at Yellowstone, and not much different in kind when it came to taking their pictures. Particularizing members of different cultures, communicating understandings of their ways of life, and creating a sense of access to their world are all difficult tasks, calling for abilities that do not develop automatically alongside photographic craftsmanship. Such abilities are based on other forms of knowledge, falling into that field of inquiry we call ethnology, which *Webster's* defines as "cultural or social anthropology."

In a comparatively even-handed assessment of Curtis's project, Lucy Lippard refers to "the monumental figure of Edward Curtis, imperfect hero of the genre and victim of the demythologizing trends of the 1980s." While taking issue with aspects of one of my own earlier favorable assessments of Curtis, Lippard states that "the alternative image that has emerged in recent years of Curtis as no more than a romantic exploiter and faker of the Indian past is also unjust. . . . [H]e was right in believing that his photographs would be invaluable (not infallible) documents of a historical process of representation. . . . [W]hen he was about halfway through his magnum opus, the Native nations began to see the importance his work might have for their own future generations."[14] Yet she resolves her own ambivalences in regard to Curtis's work by opining that "Curtis was, finally, an artist, with all the implied freedoms and shortcomings that come with that title."[15]

I think this begs the question. Edward Curtis may have been in part an artist, and some of his photographs may be considered works of art, but in the light of his own chosen presentation of his work he vigorously resists categorization as an "art photographer."[16] In commitment and by intent, Curtis was an ethnologist devoted to a long-term scrutiny of another culture, who used photography with special brilliance but as only one of several tools and methods available to him for his work. The impact of his individual photographs is such that comparatively little attention has been paid to the full context in which he embedded that imagery. Indeed, it is only recently that the reevaluation of his photographic work as ethnology has begun. It is there that controversy centers; the imagistic quality of the work is treated as inarguable, but questions arise about its informational value. John Szarkowski speaks for many, I'm sure, when he comments, "It would seem that [Curtis] wished to be, simultaneously, both ethnologist and artist, and this strikes the modern mind as an unreasonable, almost oxymoronic, ambition."[17] Or, as historian Naomi Rosenblum asks, "Can one really decide whether Curtis's views of tribal life in the United States are authentic documents or Pictorialist fictions?"[18]

This is a thorny issue, especially since Curtis worked during a time when anthropology was just emerging as a discipline, so new that it was still operating under the previous rubrics of ethnology and ethnography (the latter, a branch of the former, emphasizes the purely descriptive as against the analytical and comparative, and focuses on the material culture of its subject). There were few clear guidelines for those working in the field, virtually none insofar as graphic/photographic representation was concerned. It would not be until 1942, twelve years after Curtis's project concluded, that the book widely accepted as the first paradigm of visual anthropology—*Balinese Character,* the collaboration between Gregory Bateson and Margaret Mead—would be published.

Thus any disagreements with Curtis's procedures are, by definition, not only retroactive but essentially anachronistic. There were no established models for Curtis to follow in performing what would only later come to be called "visual anthropology." Self-taught as a photographer, he was also an autodidactic ethnologist, working (like all his colleagues in what had not yet become an academic discipline) without formal training or credentials, evolving his own *ad hoc* strategies as he went along. Some he borrowed, perhaps too uncritically, from his predecessors. For instance, one tactic for which he has been rightly rebuked (because it impeaches the reliability as "pure" data of some of his images) was his persuading some of his subjects to don garments that they no longer habitually wore—even, on occasion, to provide such garments or commission their manufacture himself.[19] Yet this had long been common practice in ethnological photography generally; photographers of the Indians from John K. Hillers in the 1870s to Curtis's contemporary Delancey Gill had garbed their subjects traditionally as a matter of course.[20]

Similarly, there is clear evidence that Curtis's assistants sometimes retouched his negatives and/or his prints—that is, altered them manually. Their motives in doing so were varied; this still-commonplace technique is regularly employed by photographers—including even such purists as the late Ansel Adams—to repair flawed or damaged negatives (Curtis's, it should be noted, were developed and proof-printed in the field), sometimes to eliminate or tone down visually distracting highlights. The technique can also be employed to alter the informational content of the image—to remove something from or add something to an image. But even Curtis's severest critic to date, Christopher Lyman, is able to muster only a baker's dozen instances of such willful tampering with the data.[21] (Lyman knowingly suppresses—or, at least, conveniently overlooks—any and all contrary evidence in which Curtis allows the image to encode elements of modernity he could easily have eliminated—e.g., Figs. 1 & 10.)

Given the extent of Curtis's photographic archive (*The North American Indian* contains some 2,500 images, drawn from a total of approximately 40,000 negatives), this is an insignificant percentage of the whole. Whatever his reasons for making these alterations, instructing his assistants to perform them, or accepting them *ex post facto,* they constitute at most a trivial shortcoming of the work. Though these instances can be construed as evidence of Curtis's willingness to fictionalize the present in his pursuit of a vision from the past, the meaning, the credibility, and the usefulness of his work do not hinge on the presence or absence of some suspenders in a crowd scene or two parasols in the background at a ritual dance. Unlike the case of hereditarian H. H. Goddard, whose 1912 book on the Kallikaks contained photographs of his subjects with features retouched to provide the necessary expressions of malignancy and moronism,[22] the oeuvre of Curtis does not represent a scientific argument invalidated by falsified evidence.

Though that small percentage of Curtis's images which are so compromised are not devoid of any informational usefulness,[23] in hindsight we might wish that Curtis had anticipated his field's later emphasis on taking things as they were found. If his sometime failure to do so is regrettable, it was one in which he was far from alone. It is worth noting that his project passed with flying colors — and, moreover, praise and encouragement — the scrutiny of a review board convened in 1907 when his work was challenged by Franz Boas of Columbia University.[24] The panel that approved Curtis's efforts up to that point and urged him to continue consisted of three of the most highly reputed scholars in the field at that time: Fairfield Osborn, curator of vertebrate paleontology at the American Museum of Natural History in New York; William Henry Holmes, chief of the Bureau of American Ethnology at the Smithsonian Institution in Washington, D.C.; and Charles Doolittle Walcott, the Smithsonian's secretary.[25] And it should be noted that he'd been supported and endorsed by ethnologists and anthropologists as diverse as George Bird Grinnell, Frederick Webb Hodge, and Robert H. Lowie.[26]

This suggests that Curtis could hardly have been photographing randomly, according to mere personal whim or the creative impulse of self-expression. That he worked within the limitations imposed by his tools and materials, selecting amidst those constraints the photographic strategies that would best enable him to describe what he thought to be important, should go without saying.[27] What is most perturbing in the current spate of debunking is its lack of technical understanding,[28] the absence of sufficient historical grounding,[29] and its assumption that, despite the current disarray and disagreement in the field, there is some fixed standard against which Curtis's work can be easily weighed and thereby impeached.[30]

For better or worse, there is no such standard. According to one source, "At the very foundation of this confusion is the lack of a coherent critical vocabulary for the field."[31] I would go further, to suggest that the problem is the field's awareness of the applicability to its actions of Heisenberg's indeterminacy principle, which proposes that concept dictates percept, and perturbation theory, which holds that observation changes the thing observed. Visual anthropologist Paul Byers puts it this way:

[T]he photographer is *always* a part of the context of the events he is photographing; he can never photograph a human behavior without being a part of it, and his photographs are necessarily a product of his interaction and his selectivity [emphasis in the original].[32]

In the words of Margaret Mead, Byers's frequent collaborator, "Photographs [are] of course heavily dependent upon the culture, the disciplinary point of view and the idiosyncratic vision of the particular photographer-analyst."[33] Sol Worth suggests, sympathetically, "Most of us simply do not want to face the fact that what we loosely call primary photographic data is . . . a structured event."[34] Derral Cheatwood and Clarice Stasz bring the lesson home: "The belief that there is an external, constant and absolute reality which can be recorded, measured, or analyzed with photography or sociology—and is therefore independent of the activity of the two fields—constitutes the reality fallacy."[35] In light of this consensus—possibly the only agreement in the field—how seriously can one take a naive critique like Lyman's, based on enduring faith in the possibility of "objective ethnographic documentation"?[36]

There is no question that Curtis's approach was not strictly schematic. Perhaps this was because his goal was so ambitious that he spread himself too thin much of the time, or perhaps because his interests in these individual tribes were so wide-ranging. Nonetheless, he channelled his varied addresses to the subject into an approach that, if not orthodox by some present-day measure, was hardly unsystematic.

In addition to the portraits, scapes, and tableaux, Curtis made several other kinds of images consistently enough to suggest a methodology. Each of these explores a different facet of that network of cultures he called "The North American Indian." One of these sets of images concentrates on the artifacts of Native American culture. These creations—baskets, weapons, costumes, tools—are treated by Curtis not simply as things but as manifestations of each culture's essence (Fig. 2). His photographs make them tactile, physical, animate, always revealing the beautifully functional shapes and textures of these works. In the portraits, Curtis generally relegated artifacts to second place in the hierarchy of content—a stylistic strategy that also represents a philosophical stance. Appositely, these still lifes permit the perusal of artifacts without the distraction of the human presence.

Another of Curtis's concerns was work—the tasks necessary to support life, and the ways in which they were performed. Fishing, reaping, weaving, along with many other skills and crafts, were explored by Curtis in a way that not only

Fig. 4. Edward S. Curtis, "Grinding Meal," *The North American Indian,* vol. 12 (1922), opposite p. 44.

recorded the significant tools and motions but also conveyed something of the attitude the task required (Figs. 4, 6, and 9). "The Fire-Drill, Koskimo" (Fig. 9), for example, is a powerful study that transmits basic craft information while also suggesting, in a direct and deeply felt manner, the fire-maker's meta-phorical relationship to materials, the earth which is their source, and mortality.

There are numerous other subgenres in the work as a whole — descriptions of daily life in the encampments, for one — that become apparent as one experi-ences the images repeatedly in their intended context. At the same time, Curtis recognized the limitations of photography as an informational system, which is why he insisted on contextualizing the images by embedding them in extensive textual environments. These writings — some generated by Curtis himself, some produced by his assistants (including George Hunt, who had trained under Franz Boas, and William E. Myers) — were all derived from first-hand observa-tion and interviews conducted under his supervision during the field expedi-

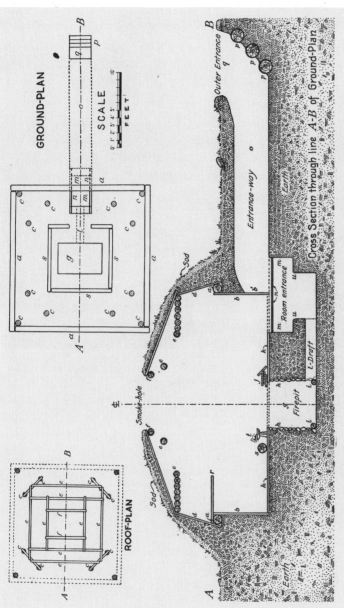

GROUND-PLAN, ROOF-PLAN, AND SECTION OF ESKIMO MEN'S HOUSE

a, Logs about pit edges; *b*, split wall timbers; *b'*, house wall; *c*, posts; *d*, split logs; *e*, rafters; *f*, smoke-hole sill; *g*, firepit; *h*, stones; *i*, small logs; *j*, planks for firepit covering; *k*, flooring; *l*, draft tunnel; *m*, room entrance; *n*, wooden hand-rails; *o*, outer passageway; *p*, log steps; *q*, square opening; *r*, bench; *s*, small log head-rests; *t*, lamp-stand and lamp; *u*, steps. Scale of ground-plan, six feet to the inch.

Fig. 5. Artist unknown, "Eskimo Men's House," *The North American Indian*, vol. 20 (1930), plate 2, opposite p. 8.

This plan is just one example of the many different kinds of contextualizing information gathered by Curtis and his assistants and contained within the Curtis project as a whole — much of it unduplicated by Curtis's predecessors and contemporaries in ethnology/ethnography.

Fig. 6. Edward S. Curtis, "Fish-weir across Trinity River — Hupa," *The North American Indian,* vol. 13 (1924), plate 459.

tions required by the project. They were then reviewed, discussed, and organized into final drafts by Curtis and his crew upon returning from the field.

Everything from tipi construction to mythology is observed, annotated, diagrammed (Fig. 5), transcribed, and discussed in these texts. Curtis and his coworkers inform the reader about dietary habits, physical characteristics, hunting procedures, religious rituals — in short, the full span of tribal specifics and activities, from the mundane to the exalted. Though he is sometimes patronizing, even — by today's standards — unconsciously racist, Curtis's biases are out on the table. By and large, he managed to convey his perceptions without condescending or moralizing. His sympathy for the Native Americans' plight is patent, as is his empathy with what he construed to be the Native American ethos; he appears to have been more open to the indigenous vision of the universe than some of his more "progress"-oriented peers.

Fig. 7. Edward S. Curtis, "Pima *Ki*," *The North American Indian,* Vol. 2 (1908), plate 45.

Additionally, Curtis gathered some 10,000 wax-cylinder field recordings of songs and ceremonies, 700 of which reportedly still survive, though their whereabouts are nowhere clearly indicated. He even produced a silent film on the Kwakiutl of the Northwest Coast—*In the Land of the Head-Hunters,* a fictional scenario—that, though a financial disaster, had a profound influence on Robert Flaherty's germinal documentary film, *Nanook of the North,* and, through it, on the ethnographic film as a form.[37]

Make no mistake about it: there may be such things as "objective" photographic documents, but Curtis's works are not among them. His body of imagery forms one man's intensely subjective report of his own responses to other people and their cultural matrix, an interpretive essay on an entire complex of cultures and their ways of life.[38]

Fig. 8. Edward S. Curtis, "Hamatsa Emerging from the Woods, Koskimo," *The North American Indian,* vol. 10 (1915), opposite p. 172.

Fig. 9. Edward S. Curtis, "The Fire-Drill, Koskimo," *The North American Indian,* vol. 10 (1915), plate 349.

Fig. 10. Edward S. Curtis, "A Nakoaktok *Mawihl,*" *The North American Indian,* vol. 10 (1915), opposite p. 176.
This is an example of an image Curtis could easily have cropped or masked along the left and right sides to eliminate all reference to the modern house immediately behind these artifacts and his human subject — yet the photographer chose (circa 1915) to leave it visible. Surely Curtis's critics have some intellectual obligation to explain such instances of full disclosure of contemporaneity — which contradict some of their charges — when advancing their cases against him.

Unquestionably, his vision—that is to say, his understanding of what he saw, above and beyond his way of seeing it—was unabashedly, even incurably, romantic, in the dictionary definition of the term: "signifying . . . the spirit of chivalry, adventure, and wonder, the preoccupation with picturesque and suggestive aspects of nature."[39] Aspects of the photographic work of Curtis could hardly be described better or more succinctly. But it can be argued that the Native American world views and theologies—which generally encouraged deeds of valor, and whose deities animated the physical world—were also quintessentially romantic; if so, that definition fit Curtis's subjects as closely as it fit the photographer himself. Certainly neither pretended to that scientific detachment and "objectivity" which had become the epistemological model of Western thought.

Because it was infused with that encompassing personal response to, and interpretation of, the subject, the work of Curtis must be understood as a simultaneous portrait and self-portrait, a blend of fact and feeling. As a present-day Native American poet, Red Hawk—who bears the same name as a man Curtis photographed long ago—has written,

> . . . *he knew enough*
> *to let his heart be in his eyes,*
> *to give everything he had for magic.*[40]

That this makes it difficult to sort out the strictly informational component of the project is true. This only means that we must develop strategies for sifting photographs so as to separate the data and information they encode from the biases of their source—or, to put it another way, to understand the relationship, in photography, between the teller and the tale. But that has always been the particular challenge presented by photography. That it's taken us this long to recognize it hardly serves to negate the totality of Curtis's project, or any other—since, as I've indicated, contemporary visual anthropologists are beginning to acknowledge, even if reluctantly, that such a blend pervades any and every photograph.

The field of anthropology as a whole, in fact, has come to acknowledge the subjectivities and biases inherent in all its operations. As Clifford Geertz has proposed, anthropology is an example of what the philosopher Gilbert Ryle has termed "thick description"—or, as Geertz puts it in his own words, "what we call our data are really our own constructions of other people's constructions of what they and their compatriots are up to."[41]

Geertz goes on to point out that "anthropological writings [and, one assumes he would add, anthropological photographs as well] are themselves interpretations, and second and third order ones to boot. (By definition, only a 'native' makes first order ones: it's *his* culture.) They are, thus, fictions; fictions in the sense that they are 'something made', 'something fashioned'—the original meaning of *fictio*—not that they are false, unfactual, or merely 'as if' thought experiments."[42] This implies that even the cultural observations of a "native" are also fictions, though generally of a higher order than those of outsiders. But to say this is not to discredit all interpretations. Geertz himself concludes,

> The claim to attention of an ethnographic account does not rest on its author's ability to capture primitive facts in faraway places and carry them home like a mask or a carving, but on the degree to which he is able to clarify what goes on in such places, to reduce the puzzlement—what manner of men are these?—to which unfamiliar acts emerging out of unknown backgrounds naturally give rise. . . . It is not against a body of uninterpreted data, radically thinned descriptions, that we must measure the cogency of our explications, but against the power of the scientific imagination to bring us into touch with the lives of strangers.[43]

Finally, to suggest that Curtis's subjects were either hapless pawns at the mercy of a White authority figure or—because he frequently paid his models—venal hirelings who would do anything for money is to misrepresent Curtis's relation with the tribes he was permitted to photograph and to propose that his subjects lacked all integrity. Neither of these notions is credible. Since Curtis had no means (much less the inclination) to force people to pose for him, and was working with equipment that required him to be fixed and visible, these images can only be understood as collaborations. Thus the combined sensibilities of all participants in these photographic acts are merged in the resulting images. If these form, in one sense, a self-portrait of Curtis, they are also, in that same sense, the visual autobiography of Native American culture "as told to" Curtis. One cannot easily determine where Curtis leaves off and the Native Americans begin, they are so entwined.

This empathy both informs the diversity of information Curtis sought out and absorbed in the process of creating *The North American Indian* and is in turn informed by it. In tandem, they are obvious components in the work's successes. They also contribute to the power and durability of his imagery, for by the time Curtis photographed anything—whether an artifact, a ceremony, a working method, or a human being—he not only had learned exactly what it was but also its history, its symbology, and its place in the gestalt of tribal life. Images made after such preparation are almost inevitably superior to those made in ignorance, when the purpose is the communicative description of specific perceptions.

So it is hardly surprising that Curtis's work presently is being treated to what James C. Faris has called an "anthropological embrace" — despite the fact that, as Faris also notes, "Strangely, anthropology has not bothered to research the Curtis photographs."[44] Without question, it will take effort for present-day workers to sift the wheat from the chaff in Curtis's epic. I will venture the prophecy that, unless the baby is thrown out with the bathwater, a large core of durable and valuable material will be identified. I will go even further, to hazard a guess that, after that has been accomplished, the field of visual anthropology will find in Curtis something of a model, even if an eccentric and probably inimitable one. John Collier has written that images made under circumstances such as those which Curtis preferred

> invariably reflect the sympathy and transfer of human feeling on the part
> of the field-worker photographer. . . . This subjectivity is an asset, how-
> ever, as well as a liability. . . . [T]he artist's perspective is likely to contain
> more of the character of the *whole view* than the disciplined scrutiny of
> [the] anthropological field workers.[45]

Indeed, some theorists seem to have come full circle, as exemplified in this statement from Darrel Cheatwood and Clarice Stasz:

> . . . aesthetic conventions of presentation, taste, and statement find their
> way into society as a whole and frame the way in which others perceive
> photographs in general. To the degree that our prints or visual images
> conform to these aesthetic tastes, we will increase our ability to reach a
> broad audience. To the degree that we are aware of these aesthetic conven-
> tions and employ them, change them, or contradict them to our own ends,
> we will increase our resources for communicating through this medium.[46]

From that credo to the work of Curtis there is only a small step. As a photographer, Curtis's accomplishment was the creation of a unified, extensive body of beautifully made images that are strong, direct descriptions of his experiencing of Native American life. As an ethnologist, his achievement was the creation of an irrefutable argument-by-demonstration that the camera was not only useful to anthropology but as indispensable as pen and paper to the full exploration and interpretation of cultures. Those were no mean feats; even today, almost ninety years after Curtis began *The North American Indian* and over forty years after his death, there is hardly anything in either field to match it.[47]

NOTES

For the captions Curtis wrote to accompany his photographs, see Picture Credits at the back of this book.

1. "Introduction: Information in and about Photographs," in Jon Wagner, ed., *Images of Information: Still Photography in the Social Sciences* (Beverly Hills/London: Sage Publications, 1979), pp. 18–19.

2. Including Beaumont Newhall's—although, in 1985, Newhall noted that he had "arranged a large exhibition of Edward Curtis's American Indian photogravures at the George Eastman House in Rochester, New York" thirty-three years previously, in 1952. See "An Appreciation," in Barbara A. Davis, *Edward S. Curtis: The Life and Times of A Shadow Catcher* (San Francisco: Chronicle Books, 1985), p. vii. Not until the fifth edition of his history, published in 1982, did Newhall see fit to include Curtis.

3. In John Szarkowski, *Photography Until Now* (New York: Museum of Modern Art, 1989), p. 141. Presumably, Szarkowski means to compare Curtis's project to Muybridge's *Animal Locomotion* and/or *The Human Figure in Motion*.

4. At an auction at Christie's in New York, October 13, 1992.

5. A. D. Coleman, Foreword to *Edward S. Curtis: The Sioux and the Apsaroke*, edited by Stuart Zoll (New York: Harper/Colophon Books, 1975), pp. xii–xiii. See also Christopher M. Lyman, *The Vanishing Race and Other Illusions: Photographs of Indians by Edward S. Curtis* (New York: Pantheon Books, 1982), pp. 147–48.

6. As early (or late!) as 1962, Margaret Mead would write, "Anthropology . . . has always been highly dependent upon photography. . . . As the use of still photography—and moving pictures—has become increasingly essential as a part of anthropological methods, the need for photographers with a disciplined knowledge of anthropology and for anthropologists with training in photography has increased. We expect that in the near future sophisticated training in photography will be a requirement for all anthropologists. . . ." From her essay, "Anthropology and the Camera," in *The Encyclopedia of Photography*, edited by Willard Morgan (New York: Greystone Press, 1963), vol. 1, p. 166.

7. For a lucid discussion of the inevitable subjectivity of scientific observation, see "The Relationship between Observation and Experimentation in the Field Study of Behavior," by T. C. Schnierla, *Annals of the New York Academy of Sciences* 51, art. 6 (November 7, 1950). Reprinted in *Selected Writings of T. C. Schnierla* (San Francisco: W. H. Freeman and Co., 1972), pp. 3–29.

8. "Visual Anthropology," in Wagner, *Images of Information*, p. 274.

9. Some photographers who might be excepted from this evaluation: Laura Gilpin, Adam Clark Vroman, Marion Palfi.

10. "Margaret Mead and the shift from 'visual anthropology' to the 'anthropology of visual communication,'" in Worth's *Studying Visual Communication*, edited by Larry Gross (Philadelphia: University of Pennsylvania Press, 1981), p. 190. In this regard, the fact that Curtis produced virtually all of the images in his project himself, rather than farming that task out to subordinates or absorbing the archives of others, results in an overall consistency to the visual aspect of the work that facilitates its reevaluation and analysis on those terms.

11. I use the term here in the sense introduced by the child psychologist Viktor Lowenfeldt in such works as *The Nature of Creative Activity* (London: Routledge & Kegan Paul Ltd., 1939). See especially Chapter IV, "Visual Perception and Haptic Perception," pp. 81–86, and Chapter V, "The Two Creative Types," pp. 87–94.

12. In addition to completing one film of his own, *In the Land of the Head-Hunters* (1914) and producing some footage in Alaska, there is evidence that Curtis may have worked as second cameraman on Cecil B. DeMille's *The Ten Commandments* (1923) and other Hollywood films. (See Mick Gidley, "From the Hopi Snake Dance to 'The Ten Commandments:' Edward S. Curtis as Filmmaker," *Studies in Visual Communication* 8, no. 3 [Summer 1982]: 70–79.) Certainly it has been established that he served as still photographer for that opus by DeMille (some examples of his work in that capacity are to be found in Davis, *Edward S. Curtis*), as well as on *The Plainsman*, starring Gary Cooper. I cannot help wondering if he crossed paths with William Mortensen, who was DeMille's still photographer a few years later on the set of *Kings of Kings* (1927).

13. A parallel (and no doubt imitative) methodology, reconstructive and directorial, was employed by Joseph K. Dixon and Rodman Wanamaker in the making of some of the images for their collaboration, *The Vanishing Race: The Last Great Indian Council* (Garden City, N.Y.: Doubleday, Page & Co., 1913). Like Curtis's, these pictures did not record history, but instead imagined and approximated it.

14. In her Introduction to Lippard, ed., *Partial Recall* (New York: The New Press, 1992), pp. 24–25.

15. Ibid., p. 25.

16. That this was understood by his contemporaries is apparent from one of the more bizarre critiques of Curtis's project, which came in 1907 from the pen of the eminent and normally astute critic of art and photography, Sadakichi Hartmann. Clearly impressed by the scope of the proposed project, Hartmann argued for the appropriateness of Curtis's choice of the camera: "[A painter] is never to be relied upon for accuracy, and accuracy is what makes Curtis's records valuable for posterity. There is no making of pictures for pictures' sake . . . every picture must be primarily an ethnographic record. Being photographs from life they show what exists and not what one in the artist's studio presumes might exist." Whereto he appended the assertion that "[the Indians] can hardly claim to be as picturesque as, for instance, the Arabian horsemen that Schreyer paints," because their clothes and decorations are "too gaudy, too loud to be truly pictorial," and proposed that the "low tones" of "black and white delineation" enabled Curtis to control what would otherwise be "too uncouth." While deprecating the imagery's significance as art photography, Hartmann endorsed it as an "ethnological document." This is a clear indication of how Curtis's work was received by one of the two most prominent critics of photography of his day. See "E. S. Curtis: Photo-Historian," in Hartmann, *The Valiant Knights of Daguerre: Selected Critical Essays on Photography and Profiles of Photographic Pioneers* (Berkeley: University of California Press, 1978), pp. 267–72.

17. Szarkowski, *Photography Until Now.*

18. Naomi Rosenblum, *A World History of Photography* (New York: Abbeville Press, 1984), p. 351.

19. Lyman, *The Vanishing Race,* p. 90 and elsewhere.

20. Joanna Cohan Scherer, "You Can't Believe Your Eyes: Inaccuracies in Photographs of North American Indians," *Exposure* 16, no. 4 (Winter 1978): 6–19.

21. Lyman, *The Vanishing Race,* pp. 70–76.

22. Stephen Jay Gould, *The Mismeasure of Man* (New York: W. W. Norton, 1981), pp. 171–73.

23. "It does say something about Indians . . . that they would allow themselves to be posed in inappropriate garb. At the least, it leads us to wonder if costumes held the meanings for Indians that anthropologists attribute to them." From Derral Cheatwood and Clarice Stasz, "Visual Sociology," in Wagner, *Images of Information,* pp. 265–66.

Paul Chaat Smith, a present-day Comanche, goes even further: "In this relationship [with the camera] we're portrayed as victims, dupes, losers, and dummies. Lo, the poor fool posing for Edward Curtis wearing the Cheyenne headdress even though he's Navajo. Lo, those pathetic Indian extras in a thousand bad westerns. Don't they have any pride?

"I don't know. Maybe they dug it. Maybe they were having fun. . . ." From his essay, "Every Picture Tells a Story," in Lippard, *Partial Recall,* p. 97.

24. An intriguing instance of the pot calling the kettle black, since "Franz Boas, respected as an objective scientist, arranged to have native Kwakiutl dress in archaic clothing and reenact outmoded customs for photographs, which he later prepared for publication by retouching out distracting details." Bill Holm, Foreword, in Davis, *Edward S. Curtis,* p. ix.

25. Victor Boesen, and Florence Curtis Graybill, *Edward S. Curtis: Visions of a Vanishing Race* (New York: Thomas Y. Crowell, Co., 1976), p. 29.

26. Lowie wrote of Curtis's work on the Crow tribe, which had been published in the fourth volume of the project in 1909, "It is an excellent piece of work and while not written either by or

for a professional anthropologist lives up to high standards of accuracy." See Lowie, *The Crow Indians* (New York: Rinehart & Co., 1935), p. 355.

27. Lyman argues against virtually all aspects of photographic craft — framing, cropping, photographing the same subject from different vantage points, selecting depth of field, even moving in for a close-up — as somehow illegitimate in anthropological photography.

28. In Lyman's critique we have a prime example of the consequences of continuing to ignore Mead's above-quoted admonition concerning the importance of "sophisticated training in photography." For instance, Lyman appears not to understand the differences between blur caused by motion of the subject or camera, lack of definition in parts of an image resulting from shallow depth of field or selective focus, and the overall diffusion created by a soft-focus lens, regularly conflating them all.

Lippard's commentary suffers from the same affliction (*Partial Recall*, p. 25), as does Rosenblum's (*World History*, p. 178).

29. The "appropriate" way to represent the world accurately has long been a subject of active debate in photography. The argument extends back at least as far as the work and writings of Peter Henry Emerson, the British physician-photographer, to whose theories and ethnological practice Curtis seems clearly indebted. Curtis's use of selective focus in ethnological work closely parallels the approach advocated by Emerson. Emerson's "scientific background led him to examine physiological factors in human vision, and on the basis of the optical theories of Hermann Ludwig Ferdinand von Helmholtz, he argued that during a momentary glance human vision is sharp only at the point of focus, whereas the camera lens produces an image that is equally sharp over the entire field; therefore, photographers should use long-focal-length soft lenses to approximate natural vision — that is, replicate instantaneous perception." (Rosenblum, *A World History of Photography*, p. 243.) Given the time frame of his apprenticeship in the medium, and his participation in the salon movement, there is every reason to suspect that Curtis was aware of Emerson's internationally controversial enunciation of these theories in his book, *Naturalistic Photography for Students of the Art* (1889), and perhaps even familiar with Emerson's application of his theories in such ethnological projects as *Life and Landscape on the Norfolk Broads* (1886) and *Pictures of East Anglian Life* (1888). Comparison between these works and Curtis's project is, to say the least, instructive. Lyman mentions Emerson's theoretical text in passing, misquoting its title (*The Vanishing Race,* p. 32), but apparently is unfamiliar with its contents and with Emerson's photographic work — or, for some other reason, chose not to pursue the obvious question of influence.

John Szarkowski at least notes the resemblance:

> "Curtis might cite in his defense the work of Peter Henry Emerson, only twelve years his senior, who in a period of five years, beginning in 1886, produced four books of photographs that described the vestigial preindustrial life of parts of England that were still relatively free of smokestacks and casual tourists. Emerson's interest in the character and quality of the lives of his subjects was surely genuine, but he saw no reason why his understanding should not be expressed with as much grace and economy as he could manage. Like Curtis, he surely posed his subjects, and it would not be surprising if he too chose not to photograph them if they were not in what he considered authentic native dress" (*Photography Until Now,* p. 141).

For more on Curtis's connections to pictorialism and the Photo-Secession movement, see Beth Barclay DeWall, "Edward Sheriff Curtis: A New Perspective on 'The North American Indian,'" *History of Photography* 6, no. 3 (July 1982): 223–39.

30. Lyman seems to take it as a given that all anthropological photographs should be in uniformly sharp focus at all distances, should be made at adult man's–eye level from the ground level of the subject, should be uncropped, and should evince no attention to pictorial quality.

31. Cheatwood and Stasz, "Visual Sociology," p. 262.

32. "Cameras Don't Take Pictures," *Columbia University Forum* 9 (Winter 1966): 31.

33. Margaret Mead and Paul Byers, *The Small Conference: An Innovation in Communication,* Publications of the International Social Science Council 9 (Paris: Mouton & Co., 1968), p. vi.

34. Worth, p. 194.

35. Cheatwood and Stasz, "Visual Sociology," p. 265.

36. Lyman, *The Vanishing Race,* p. 26.

37. Bill Holm, and George Irving Quimby, *Edward S. Curtis in the Land of the War Canoes: A Pioneer Cinematographer in the Pacific Northwest* (Seattle: University of Washington Press, 1980), pp. 29–30. The long-standing controversy over Flaherty's substitution of a bow and arrow for the then-commonplace rifle in *Nanook*'s bear-hunt sequence is directly parallel to the current critique of Curtis's occasional anachronisms.

38. One might point out that the rubber stamp Lewis Hine used on the back of his photos up through the 1920s read "Lewis W. Hine / Social Photography." Thereafter, he changed it to read, "Lewis W. Hine / Interpretive Photography."

39. Webster's New International Dictionary, second edition.

40. From a poem that appears to be a meditation on Curtis's work, "The Man Who Photographed the Indians (for Curtis and Jake)," published in *Exposure* 26, no. 1 (Spring 1988): 37.

> That Curtis's work does not readily succumb to any essentialist reading, but remains open to a multitude of interpretations, is further evidenced by the following statement:

>> We [the Puerto Rican photographers who formed En Foco, Inc., a non-profit organization in New York City] did not yet see our presence in history and there were few photographic mentors we could relate to. However, there were some photographers who possessed the *sentido* we identified with. Photographers such as Edward Curtis, Manuel Alvarez Bravo, Paul Strand, Roy DeCarava, W. Eugene Smith and Robert Frank. Their work was direct, clear documents [*sic*] of life; conventional in its humanism, obvious in its humility, sentimental in its allegiance to a better world and honest in its empathy. — Charles Biasiny-Rivera, Introduction, *A Decade of En Foco* (New York: Bronx Museum of the Arts and En Foco, 1986), unpaginated.

41. Clifford Geertz, *The Interpretation of Cultures* (New York: Basic Books, 1973), p. 9.

42. Ibid., p. 15.

43. Ibid., p. 16.

44. James C. Faris, "The Navajo Photography of Edward S. Curtis," *History of Photography* 17, no. 4 (Winter 1993): 377–87. See also the same author's *Navajo and Photography: A Critical History of the Representation of an American People* (Albuquerque: University of New Mexico Press, 1996). While Curtis is referred to regularly in discussions of the relation between anthropology / ethnology and photography, the hallmark of such discourse is the absence of direct inquiry into Curtis's project, the failure to analyze his imagery, and the substitution of an uncritical parroting of Lyman's once-trendy posturings for these scholarly obligations. See, for example, Elizabeth Edwards, ed., *Anthropology and Photography* (New Haven: Yale University Press, 1992), and Melissa Banta and Curtis M. Hinsley, *From Site to Sight: Anthropology, Photography and the Power of Imagery* (Cambridge, Mass.: Peabody Museum Press, 1986).

45. "Evaluating Visual Data," in Wagner, *Images of Information,* pp. 162–63.

46. Cheatwood and Stasz, "Visual Sociology," p. 264.

47. I have written at length about the work of Curtis on several previous occasions, most notably in my Introduction to *Portraits from North American Indian Life* (New York: Outerbridge and Lazard / E.P. Dutton, 1972) and my Foreword to Zoll, *Edward S. Curtis.* Ideas originally expressed in those essays, as well as some passages of their prose, have inevitably infiltrated this reconsideration.

The present text, previously unpublished, is a slightly altered version of a paper delivered at the conference "Images Across Boundaries: History, Use and Ethics of Photographs of American Indians," Laboratory of Anthropology/Museum of Indian Arts and Culture, Santa Fe, New Mexico, April 1993.

I am indebted to Kathy Vargas for criticism that was invaluable in the production of the final draft of this essay. All of its opinions and errors, however, are mine.

Private Lives in Public Places

THE ETHICS OF STREET PHOTOGRAPHY

> Some frowned, some smiled, some muttered to themselves; some made light gestures, as if anticipating the conversation in which they would shortly be engaged; some wore the cunning look of bargaining and plotting, some were anxious and eager, some slow and dull; in some countenances were written gain; in others loss. It was like being in the confidence of all these people to stand quietly there, looking into their faces as they flitted past. In busy places, where each man has an object of his own, and feels assured that every other man has his, his character and purpose are written broadly in his face. In the public walks and lounges of a town, people go to see and be seen, and there the same expression, with little variety, is repeated a hundred times. The working-day faces come nearer to the truth, and let it out more plainly.
>
> *Charles Dickens, The Old Curiosity Shop[1]*

In these words Charles Dickens, himself an astute observer of public behavior, gesture, and expression, described Little Nell's impressions of the streets of London. He was writing in 1841, only two years after the introduction of photography, largely uninfluenced by the new medium and certainly unaware of its future applications. Yet the urbanite fascination with the street that he presents through the innocent eyes of Nell manifested itself early in the history of photography—the genre can be traced back to Nièpce and Daguerre—and eventually became one of the medium's mainstays.

Much of the initial photography of "street scenes" was in its intent primarily informational and representational: John Thomson's *Street Life in London,* the activist photojournalism of Jacob Riis and Lewis Hine, Eugène Atget's obsessive Parisian survey. But, as this century progressed, more and more photographers took to the streets with concerns that were not those of the reporter but rather those of the novelist and poet—a search for resonant contrasts, rich metaphors, and found dramatic scenarios.

The appeal of the street to photographers is readily understandable. Blaise Cendrars wrote, "Le spectacle est dans la rue"[2]—the theatre is in the street—years before such performers as Judith Malina and Julian Beck of the Living Theatre carried it back out there again in the 1960s. As the one place in our culture where the most disparate elements are consistently thrown together in the most paradoxical juxtapositions, the street is a continually replenished source of extraordinary and surreal imagery.

Susan Sontag has argued that photography is "the only art that is natively surreal," going on to ask, "What could be more surreal than an object . . . whose beauty, fantastic disclosures, emotional weight are likely to be further enhanced by any accidents that might befall it? It is photography," she continues, "that has best shown how to juxtapose the sewing machine and the umbrella, whose fortuitous encounter was hailed by a great Surrealist poet as an epitome of the beautiful."[3] If that is indeed the case, what stage more ideal than the street could be conceived for such "chance meetings"?

Perhaps this is why Joel Meyerowitz, who began his professional career as a street photographer and has returned to the genre regularly, was quoted as saying in an interview, "I believe that street photography is central to the issue of photography — that it is purely photographic, whereas the other genres, such as landscape and portrait photography, are a little more applied, more mixed in with the history of painting and other art forms."[4]

Whether or not the form is "purely photographic" may be debatable. But there can be no doubt that such diverse photographers as Irving Penn, Berenice Abbott, Harry Callahan, Arnold Genthe, Paul Strand, Brassaï, Lee Friedlander, Charles Gatewood, Henri Cartier-Bresson, Diane Arbus, Robert Frank, Garry Winogrand, Imogen Cunningham, Walker Evans, Alfred Stieglitz, and Jacques-Henri Lartigue have chosen to address at length one or another aspect of the street at some time in their lives, while others — Weegee and Helen Levitt, to name just two — have built virtually their entire bodies of work within this form.

In so doing, they have helped to redefine and expand the street as subject, transforming it from a reportorially oriented locus of social concern to the proscenium for a surreal theatrical centered around cultural symbols. They have also stretched the parameters of "the street" itself, so that it now includes the subway (and the interior of any other mode of public transportation), the park, the beach, the café — indeed, any and every venue that can be thought of as essentially "public." This has led to a number of dilemmas, some of which can be thought of as imagistic, general, and philosophical, others of which are quite pragmatic, specific, legal, and even legislative in nature.

For instance, it could be argued that, over the past century and a half, the integration of photography into the fabric of our culture has alerted us all to the impact of photographs and our own appearance therein. Thus it seems not unreasonable to suggest that this has generated a heightened self-consciousness in regard to the aspects of ourselves that we project when being photographed. This in turn implies that we may very well modify our behavior in ways both subtle and significant whenever a camera is in our presence (or even when we think we might be photographed). Perturbation theory applies to photography as well as physics: observation changes the nature of the situation observed.

Beyond that remarkable but general effect on everyone who lives in a photographic culture such as our own, photographs made of people on the street or in other public places without the consent of the subjects raise questions of ethics as well as aesthetics. What rights do we have as citizens over the control of representation of ourselves, and what rights do photographers have in regard to making images in public situations?[5]

A decade ago, this debate manifested itself in a widely reported and much-discussed legal dispute in the courts, concerning a photograph of Clarence Arrington made by free-lance photographer Gianfranco Gorgoni. Gorgoni photographed Arrington on the midtown streets of New York City, without his knowledge or consent. Gorgoni's agency sold the image to the *New York Times*, without Arrington's knowledge or consent. And the *Times* used the image as the cover illustration for a story in its Sunday *Magazine* titled "The Black Middle Class: Making It,"[6] again without Arrington's knowledge or consent. Thus Arrington's image, in a multiple of over a million copies, was distributed by the *Times* nationwide — expropriated by the photographer, his picture agency, and the *Times* editorial staff as a symbol of the black middle-class experience.

Arrington's response, with which I sympathize wholeheartedly, was to initiate a lawsuit for invasion of privacy that slowly worked its way through the courts. Unfortunately, its eventual resolution appeared to hinge on a peculiar combination of factors, one being a technicality concerning Gorgoni's free-lance status, the other the practical problems and economic clout of the free-lance photography trade and the enormous publishing industry it services. With that as the basis on which this suit was resolved, the ethical issue could hardly be effectively addressed by the legal system. That was regrettable, because it merited (and still merits) the most serious consideration — not only by lawyers, judges, photographers, and others in the communications field, but by all of us.[7]

As I've just indicated, I think Arrington was in the right here. Despite the fact that, over the years, I've fought ardently for the rights of photographers, I also believe (in the words of Voltaire, if I recall correctly) that "your rights stop at the end of my nose." I've also had enough direct experience with photographers (particularly photojournalists and free-lancers), picture agencies, and picture editors to have a clear understanding of the emphasis most of them place on ethical considerations.[8]

So my empathy with Arrington's outrage has its roots in my personal history as well as in my critical understandings. Let me give just two examples, one of which concerns a photograph that was made, the other a photograph that wasn't.

My mother, who gave me my first box camera, retired to a ranch she bought in northern California, where my son (who's now twenty-five) and I often spent a good part of our summer vacations. There are fields and hills, cattle and peacocks, pygmy goats and horses, woods and swimming spots. It was akin to having a summer camp or dude ranch at our personal disposal — quite a pleasure, and quite a privilege.

Some years ago, during the course of a riding lesson, the saddle on the horse my son had mounted slid to the side, not having been tightly enough cinched. My son fell, breaking his arm near the elbow. Present at the time was a free-lance photographer, a close friend of ours, who was thoroughly helpful during this emergency, yet also — as much out of habit as any other impulse — took photographs of the ensuing events when time and discretion permitted. One of these showed my son just prior to going into the operating room for anesthesia, bone-setting, and the application of the cast. Dirty, tear-stained, in great pain, slumped in a wheelchair with his arm in a makeshift sling, he appeared about as helpless, woebegone, and pathetic as an eleven-year-old boy can look.

This image, on the contact sheets, made its way to my friend's stock agency, which requested a print for its files. Then, about a year later, the agency asked my friend to inquire if I would consent to a particular usage of it. Seems a textbook publisher wanted it for a volume on child abuse. Would my son or I object?

We certainly would — and did, on several grounds. The most immediate was that publication of a recognizable picture of my son identified as a battered child could have serious repercussions in our personal life and my professional sphere. Beyond that, however, there was a broader concern: such usage would be a willful falsehood, a deceitful recontexualization. All of those involved (my friend, the agency representative, my son, and myself) knew very well that on the occasion depicted in that photograph my son was a "victim" of nothing more malevolent than a combination of accident and carelessness — certainly not child abuse. Yet the agency was, in effect, asking me to permit this image to be used as visual "evidence" of an entirely different nature, so that the agency (and my friend) could make some money.

Ultimately, what upset me most was this latter issue — that, and a remarkable moral opacity on the part of the agency spokespersons, who made it very clear that they were more than willing to abide by my wishes in this particular case but were incapable of grasping the principle at stake and not especially interested in pursuing it. Consequently, to protect my son and myself, I required of the agency and my friend that in the future I would be consulted beforehand on any usage of images of us.

Thinking about it later, I realized that it was only because the agency knew of the friendship between the photographer and my son and myself that they'd bothered to check with us in the first place. Had we not been traceable, and readily available for consultation, I was convinced the requested usage would have been permitted by both photographer and agency, with no compunction, without even any second thoughts.

How many of the images we see in the mass media, in textbooks, and in other vehicles, are such spurious, falsified "factoids"? Does anyone in the field consider the consequences to the subjects of such images generated by such misuse? And, on a larger scale, the consequences to the citizenry when its informational network is thus compromised and corrupted?

Now for the photograph that wasn't made.

The night it wasn't made was several years ago. I'd had dinner in Manhattan with a photographer who was staying at my house; I was driving us back to Staten Island, where I live, across the Brooklyn Bridge. It had rained earlier in the evening. The city looked clean and bright, the air sparkled, the bridge gleamed and glistened. Traffic was crawling, with all three lanes merging slowly into the far left lane for no apparent reason.

Just over the curve of the bridge's center, the reason came into view. There, in the middle of the roadway, was a well-dressed, middle-aged woman sitting in a wheelchair, facing traffic. Behind her was a taxicab, empty, all doors open, emergency lights flashing. The scenario virtually wrote itself: the cab developing engine trouble or running out of gas, the driver heading off for assistance, the decision made to put the immobile passenger in full view to slow traffic down and prevent the rear-ending of the cab with her in it.

As we drew closer, foot by foot, I could see the woman in the wheelchair more clearly. She was alert, neatly coiffed and made up, as composed as possible under the circumstances. She also looked terribly fragile and vulnerable, alone on that metal roadway, surrounded by cars and more cars, never sure that some airhead wasn't racing toward her from the entrance to the bridge. I tried to imagine myself in her situation; it felt awful.

My companion rolled down the window on the passenger side, instructing me to slow down as we drew abreast of the scene. Watching the camera being checked and set, I suddenly saw in rapid succession five or six different versions of the potential image ahead of us, in the styles of several photographers whose work I knew well, including my companion's. They were all strong pictures. It would have been hard to miss; you couldn't have asked for a more resonant symbol of utter, abject helplessness and, at the same time, grace under pressure.

We began to pull closer to the woman. The photographer braced, ready to shoot, when the damnedest thing happened. Instead of slowing down, I instinctively put my foot on the gas and moved us out of range as quickly as I could, despite my companion's objections. There was, of course, no turning back; the scenario was behind us, the images gone.

I was surprised at myself—I do not intervene in other people's picture-making decisions. The photographer was furious. What business of it was mine? As we argued, and I thought about it, I realized that had my companion been at the wheel and slowed down to photograph, I would not have attempted to prevent it. In effect, as driver of the car I'd been asked to become complicitous in the making of that image, and had refused.

The reason for that refusal, I finally understood, was that in addition to all the pictures of that woman that I'd imagined, I'd imagined another image as well— an image of the world as that woman in the wheelchair would have seen it at that moment. There I sat, high on a bridge over the East River, a vast city sprawling away on all sides, myself crippled and unable to move. At the mercy of strangers and the world, in a situation totally beyond my control, I had to wait for what seemed like forever as car after car—hundreds of them—moved slowly past me, the faces in each one staring at me as if at some freakish spectacle. It was a nightmare, and all I had to interpose between myself and it were my courage and my poise. All I wanted was for people to pay me as little attention as possible under the circumstances, and for rescue to come soon. The last thing I needed— the thing that could shatter the delicate balance in which I held myself—was to suddenly find my picture being taken under such difficult and embarrassing circumstances by someone with a camera who'd decided that my plight was news, or art, or merely snapshot material.

Because, in that dreadful hour, when I had to entrust myself entirely to others, I would not want to know that among those others there were some who would take advantage of my helplessness by converting me into a symbol of it, to hang on gallery walls or illustrate the pages of publications or study for their own amusement. I would not want to think that there were those for whom my condition and plight meant only that I was public property, because then I might start to doubt that help would really come, and I could not afford to do that.

So I decided, for myself, not to be the shadowy figure behind the wheel in the image that woman would have registered in her mind's eye when our car rolled slowly past her with my companion busily clicking away. I've never regretted that decision. Though I don't think I was forgiven, or my motives ever understood, eventually my companion's anger at me abated. The nonexistence of that photograph — for which I hold myself absolutely responsible — does not seem to have had any negative consequences.

Though the litigation I discussed earlier was over an image made in far less dramatic and extreme circumstances, the principle involved is basically the same. The assumption that you waive your rights to control of your own image and declare yourself to be free camera fodder by stepping out of your front door is an arrogance on the part of photographers; it has no clear, absolute, and inarguable legal basis.[9] The excesses committed in its name are legion, and extreme.[10] To whatever extent the Arrington-Gorgoni case opened up this vital matter to public debate and legislative consideration on a national scale, Clarence Arrington did all of us (including photographers) a service for which the only proper repayment would have been one we'll never be able to make — the restoration of his right to a private life in public places. He'll always be the man who found himself on the cover of the *Times Magazine,* and sued.[11]

NOTES

1. *The Old Curiosity Shop* (New York: Heritage Press, 1941), pp. 329–30. (Original edition published in 1841.)

2. Blaise Cendrars, introductory note in *A. M. Cassandre: Le spectacle est dans la rue* (Montrouge, Seine: Draeger Freres, n.d.), unpaginated.

3. Sontag, Susan, *On Photography* (New York: Farrar, Straus and Giroux, 1977), pp. 51–52.

4. Lisbet Nilson, "Seeing the Light: On a Clear Day You Can See Joel Meyerowitz," *American Photographer* 7, no. 3 (September 1981): 40–53. Meyerowitz subsequently co-authored, with Colin Westerbeck, the book *Bystander: A History of Street Photography* (Boston: Little, Brown & Co., 1994). For my less-than-favorable review of that project, see *DoubleTake* 4 (Spring 1996): 142–43.

5. The only extended study I know of that addresses the sociopolitical consequences of this behavioral pattern within photographic culture is Bernard Edelman's *Ownership of the Image: Elements for a Marxist Theory of Law* (Boston: Routledge & Kegan Paul Ltd., 1979). Edelman's argument, first published in France in 1973, uses the legal rights (or lack of same) of photographers' subjects as a tool for political and economic analyses of Western culture. Edelman's reference point is the legal system of France, whose laws on this issue differ in important respects from American jurisprudence. Yet the analogies are considerable, making Edelman's inquiry a useful starting point for further exploration of this issue.

Another might be the following communique, sent across the Internet in early 1996 by the Zapatistas of Chiapas, Mexico. I suppose we could consider it their position paper on photography. I picked it up and ran it as a "Guest Editorial" in the June/July issue (No. 5) of my newsletter on the World Wide Web, *C: the Speed of Light,* where it can still be found — but do not know where else it may be archived. It is reprinted here in full, as received (forwarded on to me via e-mail by Henry Brimmer). Aside from a few unclarities and minor translation glitches, it speaks for itself:

From: tcOmjl1@corn.cso.niu.edu (lemaitre monique j) Sender: majordomo@mep-d.org
Reply-to: mexico2000@mep-d.org
Date: 96–02–10 01:17:22 EST

"Marcos in Internet" ("La Jornada," February 8, 1996)
Zapatista Army of National Liberation
Mexico
For the Photography Event in Internet
February 8, 1996

Ladies and gentlemen:

Through this medium I point out that on the date of the first anniversary of the treason brought about against the EZLN and the will for a new peace of the Mexican people and world public opinion by the government of Ernesto Zedillo Ponce de Leon, there appeared in the Lacandon Jungle (better known as rebel territories against the bad government) 2 people: 2 named Francisco Mata and Eniac Martinez, males to be more specific, who claim to be Mexican, and with the aggravating circumstances of being photographers (better known as cynical thieves), and they threatened the honorable public with their weapons (better known as photographic cameras), for which reason they were detained and handed over to the proper authorities.

They did not remain in anybody's custody aside from that of their own conscience (in a somewhat sorry state from what we can see), and they declared the following: that they come with the intention of taking pictures of Zapatista life in order to submit them to an Internet World event, and that they have no other aim than the telephoto photographers usually carry, that their intention is testimonial and artistic, that they did not receive any pay from the Zapatistas (as if we had any means to do so!) and that they did not pay the Zapatistas anything (which means that, aside from being photographers, they are stingy); that once their work in these dignified lands is over they plan to rush, rapid and swift, to their respective computers and to delight (that's what they think) the clients of Internet with their marvels (ha!).

Once the previous declaration had been taken down, the Sup (who surprisingly assumed the role of Local Private Ministry) declared guilty of the crime of image theft, with the aggravating circumstance of cynicism, since, says the Sup, the photographer is a thief who choses what he steals (which, at this stage of the crisis, is a luxury) and does not "democratize" the image, that is to say, the photographer selects the pictures, a privilege which ought to be granted to the person being photographed. Once that said, the Sup condemned them to what is explained in detail below, but before that the Sup wants to talk about the images (better known as photographs) that these photographers (better known as the guilty parties) came to take and then . . .

Now through these photographs we go back a little and we can foresee a little of the future. Through them, the photographs, we go to the old Guadalupe Tepeyac. Through them we return to the new Guadalupe Tepeyac and, between the former and the latter we see images of a rebellious dignity, that of the Indigenous people of the Mexican Southeast.

Behind the ski mask, the Sup takes the camera and his revenge. During two years he has been on the other side of the lens, he has been the object and the target, the medium and the message. But today the Sup has decided to take his revenge and he has taken the lens from the other side, from the side of the history press photographers take and, through them, the world who sees those pictures.

Now the Sup invites us to follow his pictures, to look from this side of the ski mask at what photographs don't say, at the trip they avoid, at the distance they mark.

The Sup's photographs try to build a bridge. A bridge that does not go from the "reader" of the photographs or from the photographer to the place in which the Zapatistas sometimes live, sometimes die, and always struggle. The Sup proposes you another bridge, another trip, another "reading" of the image. That is why the Sup has now picked up the camera from the angle which was forbidden to him, from the photographer's angle, from the spectator's angle.

The Sup takes a picture of the photographer taking pictures. The photographer discovers himself/herself being photographed and we can guess he is uncomfortable. Unsuccessfully he/

she tries to recompose his posture and to look like a photographer taking photos. But no, he is and continues to be a spectator. The momentaneous fact of being photographed leads him to becoming an actor. And, as always, actors must assume a role, which is only an elegant way of avoiding to say that they must chose sides, chose a faction, take an option. In the mountains of the Mexican Southeast there aren't many, and if we clear a bit the avalanche of fantastic declarations made by public officials of various kinds, we will see that there are only two options: war or peace.

There already are actors on both sides: On the side of war are the government and its army, the army which, with its war tanks and cannons, occupies the old Guadalupe Tepeyac and "protects" that hospital nobody goes to except prostitutes who "service" the garrison and the government soldiers who go there to cure themselves of the venereal deseases which are included in the "service." The government's war comes disguised as "peacemaking." For over 500 years, for the Mexican Indigenous populations "peacemaking" means death, jail, tortures, persecution, humiliation, oblivion.

On the side of peace are the Indigenous people and a national and international civil society whose existence and effectiveness is denied by the great "intellectuals" and politicians. These Mexican Indigenous people rose up in arms, declared war to oblivion and to the system which turns the lack of memory in their main capital for a new, just and dignified peace.

A new peace is peeking out of the barrels of Zapatista rifles, out of the eyes of the children, the women, the elderly and the men who have built another Guadalupe Tepeyac deep into the mountain. These men and women smile, they carry the suffering and the pain the government imposed upon them as payment for daring to rebel, for their anachronical insistence in being dignified. Nonetheless they laugh. Why? What makes these eyes who now defy the complicated equation of openings, light, speed, sensitivity and opportunity, also defy the oblivion that history promises them as their sole future? Why do these Indigenous people face the camera with the same happiness and daring with which they face the life they desire and the death they offer them? Try to ask that question. Question the images. Take them by the hand and don't let the sweet distancing they offer you vanquish you; do away with the distance's comfort or the soft indifference you derive from concentrating on the quality of the framing, the use of light and shadows, the successful composition. Force these images to bring you to the Mexican Southeast, to history, to the struggle, to this taking sides, to chose a faction.

Two sides: on one side oblivion, war, death; on the other memory, peace, life. The images of the two Guadalupe Tepeyacs, the one occupied by the government's forces and the one which, in exile, digs in its banner of dignity in the mountains of the Mexican Southeast, struggles, fights for a piece of space, demand a place in the cameras of these photographers, look for a place in the eyes who, in front of the computer screens, are witnesses to an event, and they request a piece of the world memory of a century which did the impossible to despise its own history and who is paying, day by day, the high price of not having any memory.

The Indigenous people of the Mexican Southeast, Tzotziles, Tzeltales, Choles, Tojolabales, Zoqwes, Mames, only used to appear in museum images, in tourist guidebooks, and in Indigenous art promotions. The camera's eye searches for them as an anthropological curiosity or a colorful detail from a very distant past.

The rifle's eye forced the camera's eye to look at them in a different way. They are today the example of dignity and resistance that humanity had forgotten, had lost, and has found again.

The photographed photographers haven't stopped feeling uncomfortable during the brief session of takes the Sup submitted them to. The great inquisitor that the camera's lens is was turned against its operators. Every time the diaphragm winks, the camera repeats the question that now travels through cyberspace and invades, as a modern virus, the memories of machines, men and women. The question that history always sets forth. The question which forces us to define ourselves and whose answer makes us human: On which side are you? The Sup leaves the camera in peace and takes back his rifle. He lights his pipe and bids farewell. The smoke which he leaves behind is already travelling through cyberspace proposing, asking, questioning . . .

Vale. Good health and adjust well the frame: the present is past and future.

From the mountains of the Mexican Southeast.

Subcommander Insurgent Marcos.

Mexico, February, 1996

P.D. which adjusts the focus. If the pictures come out well it will have been a mere accident. Since the time the Sup used to work as a photographer of soft porno, many years ago, he hasn't touched a camera. If they are bad, then it will be obvious that the models were awkward. It is well known that it isn't the same to shoot than to be shot at.

P.D. that foresees credit problems. The pictures' copyrights belong to whomever you want to. For me it is clear that photography prizes should be for those being photographed and not for the photographers.

(Translation: Monique J. Lemaitre)

6. Front cover, *New York Times Magazine,* December 3, 1978.

7. Less widely reported was the case of construction worker Carl De Gregorio, who was filmed walking along Madison Avenue holding hands with a female co-worker. Despite his appeal to the film crew, this footage was broadcast on CBS-TV in a May 1982 news segment on "Couples in Love in New York," identifying the pair as "hard-hat lovers." De Gregorio's thirty-year marriage collapsed as a result. His $1.6 million suit against CBS was dismissed because the broadcast named neither party and they were "filmed in a public place and can have no expectation of privacy in that location." See Katharine Lake, "Wrenching end to hard-hat's suit," New York *Daily News* (March 17, 1984): 9.

8. One indication comes from the American Society of Media Photographers, the oldest and largest professional organization for such working photographers. The ASMP's "Code of Ethics" deals *exclusively* with how much photographers are entitled to charge for their work.

As for the moral competence of picture editors, consider that Ruth Ansel — the *New York Times Magazine* art director who assigned Gorgoni to make the cover shot — told him that any well-dressed black person on the street would serve to represent the black middle class. (Does this mean they *still* all look alike?) Then, finding the initial court decision in favor of Arrington "a little outrageous," she explained, "I don't think there was any intent to classify him in any denigrating manner [by making him into a symbol of black yuppification in an internationally circulated periodical!]. *As a matter of fact, I thought it was a good photographic image."* (Emphasis added.) Quoted in T. Malyon, "The Fateful Photograph," *Camera Arts* 2, no. 5 (October–November 1982): 26ff. For which, read: So long as we present an attractive image of you, it's none of your business what we make you represent . . .

9. See photography historian Bill Jay's fascinating essays, cited below, for a discussion of the early response — public, journalistic, and legislative — to the introduction of photographic activity into European and British public life during the middle and late 1800s: "The Photographer as Aggressor," in David Featherstone, ed., *Observations: Essays on Documentary Photography* (Carmel, Cal.: Friends of Photography, 1984), pp. 7–24; and "The Amateur Photographic Pest," *Daytona Beach Community College Newsletter* (Spring/Summer 1986): 16–18. See also Robert E. Mensel, "'Kodakers Lying in Wait': Amateur Photography and the Right to Privacy in New York, 1885–1915," *American Quarterly* 43, no. 1 (March 1991): 24–45. According to Mensel, "The evidence . . . indicates that amateur photographers played an important role in provoking the outrage among editorial commentators, judges and legislators which eventually helped lead to the recognition of the right of privacy in New York." Ibid., p. 25. Ironically, he cites a *New York Times* editorial from August 23, 1902, in support of laws safeguarding the public from photographers: "If there be . . . now no law to cover these savage and horrible practices . . . then the decent people will say that it is high time that there were such a law."

10. In consideration of that fact, but taking also into into account the concerns of photogra-

phers, I proposed in 1989 the creation of "photo-free" and "auto-release" zones in major urban centers, the former to be public spaces where all photography was prohibited, the latter public spaces wherein no permission would be needed to photograph. See my contribution to "Forum: Back to the Future: Photography in the 80s and 90s"/"Zuruck in die Zukunft: Fotografie in den 8oer und 9oer Jahren," *European Photography* 40, vol. 10, no. 4 (October–December 1989): 16–18.

11. The drafting of this essay was proposed by the reconsideration of a much briefer, much earlier meditation on the same subject, "Street Photography: A Question of Direction" (*The New York Photographer*, no. 2, 1971). A few passages from that text have been incorporated into this one. In approximately its present form, this essay was first published as "Private Lives, Public Places: Street Photography Ethics," *Journal of Mass Media Ethics* 2, no. 2 (Sring/Summer 1987): 60–66.

Epilogue

You might think it eccentric of me to propose that a course in Eisenhower-era stereotypes of Mexico and other countries in the Southern Hemisphere would be sensible preparation for a career in art photography. Yet there's something here for those with a nose for the ironic, for what afflicts North American art photography today is a complex of conditions that we gringos are more prone to attribute to the social dilemma depicted in those condescending 1950s over-simplifications of Third World realities. That is, North American art photography today is produced by a migrant-labor caste that cannot escape its condition because it is politically uneducated, only marginally literate, and addicted to its religion and its lotteries.

This migrant-labor caste, from which emanates what one recent anthology optimistically labels "new American photography,"[1] is composed almost exclusively of men and women under the age of forty with master of fine arts degrees granted by photography programs housed in colleges, universities, and art institutes. This M.F.A. degree is considered to be a "terminal degree"—that oddly named highest form of academic certification available to the studio artist.

As almost anyone who has bought one will agree, the M.F.A. degree has only one practical application: it is a work permit that qualifies its possessor to seek employment in the academic-photography sector of the photographic-art establishment. For several decades now, that establishment has actively encouraged thousands upon thousands of young people to enter a program of studies in order to acquire a credential that would only certify them as potentially capable of teaching what they had been taught. They were lured by promises of full employment and work situations that would leave them ample time to pursue their art-making inclinations.

For various reasons, this agenda was attractive to a certain sector of the North American public: white, middle-class, untypically close to parity in its gender distribution—a privileged group, in short. Politically uninformed, unaware even of what would constitute its own enlightened self-interest, this caste bred so rapidly that it soon flooded the labor pool. This, along with that caste's reliance on movies and television for its sense of history and its relation to language, enabled management (in our case, the academic-art establishment) to use this labor force against itself. Erosion of the tenure system, in opposition to which there are indeed numerous sensible arguments, was the first step. Then came the elimination of long-term contracts. With the Yeshiva University decision of a decade ago, in which the Supreme Court declared faculty of private institutions of higher learning to be management, thus ineligible for collective bargaining, this marginalization was virtually complete. More and more, teaching artists and art teachers (these are not synonyms) work under short-term contracts of two years or less, moving continuously from job to job. Their tenuous hold on stability is further undermined by the evolution of an underclass of free-lance pieceworkers: part-time teachers willing to work for next to nothing, with no protection or benefits—even willing, in their desperation, to serve as levers for the removal of anyone who complains, since there are dozens, indeed hundreds, ready to jump into any abandoned niche without asking difficult questions.

Fortunately for the power structure, it has not been necessary to shatter a spirit of community or a sense of working-class solidarity in achieving this control: those attitudes were already alien to this caste. However, two forces traditionally used to keep migrant labor from rebelling against its oppression are in active operation here.

One is religion. In this instance, the belief system begins with faith in the status of artist as a privileged, even transcendent position in our culture. This is encouraged by the training schools in which academic artists are bred. So too, of course, is the notion that their degree certifies not only that they are artists but, magically, good artists; and, even more amazingly, that at the ripe age of twenty-four or so they have something to teach to others.

(By the way, there is rumor that some schools, unable to guarantee employment to their M.F.A. graduates, are planning to invent a *new* terminal degree, the Doctor of Fine Arts or D.F.A. This would instantly render obsolescent all M.F.A. degrees, forcing the entire labor pool back into school for job retraining, thereby temporarily alleviating the pressures of unemployment. A brilliant stroke, no?)

Like state-run religions, state-run lotteries are invariably counterrevolutionary. If religion promises pie in the sky when you die, transcendence in the afterlife, the lottery seduces one into gambling for a piece of the action, upward mobility here on earth. Paradoxically, lotteries are a form of taxation of the poor yet also a means for calming them; no one with a ticket for a sweepstakes in her pocket is likely to work wholeheartedly to change the system.

The myth of the specialness of the artist is this migrant-labor caste's religion. What are its lotteries? Why, the National Endowment for the Arts grants to individuals, along with such other sources of selective support as the Guggenheim Foundation and the New York State Council on the Arts, for one. Another is the gallery-museum network, with its star system, sometimes plucking the to-be-anointed right out of their graduate-school thesis seminars.

Almost all contemporary artists play these lotteries, even if warily or cynically; very few abstain on principle. The younger ones seem unaware that it was once considered possible to be an artist without ever getting a grant. Like welfare clients, they have become enmeshed in a psychological cycle of dependency on the dole, unable to conceive of a creative project that does not require outside funding or to initiate one that does not receive it.

All this is a not-unpredictable consequence of following one particular model of artistic activity. Is there an alternative?

Consider this statement from the Mexican photographer Manuel Alvarez Bravo, made in 1968. It is intended to describe Mexican mural artists, but I think it also limns a radically different artistic attitude and a different type of artist altogether. (Although I suspect he would not say so himself, I've always taken it to be the photographer's self-description and credo as well.)

> Popular Art is the art of the People. A popular painter is an artisan who, as in the Middle Ages, remains anonymous. His work needs no advertisement, as it is done for the people around him. The more pretentious artist craves to become famous, and it is characteristic of his work that it is bought for the name rather than for the work — a name that is built up by propaganda. . . . The art called Popular is quite fugitive in character, of sensitive and personal quality, with less of the impersonal and intellectual characteristics that are the essence of the art of the schools. It is the work of talent nourished by personal experience and by that of the community — rather than being taken from the experiences of other painters in other times and other cultures, which forms the intellectual chain of nonpopular art.[2]

I know of no more succinct description of that black hole which is the current North American photo scene — a voracious vacuum into which crop after crop of highly touted new stars have simply disappeared, a vacancy that threatens to suck all the life out of this so recently young and vital medium. Impersonal, intellectualized, egocentric, detached from the context of its own time and place, sustained by hype: these are the same phrases so many of us mutter as we walk through museums, galleries, the corridors of graduate programs across the country, or thumb desperately through monographs and magazines, looking for anything worth looking at twice.

If this is, unintentionally and by indirection, a description of the way things are here, it is also (again by indirection) a prescription for how things might be changed. Piecing together the clues imbedded in Alvarez Bravo's statement, I would extrapolate a set of understandings in the shape of an agenda that I offer for the contemplation of anyone who, like myself, finds the "new American photography" stillborn.

- If you would be an artist whose work truly matters to any group of people, you must live as one of them, speaking their language, sharing their experience, their air, their food, their water, addressing your mutual concerns. Therefore, the first rule is: *Stay put*. Grow roots; allow the soil to feed you.

- Dig in your heels. Do not accede to any system that would shunt you aimlessly, constantly, from one context to another. Such systems are hostile to your survival. Develop versatility; there are alternative means for supporting yourself. Learn to thrive in the cracks.

- If you live in an art ghetto, you will think like a herd animal; if you live as a hermit, you will make hermetic art. Find some middle ground where there is room to breathe and time to think, where no one knows of any reputation you may have acquired. Try to keep it that way.

- Make a home for yourself. Heed the rhythms of intimacy. The artist must learn to be at home in his or her own work, to invite others in and make them feel welcome.

- Know history, especially your particular history, that of yourself and your people, whoever they are. You must be aware of all that has brought you to this moment. Only then can this moment, or any other, be truly yours.

- You are a worker, a producer of objects, a citizen in the polity. Be aware of your class origins, your class position, your class aspirations. Never allow yourself to believe — as did Ernest Hemingway — that the only difference between the rich and the poor is that "the rich have more money."

- Speak—and make art—when you have something to say. Otherwise, teach yourself to shut up. Accept the natural rhythms of your own fallow and fertile cycles. Do not produce work merely to prove or reassure yourself. Artists are artists even when not making art.

- Put your own work on view in your home and studio, where you must live with and confront it daily. If your images cannot nourish you and sustain your own interest at length, they are unlikely to be of use to anyone else.

- Hone your craft. There is always a deeper level of communion with your tools, materials, and processes to work toward. You must find ways to make even pain and ugliness engage the senses; otherwise who will be persuaded to look at length—and why else make a picture in the first place?

- There are many ways to learn your craft. Be neither proud nor ashamed of the sources of your knowledge. But no matter what form your education took—the academy, apprenticeship, self-teaching—you must recognize your student work as such and put it behind you; otherwise you will make student work all your life. Only then can you begin to build a poetry of your own. This will take years. Be patient with yourself.

- With perseverance and good fortune, you will find your true subjects— or they will find you. In either case, be prepared to be surprised: one does not choose one's obsessions.

- If economic security is your goal, you are in the wrong profession. Frugality is one of the artist's tools. If you're lucky, such economic success as comes your way will arrive in increments that enable you to go on working without ever forgetting the experience of hunger. In that way your work may continue to speak to the hungry, who form the largest audience in the world.

- If recognition—or, even worse, fame—is your goal, you are again in the wrong profession. Modesty is another of the artist's tools. If you're lucky, any recognition you gain will be merely commensurate with your achievement, and any fame that afflicts you will pass quickly, leaving your sense of self undamaged, so that you can get on with your work.

- And, finally: Get on with your work.

I do not know what North American photography would look like if a generation of its photographers followed this advice. I can only assure you of this: It would not look anything like it does at present.[3]

NOTES

1. Kathleen McCarthy Gauss, *New American Photography* (Los Angeles: Los Angeles County Museum of Art, 1985).

2. Quoted in Emily Edwards, *Painted Walls of Mexico: From Prehistoric Times Until Today* (Austin and London: University of Texas Press, 1968), p. 145.

3. This essay is a slightly revised excerpt from "Meditations on a Set of Hypotheses Extrapolated from the Work of Manuel Alvarez Bravo," the text of the Brehm Memorial Lecture in honor of Manuel Alvarez Bravo, delivered at Ingle Auditorium, Rochester Institute of Technology, April 10, 1986.

The value of a book is not in the book, it is in the subsequent behavior of its readers.

Wendell Johnson, People in Quandaries (1946), p. 206

Publication Credits

"The Destruction Business: Some Thoughts on the Function of Criticism" first appeared, in considerably different form, as a two-part series in my column, "Depth of Field," for *Darkroom Photography/Camera & Darkroom*. The first half, titled "The Destruction Business," was published in *Darkroom Photography* 12, no. 12 (December 1990); the second part, titled "Shooting Iago from the Balcony: Critical Distance and Feedback Loops," appeared in the next issue of the same magazine, 13, no. 1 (January 1991), which had then changed its name to *Camera & Darkroom*. This much revised and expanded version is previously unpublished.

"On Redaction: Heaps and Wholes, or, Who Empties the Circular File?" first appeared in the Canadian journal *Photo Communiqué* 10, no. 2 (Summer 1988), and subsequently — both in English and Danish — in *Katalog* (Denmark) 2, no. 4 (June 1990). A shortened and considerably different version of it appeared under the title "Heaps and Wholes, or, Who Empties the Circular File?"in my column, "Depth of Field," for *Camera & Darkroom* 14, no. 7 (July 1992). A slightly different version from the final one appeared in *LensWork Quarterly* 11 (Fall 1995).

"Documentary, Photojournalism and Press Photography Now: Notes & Questions" first appeared, in considerably different form, as a three-part series in my column, "Light Readings," for *Lens' on Campus*: "Information, Please!" 7, no. 1 (February 1985); "Most Photojournalism Isn't," 7, no. 2 (March 1985); and "Who Profits?" 7, no. 3 (April 1985). In approximately its present form, but under the title "Documentary and Photojournalism Now: Notes and Questions," it appeared subsequently in *Fotokritik* (Germany), 20 (December 1986), in both English and German.

"The Image in Question: Further Notes on the Directorial Mode" originated as a catalog essay for the traveling survey exhibition *True Stories and Photofictions,* organized by the Ffotogallery, Cardiff, Wales, which opened in May of 1987. A revised version of it then appeared, under the title "The Image in Question" and in considerably different form, in my column, "Light Readings," for *Imaging On Campus* (the successor to *Lens' On Campus*) 1, no. 3 (October 1987). Its first appearance in approximately its present form, and under its full title, took place in the *Center Quarterly #36*, vol. 9, no. 4 (Summer 1988). Subsequently it was reprinted in *Katalog* (Denmark) 1, no. 4 (June 1989), in both English and Danish, and anthologized in *Esthetics Contemporary*, edited by Richard Kostelanetz (Buffalo, N.Y.: Prometheus Books, 1989). Most recently it appeared, in both English and Portuguese, in *A Fotografía na Arte Contemporanea,* edited by Manuel Vilariño, the proceedings of a 1994 conference at the University of Santiago de Compostela, Spain (Coruña: Centro Galego de Artes da Imaxe, 1995). That final version, the one presented here, incorporates passages of another essay, "Collaborations Through the Lens: Photography and Performance Art," in *DOC·U·MEN·TIA,* edited by f-stop Fitzgerald (NY: Post Contemporary Publishers, 1986).

"Mutant Media: Photo/Montage/Collage" originated as a catalog essay for the survey exhibition *Montage,* organized by and presented at the Hillwood Art Gallery, Long Island University, N.Y., November–December 1988. A revised version thereof appeared as a two-part series in my column, "Depth of Field," entitled "Mutant Media: Photomontage and Photocollage," *Camera & Darkroom* 15, no. 3 (March 1993), and "Photomontage/Collage: Media Prophecy for the 21st Century," 15, no. 4 (April 1993). This much revised and expanded version is previously unpublished.

"The Vanishing Borderline: Sketch for a Manifesto on the 'Democratization' of Art" first appeared, in considerably different form, as a two-part series in my column, "Light Readings," for *Lens' On Campus*: "Democratizing Media," 8, no. 5 (October 1986), and "The Vanishing Borderline," 8, no. 6 (November 1986). Shortly thereafter, in approximately its present form, it appeared in *The Structurist* (Canada) 25–26 (Winter 1986–87). Sometime thereafter, simply titled "The Vanishing Borderline," another version of it appeared in *A Critique of America* (June–July 1988).

"Conspicuous by His Absence: Concerning the Mysterious Disappearance of William Mortensen" first appeared, under the title "Disappearing Act" and in considerably different form, in *Camera Arts* 2, no. 1 (January–February 1982). This much revised and expanded version is previously unpublished.

"Lentil Soup: A Meditation on Lens Culture" first appeared, in considerably different form, as a two-part series in my column, "Light Readings," for *Lens' On Campus*: "Lentil Soup," 6, no. 2 (March 1984), and "Lentil Soup Again," 6, no. 3 (April 1984). In that same form, and under those same titles, it appeared next in *European Photography* #20, vol. 5, no. 4 (October–December 1984), and #21, vol. 6, no. 1 (January–March 1985), in both English and German. Its first publication in footnoted form came in *Et Cetera: A Review of General Semantics* 42, no. 1 (Spring 1985). It next appeared under the title "Lentil Soup: A Cultural History of the Lens" in the Canadian journal *Photo Communiqué* 8, no. 1 (Spring 1986). Under its present title (or translations thereof), it then appeared in *Impact of Science on Society* 142 (Fall 1986), first in English, and subsequently in that journal's Russian, Chinese, Korean, French, and Arabic editions. Subsequently it appeared, in Italian, in the Italian journal *Fotologia* #12 (Spring–Summer 1990). Finally, yet another version of it appears in volume 4 of *Studies in Communication: Communication and Culture: Selected Proceedings from the Sixth International Conference on Culture and Communication, Temple University, 1986,* edited by Sari Thomas (Norwood, N.J.: Ablex Publishing Corp., 1990). This is its first publication in this final form.

"Edward S. Curtis: The Photographer as Ethnologist" first appeared, in somewhat different form, in *Katalog* (Denmark) 5, no. 4 (June 1993). This much revised and expanded version is previously unpublished.

"Private Lives in Public Places: The Ethics of Street Photography" first appeared, in considerably different form, as a two-part series in my column, "Light Readings," for *Lens' On Campus*: "The View From Street Level," 5, no. 1 (February 1983), and "Private Lives in Public Places," 5, no. 2 (April 1983). In approximately its present form, it appeared shortly thereafter in the *Journal of Mass Media Ethics*, 2, no. 2 (Spring–Summer 1987).

"Items for An Agenda" first appeared in my column, "Light Readings," for *Lens' On Campus*: 8, no. 4 (September 1986).

Picture Credits

William Mortensen photographs copyright © Deborah Irmas, reproduced by permission of the Center for Creative Photography, University of Arizona, Tucson.

Cartoon by Gahan Wilson, p. 115, copyright © 1972 *Playboy* magazine, reproduced by special permission.

Cartoon by Rouson (John Henry Rouson), "Boy and Girl," p. 116, copyright © 1972, *Los Angeles Times* Syndicate, reproduced by permission.

Edward S. Curtis photographs reproduced by permission of the New York Public Library.

Below are Edward S. Curtis's captions for several of the images reproduced elsewhere in this book:

Frontispiece. "Principal Female Shaman of the Hupa," *The North American Indian,* vol. 13 (1924), plate 467. Many Hupa shamans were women. They acquired the power to cure disease. They were credited with the ability to inflict mysterious sickness by sorcery, and only they could relieve the victim of such magic.

Fig. 2, p. 138. "A Haida Chief's Tomb at Yan," *The North American Indian,* vol. 11 (1916), plate 397. The remains of the chief rest in a niche cut into the top of the transverse beam. This tomb is of unusual form, and must have been erected at enormous cost to the dead man's family.

Fig. 3, p. 139. "Coming for the Bride," *The North American Indian,* vol. 10

(1915), plate 337. In the bow Qúnhulahl, a masked man personating the thunderbird, dances with characteristic gestures as the canoe approaches the bride's village.

Fig. 6, p. 146. "Fish-weir across Trinity River — Hupa," *The North American Indian,* vol. 13 (1924), plate 459. Each summer a substantial structure of this kind is thrown across the river, the southern and the northern divisions of the tribe alternating. The weir remains in place until the spring freshets carry it away. A fisherman stands on each of several platforms erected below an equal number of openings in the weir, and lowers and draws his dip-net at random. As the construction of a weir is a communal undertaking, the catch is divided each evening according to the requirements of the various families.

Fig. 7, p. 147. "Pima *Ki,*" *The North American Indian,* Vol. 2 (1908), plate 45. The old-time dwelling of the Piman tribes. The *Ki* was usually about fifteen feet in diameter. As the winter climate of southern Arizona is very mild, only a small fire was needed to keep the *Ki* warm in even the coldest weather.

About the Author

Named one of "the 100 most important people in photography 1998" by *American Photo* magazine, and "considered by many to be the dean of U.S. photo critics" (according to the Japanese magazine *Art and Collector*), media commentator and educator A. D. Coleman lectures, teaches, and publishes widely both here and abroad. Since 1967, Coleman has published more than 170 columns in the *Village Voice*; 120 articles in the *New York Times*; features in such diverse publications as *ARTnews, Art in America, Collections, Dance Pages, France, New York,* and *ArtLook*; and introductions to several dozen books. His widely read Internet newsletter, *C: The Speed of Light,* appears bimonthly on the World Wide Web in The Nearby Café, a multi-subject electronic magazine of which he is executive director (at http://www.nearbycafe.com).

A member of PEN, the Authors Guild, the National Writers Union, and the American Society of Journalists and Authors, Coleman served for years as executive vice-president of AICA USA, the international association of critics of art. He received the first Art Critic's Fellowship ever awarded in photography by the National Endowment for the Arts in 1976, a Logan Grant in Support of New Writing on Photography in 1990, and a major Hasselblad Foundation Grant in 1991. He was a J. Paul Getty Museum Guest Scholar in 1993 and a Fulbright Senior Scholar in Sweden in 1994. In the winter of 1996–97 Coleman was honored as the Ansel and Virginia Adams Distinguished Scholar-in-Residence at the Center for Creative Photography in Tucson, Arizona, where a twenty-seven-year bibliography of his writings on photography is currently in production.

His book *Critical Focus* received the International Center of Photography's Infinity Award for Writing on Photography in 1995; both that volume and

Tarnished Silver were singled out for honorable mention in the 1996 Kraszna-Krausz Book Awards.

From 1988 to 1997 Coleman served as the photography critic for the weekly *New York Observer*; his syndicated columns appear regularly in *Photo Metro, Photography in New York, European Photography* (Germany), *Foto* (Hungary), *Foto* (Holland), *Fotografie* (Czech Republic), *La Fotografia* (Spain), and *Juliet Art Magazine* (Italy). Under his full name, Allan Douglass Coleman, he publishes poetry, fiction, and creative nonfiction. His work, which has been translated into nineteen languages and published in twenty-six countries, is represented by Image / World Syndication Services.

Index

Cohen, Stephen, 75
Collage, 67, 68; Cubist, 65; montage and, 77
Collier, John: on visual anthropology, 135, 153
"Comanche, A" (Curtis), 132; reproduction of, 132
"Coming for the Bride" (Curtis): reproduction of, 139; Curtis caption for, 183–84
Commanday, Robert, 6
Command to Look, The (Mortensen), 94, 110n8
Communication, 13, 47; communication about, 120; effectiveness of, 14; lens and, 131n42; Other and, 14; photography and, 82, 84; visual, 113; writing and, 84
"Composite Imagery and the Origins of Photomontage" (Sobieszek), 67
Compound lens, 120, 121, 123; invention of, 119
Computer culture, 82, 87, 88–89
Consilvio, Tom, 28
Contact: Theory, 31
Conversations With The Dead (Lyon), 42
Cooper, Gary, 154n12
Copernicus, Nicolas, 121
Corpron, Carlotta, 75
Cowin, Eileen, 59
Creative impulses, 76
Crimp, Douglas, 54–56
Crisis: Chinese ideogram for, 8; criticism and, 7–8
Critical discourse, 11, 12; thoughts on, 5–7
Critical distance: establishing, 7; lack of, 5–6
Critical tradition, establishment/continuity of, 9–10
Criticism, 22n16; giving/receiving, 16; root of word, 7; thoughts on, 1–21
Critics, 5, 8, 22n12; dissident, 19; and mosquitoes compared, 12; obligation of, 11–12; reading, 10–11; unpopularity of, 9
"Crown" glass, 119
Cultural symbols, 160
Cultural *zeitgeist*, 15
Culture, photograph and, 136, 160
Cumming, Robert, 59
Cunningham, Imogen, 31, 160
Cunningham, Merce, 23n31
Curtis, Edward Sheriff, xix, 37, 157n40; anthropology and, 141, 142, 152; anthropology/photography and, 157n44; as art photographer, 141; ethnology/

photography and, 157n44; frontispiece, 132; landscape photography by, 137–38; models for, 152; Native Americans and, 134, 135–36, 141–42, 144–46, 147, 152; photo by, 138, 139, 144, 145, 146, 147, 148, 149, 150; recordings by, 147; visual anthropology and, 135, 153; work of, 134–37, 143–44, 147, 151, 153, 157n40

Da Capo Press, 31
Dadaists: montage and, 78n6; photomontage and, 65, 66
Daguerre, L.J.M., 159
Daguerreotype, 83, 117, 126, 130n34
Davenport, John L., 111n34
"Death of Hypatia" (Mortensen), 99; reproduction of, 100
DeCarava, Roy, 42, 49n13, 157n40
Defining technology, 113
De Gregorio, Carl: suit brought by, 168n7
DeMille, Cecil B., 97, 154n12
Democritus, 118
Department of Photography (Museum of Modern Art), 96
Deren, Maya, 55
Descartes, René, 118
"Desert Cantos: The Playboys" (Misrach), 75
Destruction, 2, 7, 8, 20
D.F.A. degree. *See* Doctor of Fine Arts degree
Diaphana (Maurolycus), 119
Dickens, Charles: quote by, 159
Dickinson, Emily, 9
Digges, Leonard: compound lens and, 119; lens culture and, 120
Digital-camera systems, 86–87
Dioptrice (Kepler), 122
Directorialism: *auteurism* and, 56; manifestation of, 60
Directorial mode, xviii, 54, 57, 59, 60n9, 97, 138
Directorial photographers: artifacts and, 58–59; performance evoked by, 59–60
Direct-positive process, 83
Disasters of War (Goya), 104
Disbelief, suspension of, 58
Disfarmer, Mike: "Heber Springs Portraits" project and, 30
Dixon, Joseph K., 155n13
Doctor of Fine Arts (D.F.A.) degree, 172
Docudrama, 133

Metacommunication, 120, 124

Metzker, Ray, 76

Mexican Indigenous population, 167n5

Meyerowitz, Joel: on street photography, 160, 165n4

M.F.A. degree, 171, 172

Michals, Duane, 58, 59, 97; montage process and, 72

Microfiche, documentary and, 46

Microscopes, 117, 126; impact of, 122, 124; references to, 122–26

Minamata (Smith and Smith), 41, 42

Mise-en-image, 58, 97, 138

Misinterpretation, problems with, 13

Misrach, Richard, 75

Moby Dick (Melville), 93

Model, The (Mortensen), 94

Moholy-Nagy, Laszlo, 73, 90n14

Mohr, Jean, 46

Molinier, Pierre, 76

Monsters and Madonnas: A Book of Methods (Mortensen), 94, 96, 109n8

Montage, 66, 68; collage and, 77; film editing and, 71; media, 77

Montage and Modern Life (Phillips), 69

Moore, Henry, 97; on critics, 5, 22n13

Morgan, Barbara, 72, 79n36; photomontage and, 73, 74

Mortensen, Myrdith, 111nn33, 39

Mortensen, William, 79n35, 111n26; directorial mode and, 97; essay on, xviii, xix; exile of, 93, 106–7; influence of, 94–95, 108–9,109–10n8; photo by, 98, 100, 101, 102, 103; propaganda and, 104,105; purism/pictorialism and, 95; work of, 96, 97, 99, 105, 111n39

Mortensen on the Negative (Mortensen), 94

Mortensen School of Photography, 94

Mueller, Thomas, 49n3

Müller-Pohle, Andreas, 60n4

Munari, Bruno, 79n24

Murillo, Rosario, 90n17

Murmurs of Earth (Sagan), 126

Muses, 2, 16; critics and, 1

Museum of Modern Art, 96; Heartfield at, 66; press release by, 27–28

Muybridge, Eadweard, 133

Myers, William E., 144

Nagatani, Patrick, 59

"Nakoaktok *Mawihl*, A:" (Curtis), 150; reproduction of, 150

Nanook of the North (Flaherty), Curtis and, 147, 157n37

National Endowment for the Arts, 17, 173

Naturalistic Photography for Students of Art (Emerson), 156n29

Negative sandwiches, 72, 75

Neruda, Pablo, 88

New American photography, 171, 174–75

New Columbia Encyclopedia, The, xvii–xviii, xix

Newhall, Beaumont, 108, 110n14; Curtis and, 154n2; exhibits and, 96; Mortensen and, 93–94, 95, 107, 109, 111n34; on photomontage, 68–69

Newhall, Nancy: Mortensen and, 94, 95; pictorialism and, 96

Newman, Arnold, 59

New Museum for Contemporary Art, 39

New York Observer, 3, 4, 18

New York Review of Books, The, 4, 22n6

New York State Council on the Arts, 173

New York Times, 161, 165; on Curtis, 134

Nicaragua (Meiselas), 40

"Nicaragua Media Project, The," 39–40

Nicolson, Marjorie: on microscope, 123; on telescope, 122, 125

Nièpce, Joseph Nicéphore, 126, 159

Nietzsche, Friedrich: on critics/mosquitoes, 12

Nin, Anaïs, 73

Norris, Frank, 43

North American Indian, The (Curtis), 37, 133, 152, 153; images in, 143–44; making of, 135–36

Nouveaux Realistes, 74

Nystrom, Christine L., 131n43

Objectivity: journalism and, 47; photography and, 50n24, 151

Obscura, 111n32

Observation, verification of, 125

Ochs, Adolph, 50n24

Oeuvre, 32, 88; contents of, 31; defining, 30

Old Curiosity Shop, The (Dickens), quote from, 159

Oliveros, Pauline, 89

O'Neill, Eugene, 97

Ortega, Daniel, 90n17

Ortega y Gasset, José: on decline of quality, 88

Ortiz Echagüe, José, 111n24

Osborn, Fairfield, and Curtis, 142

Other, communication and, 14

critical discourse and, 18; financial success for, 23n31

Projection Control (Mortensen), 94

Propaganda, 104, 105

Ptolemy, 118, 121

Public discourse, 9, 19, 22n4; quality/quantity of, 2

Purism, 110n10; pictorialism and, 94–96, 105–7

"Quest for Pure Form, The" (Mortensen), 99; reproduction of, 101

Radical, criticism and, 8

Radio telescope: 126, 130n41; message reproductions of, 127, 128

Ramirez, Sergio, 90n17

Rauschenberg, Robert, 76

Ray, Man, 79n28; on criticism, 7, 12; on nonphotographic elements, 71

Reagan, Ronald, 40

Realism, photocollage/photomontage and, 73

Reality, reproduction of, 57

Recontextualization, thoughts on, 162–63

Redaction, 27, 29, 30–31

Red Hawk, 151

Reflections upon Ancient and Modern Learning (Wotton), 123

Reissman, W., 79n26

Rejlander, O. G., 69, 79n22; directorialism and, 60; photomontage and, 67, 73

Religion, artists and, 172–73

Representation, defining, 36

Reproduction quality, 39

Resurrection City (Freedman), 42

Richards, Eugene, 50n18

Richards, I. A., 15

Riefenstahl, Leni, 18–19

Riis, Jacob: documentary and, 40; photojournalism and, 159

Ritchin, Fred, 43–44, 49n16

Rizzuto, Angelo, 30

Robinson, Henry Peach, 69, 79n22; directorialism and, 60; photomontage and, 67, 73

Rodriguez, Sebastian, 50n18

Rogovin, Milton, 42

Rosa Ursina sive Sol (Scheiner), 122

Rosenbaum, Ron: on self-parody, 52n25

Rosenberg, Harold: on criticism, 16–17

Rosenblum, Naomi, 69; on Curtis, 140;

Mortensen and, 109; on photomontage/photocollage, 67

Rosler, Martha, 51n25, 77n3

Rouson, John Henry: cartoon by, 115–16; reproduction of, 116

Rubin, William, 69; on photomontage/photocollage, 67

Ryle, Gilbert, 151

Sackrey, Charles, 88

Sagan, Carl: on radio telescopes, 126

St. Augustine, 118

Salgado, Sebastiao, 44

Sander, August, 37, 41

Sartre, Jean-Paul, 42

Scharf, Aaron: on Ernst/Heartfield, 67

Scheiner, Christophorus, 122

Scholarship, xx–xxi, 31, 32

Schulze, Johann Heinrich: image-making and, 124

Schwarz, Heinrich: on photography, 124

Science, photography and, 82, 117, 126, 151

Scully, Julia, 30

Seagram's "Courthouse" project, 48n2

"Seeing Straight" (exhibit), Newhall and, 109, 110n15

Sekula, Allan, 51n25

"Selections from the Collection: Dada and Surrealism" (exhibit), 66

Self-criticism, 7

Self-expression, 13, 14

Serra, Richard, 16, 17

Serrano, Andres, 17, 23n32

Shakespeare, William, 93

Shavelson, Lonny, 50n18; on photography, 27

Sherman, Cindy, 56, 60n10; directorial and, 60n9

Siderius Nuncius (Galileo), 121, 130n18

Sight gags, 115

Silk, Gerald, 79n24

Simmons, Laurie, 58

Sinclair, Upton, 43

Siskind, Aaron, 31, 75

Sitney, P. Adams: on criticism, 6, 7

60 Minutes, photojournalism and, 49n5

Sketchbooks, computer-imaged, 88

Skoglund, Sandy, 59

Smith, Aileen, 41, 42, 51n25

Smith, Paul Chaat: on Curtis, 155n23

Smith, W. Eugene, 41, 44, 49nn9, 12, 50n23, 51n25, 61n17, 97, 157n40; on journalism/